le corbusier

preface and acknowledgments

For over half a century Le Corbusier was one of the most controversial figures, not only of modern architecture, but of all Western
culture. Six years after his death he is by no means in eclipse. On
the contrary, he is still both reviled and worshipped. He is still
accused of ruining our cities, but he is also compared with Michelangelo and Leonardo. Whichever assessment ultimately prevails
he will certainly remain one of the most fully documented figures
in the history of art. His biographer—and the present biography
can be no more than a sketch—is faced with an immense amount
of material. Inevitably much of this is no more than ephemeral
journalism, useful mainly as showing what was thought of Corbu
at some particular date. Some of this material is from his own pen
— again mainly journalistic stuff, although of a pretty explosive
kind, written to propagate his ideas, theories and the cause of
modern architecture generally. This dates mainly from the earlier
years when patrons were lacking, and when there were still walls of
prejudice to be battered to the ground. Apart from Corbu's
journalism, however, there were his more enduring written works.
These included the famous *Ville Radieuse* of 1933, a seminal work
in its way; and the *Mon Œuvre* of 1960, valuable for Le Corbusier's
own comments on his buildings and patrons. They also include that
extraordinary mixture of autobiography, philosophy and mathematics, *Le Modulor*.

Apart from journalism and Le Corbusier's own books, anyone
who writes about him at all must necessarily pay a very high
tribute to Mr W. Boesiger who has, through the years, edited the
Œuvre Complète—a unique literary edifice wherein all his architectural drawings, from the mere doodle to the great plans, are
collected together and annotated in three languages. This *Œuvre*

Complète is now available in eight magnificent volumes. The whole work is a great monument to Le Corbusier, such as few artists have received in their lifetime, or even afterwards.

I must also acknowledge my great debt to Mr Peter Blake, whose *Le Corbusier: Architecture and Form* has provided me with many facts, ideas and felicitous phrases. Mr Blake also tells fully for the first time the real story of Le Corbusier and the United Nations Buildings. Sincere thanks are also due to Mr Anton Henze for his admirable little book on the Monastery of La Tourette, particularly for his account of the Dominican Order and of the way in which that Order dealt with the problem of building a modern monastery. Upon this account I have drawn quite shamelessly since it contained material which could not be available elsewhere. Finally to Miss Norma Evenson thanks are due for her scholarly and perceptive book, *Chandigarh*, without which I could not have written of the genesis of that city, both before and after Le Corbusier came on the scene. I am also most grateful to Mr Kenneth Allinson for the excellent work he has done on the Appendix and Bibliography.

The photographic credits are listed separately, but I should like to record my thanks to all those who have provided illustration material.

I hope that I have duly acknowledged all quotations in the textual notes, but I am also glad to be able to list them here. My thanks, therefore, to the following publishers, authors or other holders of copyright for permission to quote from the books listed below. For convenience the name of the English publisher is also given in parentheses whether he is the holder of the copyright or not.

Artemis Verlag und Verlag für Architektur: Zürich.
> Edited by W. Boesiger: *Œuvre Complète*. Eight volumes.
> (*Complete Architectural Works*: Thames and Hudson, London.)

La Fondation Le Corbusier: Paris.
> Le Corbusier: *Mon Œuvre*. 1960.
> (Le Corbusier: *My Work*. Trans. James Palmes. Architectural Press Ltd, London, 1960.)

Faber and Faber Ltd, London.
> Le Corbusier: *La Ville Radieuse*. Vincent, Fréal et Cie, Paris, 1933.
> (Le Corbusier: *The Radiant City*. Faber and Faber Ltd, 1967.)

Faber and Faber Ltd, London, and Harvard University Press.

> Le Corbusier: *Le Modulor*. 1949.
>
> (Le Corbusier: *The Modulor*. Trans. Peter de Francia and Anna Bostock. London, Faber and Faber Ltd; Cambridge, Mass., Harvard University Press. Copyright, 1954, by Charles Édouard Jeanneret.)

The Harvill Press, London.

> Le Corbusier: *L'Unité d'Habitation de Marseille*. 1950.
>
> (Le Corbusier: *The Marseilles Block*. Trans. Geoffrey Sainsbury. The Harvill Press, 1953.)

Peter Blake.

> Peter Blake: *Le Corbusier: Architecture and Form*. (Penguin Books Ltd, 1963.)

Verlag Gerd Hatje, Stuttgart.

> Le Corbusier: *La Chapelle de Ronchamp*. 1955.
>
> (Le Corbusier: *The Chapel at Ronchamp*. Architectural Press Ltd, London, 1957.)

Josef Keller Verlag, Starnberg.

> Anton Henze: *La Tourette*.
>
> (Anton Henze: *La Tourette: the Le Corbusier Monastery*. Lund, Humphries, London, 1966.)

University of California Press. Berkeley, California

> Norma Evenson: *Chandigarh*. 1966.

Thanks are also due to Whitney Publications, Inc., of New York for permission to quote from articles that have appeared from time to time in *The Architectural Forum*, and to *The American Architect* for the use of a quotation from an issue of 1936. Mr Clive Entwistle, one of Le Corbusier's most distinguished translators, has been most helpful.

contents

illustrations

plates

in text

Figures 1, 2, 3, 8, 9 from *Œuvre Complète*, by permission of Artemis Verlag,
  Zürich
Figures 4, 5, 6 from *La Tourette* by Anton Henze and Bernhard Moosbrugger,
  by permission of Josef Keller Verlag, Starnberg
Figure 7 by the author

Many years ago Le Corbusier wrote a dedication. As this is his biography I cannot do better than use his words:

In gratitude to my wife for the years of wonderful devotion, for surrounding me with the blessing of quiet, affection and happiness.

functionalist

This frightful word was born under other skies than those I have always loved—those where the sun reigns supreme.

Le Corbusier

One

apprenticeship

'The Lodestar of his generation.'
Jane Drew

When Le Corbusier* was born near Geneva in 1887 there was no such thing as 'modern architecture'. When he died in 1965 there was, for many of us, nothing else. Modern architecture had become one of the great established facts of the world, as Gothic, Classic or Baroque before it. That modern architecture should now have become more different from these historical styles than they ever were from each other, is an additional fact, an important fact which must emerge from any study of Le Corbusier.

The very nature of modern architecture is due largely, although not wholly, to four men: Frank Lloyd Wright, Walter Gropius, Mies van der Rohe and Le Corbusier; and to such engineers as Maillart, Ove Arup and Luigi Nervi. All these men, in their very different ways, responded vigorously, intelligently, imaginatively and, to some extent, romantically, to the world in which they found themselves. That is to be a man. It is quite true that in the final analysis modern architecture has been above all things the product of catastrophic changes in technology and society. In quality, however, like all the architectures there have ever been, it has been good or bad only in accordance with the capacity with which men have faced these changes, not regretting them but, rather, exploiting them to make a great art.

---

* *His real name was Charles Édouard Jeanneret. He changed it to Le Corbusier— the 'crow-like one'—in 1923, when he published his first book,* Vers Une Architecture. *For convenience he is always referred to here as Le Corbusier, the name he immortalized.*

To understand modern architecture and to understand how, over the last hundred years, it has differentiated itself so markedly from all previous styles is a very necessary preliminary to any understanding of Le Corbusier himself. Let us, therefore, look at the architectural scene when Le Corbusier was young. That scene, as beheld by the young Swiss art student at the beginning of this century, was complicated and confused, even rich, not inspiring. Here and there, and very tentatively, the seeds of a better, or at any rate a different, architecture had been sown, almost inadvertently, by the Victorian engineers; more self-consciously by such things as the tiny Arts and Crafts Movement in England and Northern Europe; in the realm of theory by some such rare prophet as William Morris in England, Viollet-le-Duc in France. Such tender seeds had borne little fruit and been little noticed. When Le Corbusier was a boy, architectural design throughout the Western world was at its lowest point—even the brash self-confidence of High Victorianism and of the Second Empire had passed—while the design of cities was virtually non-existent. To realize the impact of this sombre scene upon Le Corbusier and ultimately the impact of Le Corbusier upon the scene, it is necessary to glance first at the whole architecture of Europe and America.

Le Corbusier was Swiss, but he was French-Swiss and by early adoption a Parisian. First, therefore, it is the French scene that we must consider. Le Corbusier's greatest enemies were French architects. Le Corbusier and the 'official' architectural profession in France were eternal protagonists in a bitter and often absurd drama, a drama compounded partly of jealousy, partly of fear, partly of arrogance, but far more of utter incompatibility—two different views of life itself. The greatest single obstacle to the development of modern architecture everywhere during the last hundred years, and to Le Corbusier's work and teaching in particular, has always been the architects of France. Socially and officially the status of the architectural profession was high, still much as it had been ordained by Louis Quatorze and then, at that point, frozen into a ghastly living death.

Stylistically and structurally, throughout the nineteenth and twentieth centuries, architecture in France was quite static. It was not an art; it was a rite. Yet so great was its past prestige, its academic authority, that disastrously it became the model for Europe and America. Even in the present century, when some sort of formal training had at last replaced the apprenticeship system, the architectural schools within the American universities, and such schools as there were in Britain or Germany, based their curriculum and even their jargon almost wholly upon that of the École des Beaux Arts. It was not an education; it was a ritual. Architecture was a 'Fine Art', an academic thing in which classic correctitude was all, in which the 'rendered' drawing mattered more than the actual building, in which every move in a high game was preordained. Engineering, on the other hand, was merely useful, necessary and commercial. Any originality or creativity was heretical. Any suggestion that architecture might conceivably change in response to new methods of construction, or new ways of life, was blasphemy. The very few architects who had dared to build in iron, for instance—even in iron Gothic— men such as Labrouste (1801–75) who built the elegant Bibliothèque Sainte-Geneviève in the Place du Panthéon, or L. A. Boileau (1812–96) who built Saint-Eugène in Paris and Notre-Dame-de-France off Leicester Square in London, were virtually ostracized, beyond the pale. The work of great engineers such as Joseph Paxton (1803–65), Gustave Eiffel (1832–1923) or Robert Maillart (1872–1940), whose Swiss bridges are still among some of the most delicate in the world, was never thought of as having anything whatever to do with architecture. Théophile Gautier, as a poet, could say what he liked, but his statement, made one year before Paxton built the Crystal Palace, that 'Mankind will produce a completely new kind of architecture ... as can be seen in railway stations, suspension bridges and conservatories', bore all the stigma of academic blasphemy. Strangest of all, and far more significant, was the curious case of Viollet-le-Duc (1814–79).

Viollet-le-Duc was one of the great architectural theorists of history. He can hardly have expected to see his theories interpreted in terms of real building, but coming just at the time when the whole Romantic Movement was passing from the poets and the dreamers to the hard realists, from fantasy to iron, those theories were of immense importance. The younger Viollet-le-Duc, with a reputation based mainly upon the work of mediaeval restoration and upon the extraordinary extravaganza of the château at Pierrefonds, might long since have been forgotten— a rather jejune figure of the Gothic Revival, a minor Victor Hugo of architecture. By the sixties, however, he was quite firmly anti-Establishment, anti-clerical, ardently republican and a regular contributor to Left-wing journals; a sort of architectural Sainte-Beuve. It was in his famous *Entretiens sur L'Architecture*, the first volume of which appeared in 1863, that Viollet-le-Duc developed his theme. Architecture itself has nothing to do with the past; one may learn by studying the past—more particularly by the study of Gothic—how to analyse a great building, how to synthesize and how to reason, but not how to copy. The greatest buildings of ancient or of mediaeval times now exist only that they may be analysed. Reduce that analysis to a rational argument, and then apply that argument to some modern problem.

This thesis, like the poet Gautier's statement that mankind would one day produce a new architecture, was sheer heresy. This time, however, it came not from a poet, who had the poet's licence to say what he pleased, but from an architect. Consequently most of Viollet-le-Duc's later life was passed in violent opposition both to the Academy and to the École des Beaux Arts. The École was, and still is, a place where students are trained by the Government, efficiently and rigidly, to produce in accordance with a formula variations upon the theme of the Grand Manner, a theme which was always formal, classical, symmetrical, with every part of the plan 'developed along an axis, every minor *motif* designed in accordance with a rule, the sum total magnificent upon paper . . . quite regardless of function, quite regardless of structure, quite regardless of life'. Viollet-le-Duc, since he could hardly be ignored, did in fact give half a dozen lectures at the École des Beaux Arts, to the accompaniment of hisses and boos. Only once, when he said that as the Greeks had given architectural expression to their mythology, so must the nineteenth century give architectural expression to such concepts as the power of steam or electricity, only then, for those few moments, did he hold his audience in silence. John Summerson has suggested that in that silence of the École des Beaux Arts lecture hall modern architecture may have been born.

One would like to think so, but at any rate so far as the École des Beaux Arts is concerned, the baby was born dead. Also, there were many other moments for which one might make such a claim. There was, for instance, the one in England in 1883 when William Morris asked 'what business have we got with art at all unless we can share it?' There was that moment in America in 1901 when Frank Lloyd Wright, looking out over the towers of Chicago by night, said that 'if all this power must be uprooted that civilization may live, then civilization is already doomed'. There was the moment in Brussels in 1894, with Van de Velde asking 'why artists who build palaces in stone should rank higher than those who build in metal'. In Vienna in 1910 it was Adolf Loos who said that 'the engineers are our Hellenes, from them we receive our culture', while in Munich in 1913 it was Walter Gropius who shocked the Germans by speaking of 'the un-acknowledged majesty of the American silos'. Above all there was the famous moment in the nineties when Louis Sullivan realized that one might actually hang the stone on the steel—instead of building walls—and the Chicago skyscraper was born.

Those pioneers of the Modern Movement were a very small élite, but they were everywhere, knowing that in architecture as in painting, as in life itself, it was time for a new world to come into being. Those moments, those visions, proclamations and manifestos were clearly the birth pangs of a new culture, which some disliked and feared, and which none could see clearly. In themselves they may have been mainly symbolic, but for Le Corbusier the doctrine of Viollet-le-Duc, the greatest historical authority in French architecture, was perhaps the most signi-ficant part of his inheritance. Viollet-le-Duc died a few years before Le Corbusier was born, but that and the fact that there should be no actual resemblance between Viollet-le-Duc's rather weird pseudo-Gothic and Le Corbusier's work is neither here nor there. Viollet-le-Duc, in his own time, could hardly be expected to produce modern buildings; it was more than enough that he should repudiate a suffocating academism, and that he should state quite clearly that the world needed a new spirit and a new architecture. For the young Swiss student that was not only enough, it was a shattering realization.

In the generation before that of Le Corbusier, France, more than any other country, exemplified for the Western world the nature of Western culture. It did so rather paradoxically: the paradox of freedom within the rule of law, of unlicensed freedom embedded in a setting of almost compulsive coventionality; virtually perhaps the intellectual liberation of 1789 living side by side with the cultural rigidity of the *ancien régime*. It is a paradox that has been the strength of Europe. To rebel might be eccentric, but was never forbidden. Nevertheless the true rebel such as Viollet-le-Duc, a man of distinction condemning the socially acceptable, was rare at the end of the nineteenth century. Why should it be otherwise when the socially acceptable was so completely formulated? Rebellion, dissent, even originality, were permitted—for that too was part of the tradition—but were considered ill-mannered, gauche, at the very least unnecessary and strictly, so to speak, for the Left Bank. The Establishment, after all, provided everything: there was the Opera, the Conservatoire, the Academy, the Salon, the École des Beaux Arts; there was everything. Why rebel? And yet—for these very reasons—France was the country of revolutions, the country of the Salon des Refusés, the country where, in Le Corbusier's youth, Picasso could paint his first picture and Proust could write his first novels. Always, it was necessary that a man should sometimes breathe the air of freedom. One must not stifle and die.

So far as modern architecture is concerned, whether in the refined skill of a Mies van der Rohe or in the pedagogic ability of a Gropius, it is always possible to smell the air of Central Europe. Equally in the 'organic' architecture of Frank Lloyd Wright one can discern the English vernacular re-interpreted through the mid-Western romanticism of Walt Whitman. The pure geometry and clean Hellenic purity of a naked steel frame in the Teutonic manner of Mies, as also the cosy craft revivalism in the English manner of William Morris or Philip Webb, were both clean outside Le Corbusier's purview; they are irrelevant to this story. To try to link Le Corbusier with these other facets of twentieth-century architecture is to misunderstand his whole historic position. It is to falsify the nature of things. In England he was asked what he thought of Lutyens. The reply was uncompromising: '*Qui est-il?*' Between the architect of New Delhi, capital of British India, and the architect of Chandigarh, capital of the Punjab, there was not, and never could be, any common ground whatsoever. Le Corbusier was destined to build in Russia, in the Punjab, in Japan, in Algiers, in Massachusetts. His buildings were always magnificently appropriate, and yet in some odd way—although official and academic France remained the eternal enemy—Le Corbusier's world could never have been conceived except by a Frenchman; it was only France, Paris, that could have given us Le Corbusier. Here indeed was a Frenchman.

And yet in France itself, at the end of the last century, Le Corbusier beheld a dead world. He beheld a dead architecture, wholly classical and formal, crammed with Baroque motifs and stylistic trappings. Its saving grace was that it probably owed

6

more to Imperial Rome than to Baroque Italy. First- and Second-Empire Paris was, after all, a very Roman city. There was never anything Teutonic about it. It was of the Mediterranean, conceived long ago in lands of marble and on golden promontories, rather than in the lands of the conifer. Le Corbusier's architecture, even more his conception of the city, was again superficially quite different; but it too was of the Mediterranean—well-ordered masses in the sunlight.

It was mainly, however, against the sterility of nineteenth-century architecture—its irrelevance to modern life and to all technology—that not only Le Corbusier but the whole modern movement were so utterly opposed. This almost savage opposition to academic tyranny—and the mere use of steel and glass and concrete was only a facet of it—was what united the first generation of pioneers. It was perhaps, to start with, a rather negative sort of opposition, but the whole ethos of the École des Beaux Arts was so universal and so suffocating that those pioneers, perhaps inevitably, came to regard themselves as an international élite, as something wonderfully new and fresh, almost as messiahs of a new order.

To such thinking there must always be one proviso. However marvellous or 'international' an architecture may be—and the same applies to almost anything from cooking to grand opera—always some curious residue of national quality and character will persist. Both Gothic and the Renaissance were in the fullest sense international styles; but whether any particular Gothic or Renaissance building is in fact Italian, French, Flemish or English is seldom in doubt. At the moment we need not concern ourselves with whether the cause of this is historical, climatic or cultural; we are concerned with it as a reality. It was a reality which made of Le Corbusier not only a great international figure, building all over the world, but also a great Frenchman. Modern architecture has certain basic techniques—the use of steel and so on—which are much the same everywhere. From its very inception it has been an avowedly international style; it has never succeeded in evading the stamp of its own parish. One has only to think of, say, a Philip Webb building in Paris or of a Frank Lloyd Wright building in Rome, to get the point. Late in his life, building at his greatest in the Punjab, Le Corbusier was mysteriously but quite definitely French, as well as Indian. The Ethiopian, even if he is a genius, cannot change his skin, nor the leopard change his spots.

7

But of course it was only one particular aspect of 'Frenchness' that Le Corbusier made his own, and even that was probably a subconscious process. Le Corbusier, whose life may be seen as a perpetual battle against French orthodoxy, emerges ultimately not only as the famous 'Corbu' of the Modern Movement but also, curiously enough, as the last exponent of France's great Roman grandeur. It is not, after all, for nothing that one reaches maturity in Paris. Swiss by birth, Parisian by adoption, one is tempted sometimes to write him down a Provençal, only to remember that it was indeed at Marseilles, between the mountains and the sea, that he first fully realized himself on a gargantuan scale, Roman and Mediterranean, almost Cyclopean.

At no time in history could a man like Le Corbusier have built the Paris Opera House; for all its brilliant plan, its architecture was that of fashion. But one can quite easily imagine him having built the Pont du Gard at Nîmes, that splendid and wholly functional creation of the Roman sappers. For the nonsense of the Second Empire and what followed, for such monuments of pretension and futility as were new when he was young—the Opera House, for instance, finished in 1874, or the Petit Palais finished in 1900, and a score of others—he naturally had no use whatever. But somehow, deep in his subconscious mind, there must have been planted a permanent memory of the great classic spaces of Paris—the Arc de Triomphe, the Madeleine, the Louvre, the Chambre des Députés—like huge milestones demarcating the central area of the city; or of the avenues and canals and great steps of Versailles and Vaux-le-Vicomte; or of the small classic city of Nancy. These things, not in their outward or stylistic guise but in their essence and their basic form and scale, did become part of his inheritance, the inheritance of a great European. In the vast plan for Chandigarh, or in the ill-starred project for St Dié there stalks the ghost of Paris. After all, such cities and such monuments, no less than fine modern architecture, conform to Le Corbusier's famous, if untranslatable, definition: *L'architecture est le jeu savant, correct et magnifique des volumes assemblés sous la lumière.*

In considering the architectural world of Le Corbusier's youth it is very necessary to remind ourselves of this Roman or Mediterranean streak in his make-up. In the larger perspective of modern architecture's fight for recognition and of its concern for modern life it is so easily forgotten. And yet in the long run, in the later and larger and grander works, it became paramount. This Grand Manner, the 'high-game' of Baroque—whether in the design of buildings or cities—has been so associated with both Imperial Rome and Papal Rome that it is necessary to remember that it is in actual fact something quite independent of style or period. One can see it in Napoleonic Paris, at Luxor or at Brasilia. It is something *sui generis*, an affair not only of form but of spirit, something compounded of proportion, scale, poetry and generosity.

At the beginning of this century—except in the whole new world of the machine—there was nowhere any true inspiration for a young architect apart from this grand and organic architecture of the soil. Frank Lloyd Wright found it in the prairies and the pine or birch forest; Le Corbusier found it in the play of sunlight upon concrete and marble, so that sometimes 'aridity' becomes an almost positive quality in his work. Apart from this one almost intuitive inspiration from an older world, Le Corbusier, in his years as an art student, could look out only upon the art and architecture of a dying culture.

It is true that in England, although few Englishmen recognized it at the time, he might conceivably have looked instead upon that considerable prologue or 'pre-history' of the Modern Movement—the Railway Age. Only in those countries, such as England and America, where the industrialism of iron and steam had come soon enough to be touched by the magic wand of the Romantic Movement, could there be this possibility of discovering the basis for a fresh start, for the creation of a new spirit and for the repudiation of old styles. This discovery was made in the end by Le Corbusier, as it was by every modern architect; but not until years later, not until he was nearly forty, could he bring himself to write *Vers Une Architecture*. Meanwhile it was difficult for anyone, a Frenchman above all, to recognize the new spirit of a new age even when it was under his nose, to recognize it beneath the grime and the soot and misery of Victorian England. Nevertheless, in the two generations before Le Corbusier much of this 'pre-history' of the Modern Movement was being written in England, and in a big way. It was to be seen in the viaducts, stations, canals, docks and warehouses. It was even to be seen, as early as the middle of the century, respectably married to Ruskinian Gothic as, for instance, in such a striking example as the Gothic iron roof of Dean and Woodward's Oxford Museum.

For Le Corbusier, however—the Swiss art student still intent upon discovering Paris and Vienna—this English Railway Age, this amazing mixture of function and style, was non-existent. His mind was lively enough, but it gazed upon the world, for better or worse, through French spectacles. This still meant to him that to some extent orthodoxy must prevail or at least, in some things, that the Latin Rule of Law must prevail. Industrialism was a commercial aberration, a matter for engineers and contractors; if romanticism was to be permitted at all, then, like Classicism, it must presumably assume the form of some recognizable style such as Gothic—peculiar but respectable. If, on the other hand, romanticism should prove rebellious—as was its nature—and spawn some totally new kind of architecture, then that of course would not be architecture at all. Le Corbusier's formative years led to the discovery of this fallacy; his life was devoted to its destruction.

Some brave spirit, invited to lecture at the École des Beaux Arts on the subject of concrete, was howled down by the students as a 'mere contractor'. Ruskin, with Paddington and St Pancras under his eyes, could ask what separated a rat-hole from a railway station; until quite late in life Viollet-le-Duc could dismiss these stations, as well as the new French markets with their wonderful steel roofs, as 'mere sheds'. It was Viollet-le-Duc, however, who ultimately, in his *Entretiens sur l'architecture* (1863–72), dared to point to a new road. Indeed, after the undeniable success of the Crystal Palace in 1851, Ruskin, Gilbert Scott and Viollet-le-Duc all began to veer a little, very cautiously, towards the possibilities of iron and glass. 'That there might have to be a new kind of architecture one day' was about all it amounted to. Nobody dreamt for one moment that that architecture was already around them. How could it be when it was called 'engineering'? The idea that the machine itself might be beautiful as well as efficient, and—the corollary—that a new architecture might be born in the same spirit, was something that was too much to grasp; it was something that had to await the publication in 1923 of *Vers Une Architecture*, possibly one of the greatest architectural books ever written, certainly the most significant and influential.

If the farce of the academic game was only beginning to dawn upon him in his student days, and if the full impact of the Railway Age and of the Machine was not immediate, the mind was stirring

and the eye was observing. There was also one important movement at the turn of the century which neither the Swiss student
nor the young Parisian could entirely ignore. This was *Art
Nouveau*. *Art Nouveau* was more than a fashion but a good deal
less than a revolution. It is seen now to have been ephemeral,
but those were the days when, at any rate in Chelsea or on the
Left Bank, anything new seemed to be better than nothing.

So far as Le Corbusier and *Art Nouveau* were concerned there
must obviously have been some curiosity and interest. He was,
in those early years of the century, living in the world of Horta,
Beardsley, Guimard, Endell, Mackintosh and the rest. Sometimes
one thinks that there are traces of it in his work—certainly of
Gaudi—but in the end Le Corbusier rejected *Art Nouveau* almost
completely. That was inevitable. That rejection was also important
both for the sake of his own development and, in the long run,
for the sake of modern architecture and the world's cities. *Art
Nouveau*, in its own rather small way—mainly as *décor*—had its
great moments. The thought of an *Art Nouveau* Ronchamp or
Chandigarh leaves one speechless. All the same there are many
touches—the candlesticks and stained glass at Ronchamp, the
murals in the High Court at Chandigarh, the 'roofscape' at
Marseilles—which would all be a little different if *Art Nouveau*
had never been. *Art Nouveau*, whatever its faults and its super-
ficiality, had its own brilliant exponents, mainly Gaudi and
Mackintosh. It is still fascinating to the dilettante, but—like most
things fascinating to dilettanti—it was decorative rather than
structural. An *Art Nouveau* Le Corbusier would have been a
disaster, like a rococo Michelangelo. How narrowly did we escape
It?

Le Corbusier had entered the Art School at La Chaux-de-Fonds,
near Geneva, when he was only fourteen, in 1901. Outwardly it
was a sound technical school concerned mainly with the watch-
making industry, but Le Corbusier was to describe his teacher,
Professor L'Eplattinier, as having 'opened to me all the gate-
ways to the world of art'. L'Eplattinier also started a course for
murals and sculpture, of which Le Corbusier became a member.
In 1906, scarcely more than a student, he was commissioned to
build a villa for one of the School trustees. This villa was not in
itself very important, although competent, but the fees enabled
the young architect to travel via Budapest and Munich to Vienna.
Vienna was his first real contact with this fresh and fascinating

style, *Art Nouveau*, fresh and fascinating but, as he very soon realized, a dead end.

What was *Art Nouveau*? It was a most curious chapter in the history of taste. For a time it was everywhere. It was not only everywhere, it was everything: decoration, literature, painting, costume, theatre, typography. The English called it *Art Nouveau*, imagining it to be French. The French, who knew that it came from Brussels, called it simply 'the modern style'. The Germans called it *Jugendstil*, while the Italians, borrowing the name of a London shop, called it *stile Liberty*.

Architecturally, like functionalism which came after it, *Art Nouveau* was a revulsion against stylism, but in a totally different way. It still clung, for instance, to the Ruskinian doctrine that architecture was ornamented building, therefore ornament there must be. Ornament could not, however, any longer come from the history books—that was quite unfashionable—and so *Art Nouveau* invented its own ornament. It was a great liberation, almost an intoxication. *Art Nouveau* ornament could be almost anything provided it was without historical precedent. Swirling, swooning lines expressive, so it was said, of emotions such as joy, strength, lassitude; attenuated plants and maidens; exaggerated and conventionalized forms: these were the things that became the hallmark of the style, whether in wood, stone, iron, stained glass or, as so often, beaten copper. The only precedent may perhaps be detected faintly in Rossetti's phthisic girls. The full explanation of this whole curious phenomenon in the arts goes rather deeper than might be supposed. Psychologically *Art Nouveau* was seldom obscene, but it was certainly selfconsciously and deliberately decadent, a *fin-de-siècle* expression of hedonism, a revolt. Beardsley, Wilde, Swinburne, Baudelaire, Verlaine, Proust, Ibsen, Toulouse-Lautrec all came within its scope. So for that matter did the Gibson Girl, the Eiffel Tower and the early houses of Frank Lloyd Wright.

Now Le Corbusier, who was sophisticated but never decadent, must have added all these things together in his acute mind, only to find that the sum total was not architecture. For him architecture would always be the massing of great volumes in the sunlight, within the rules of structure. And nowhere in the whole of *Art Nouveau* could he ever have found *that*, except just possibly in the Glasgow buildings of Charles Rennie Mackintosh whose work Le Corbusier never saw. Horta's pioneering work in

Brussels was mainly ornament based upon those excessively languid curves so typical of *Art Nouveau*. In America there was Sullivan's truly lovely *Art Nouveau* ornament in ductile steel; mere surface decoration on those first skyscrapers which mattered so much more than their ornament. The iron and glass *magasins* in Paris, such as the *Samaritaine*, and Hector Guimard's bizarre ironwork at the entrances to the Paris Metro stations, must equally have left Le Corbusier unmoved. That meant that there were only Mackintosh's Glasgow Art School, Scottish, dour and hardly stylistic at all—the 'first modern building'—and Gaudi's marvellous pseudo-Gothic extravaganzas in Barcelona, probably the first revelation to Le Corbusier of the potentiality, the sheer plasticity, of concrete. Mackintosh and Gaudi, the two poles of *Art Nouveau*, the stern functionalist and the magnificent lunatic, neither of them quite conforming to Le Corbusier's definition of an architect.

It was in Vienna, in 1908, that he first encountered *Art Nouveau* personally as it were, on the drawing-board. This was in Josef Hoffmann's *Wiener Werkstätte* (Viennese Workshops). Hoffmann was, by the standards of his time, quite an advanced, even sophisticated designer. He may even have been feeling his way towards some manifestation of steel or concrete, but was never really quite equal to this challenge of the modern world. True, he sought inspiration in the forms of the machine and of structure; it was the only fashionable thing to do. But it was some new inspiration for ornament that he was seeking in vain, never realizing that structure itself would supply that inspiration, that a new form of structure was, in effect, an architectural revolution. The possibility of such a revolution, the possibility of a totally new kind of architecture, not merely a new style, was brought home to Le Corbusier in those formative years, not by Hoffmann but almost wholly by two men: Peter Behrens in Berlin and, more important, Auguste Perret in Paris.

It was not until 1910 that Le Corbusier actually met Peter Behrens, the year after Behrens had completed his famous Turbine House for A.E.G. in Berlin, an early landmark of the Modern Movement. That Turbine House was the most magnificent of the 'sheds', a delicate framework of glass and steel clipped between massive pylons of masonry. It is easy now, with hindsight, to say that those massive pylons were functionally unnecessary, a spurious Egyptological attempt to express 'power'.

That the light steel frame could stand alone, like some huge birdcage, and be beautiful, was still unthought of. It was for the next generation to discover that the 'wall', in every traditional sense of the word, had become obsolete, as, for instance, at Gropius's Fagus Factory at Alfeld on the Leine (1911) or in Le Corbusier's own *Pavillon de L'Esprit Nouveau* in the Exhibition of Decorative Arts in Paris (1925)—two buildings without walls, structurally unprecedented but undeniably architecture.

Meanwhile in 1909 Behrens's Turbine House had pointed to the inadequacy of Hoffmann, or at least to his inadequacy in the eyes of Le Corbusier. Hoffmann, like so many of his *avant garde* contemporaries, was content to express himself mainly through panels of *Art Nouveau* ornament laid on the walls of the building—what Le Corbusier called contemptuously 'Hoffmann's doilies'. It was Le Corbusier's experiences with Perret and with Behrens that convinced him that his half-formed theories about a new kind of architecture were fully justified, that old Viollet-le-Duc, years ahead of his time, had not been wrong. Hoffmann wanted to come to some permanent arrangement with this brilliant young student. Le Corbusier remained in the Wiener Werkstätte for only a few months; those 'doilies' were too much for him. He then fled to Paris, the great city of his destiny.

Therefore 1908 was the year in which for the first time— whether in Vienna or Paris—Le Corbusier first glimpsed the big world, the world beyond the Art School at La Chaux-de-Fonds. After leaving Hoffmann, Le Corbusier worked for fifteen months in the studio of Auguste Perret, a very great French architect. Those fifteen months were a most fundamental part of Le Corbusier's development. They were his real apprentice-ship.

It was a good year, a good moment in history, for a young man to be discovering Paris. 'Paris,' he wrote more than fifty years later, 'Paris is the town which I have loved and which I covered in every direction when I was twenty! Paris, whose fate today makes one shudder, victim of minds as trivial as they are venal, sapping her very life-blood.'[1] Le Corbusier could sense in the very streets, let alone the cafés and galleries, the spirit of a new age: *l'esprit nouveau*, the title, as it happens, of the magazine which twelve years later he would be editing in partnership with the poet Paul Dermée, a magazine of which the theme, in the broadest sense, was *l'esthétique de la vie moderne*. It was a good

year ... Picasso had just painted 'Les Demoiselles d'Avignon'
and had it dubbed with the new name of 'Cubism'. Braque, too,
was painting in this new manner, while Cézanne was trying to
show that natural forms had a geometric basis, that they were
derived from the cone, the sphere or the cylinder. All this was at
least an escape from the enervating nonsense of so much of *Art
Nouveau*, let alone the old academism which was dying so hard.
This new art was also a species of unsentimental realism, an art of
logical form more likely to be found among engineers or architects
than among poets or painters.

In the generation older than himself Le Corbusier had been
able to see only Viollet-le-Duc as the prophet and the theoretician;
among a younger generation he could now, in 1908, see the theory
being put into practice—and moreover without any *Art Nouveau*—
only by Peter Behrens in Germany and by Auguste Perret in France.

Perret was the more important. Behrens, in a sense, merely
continued that 'pre-history' of the Modern Movement—the
Railway Age—into the new century. He used steel and glass
functionally and his buildings were industrial; to ornament them
or to build in some historic style would have been merely perverse;
he merely maintained, rather splendidly, the tradition of Brunel.
Perret, on the other hand, saw that all types of building—flats,
offices, churches—must be of reinforced concrete, and that that
in itself meant a totally new kind of architecture. If, for Le
Corbusier, Viollet-le-Duc was a great prophet, the Forerunner,
then Perret was the Messiah.

For every reason—functional, technical and aesthetic—it
seemed as if reinforced concrete must be the medium for this
architecture of the new age. Moreover Gaudi had shown that
for the imaginative designer reinforced concrete had an even
greater potentiality than steel. It was strong, light and completely
plastic; in theory at least one could build almost anything.
Perret realized all this and had the courage to use this new
material, this new structural system, with honesty, skill and
artistry, as it should be used. Twenty years later Le Corbusier,
whose praise was never lightly bestowed, was wondering whether
anyone realized 'what an heroic part Perret had played in those
years'.

It was to be nearly thirty years before they condescended to
make Perret a professor of the École des Beaux Arts. His pioneer
works, the merits of which were spotted by Le Corbusier, are only

now finding their way into the text books. Perret is more generally known for his rather lifeless rebuilding of Le Havre after the Second World War, when he was over seventy. More famous is his church at Le Raincy, near Paris (1922–3), where he took his inspiration from such mediaeval lantern churches as, say, King's College Chapel, Cambridge, or the Sainte-Chapelle, and gave them back to us in reinforced concrete: the entire wall becomes a concrete grille filled with coloured glass, and the roof a smooth vault of flat segmental curve—hardly possible in stone—supported on extremely delicate columns. This church at Le Raincy was a noble conception but also, perhaps, a rather too obvious reinterpretation of history in a modern material.

Far more significant, if superficially less sensational, was the work done by Auguste Perret in the opening years of the century. It was this work that so attracted Le Corbusier. He was right. These Paris apartment houses, ordinary enough at first glance, were actually full of structural enterprise and originality of a most pregnant kind—the first comprehension, apart from Gaudi, of the real nature of reinforced concrete. Besides their structural significance, however, these buildings show also the 'heroic part' played by Perret in his great restraint. Reinforced concrete, apart from its structural importance, gave endless opportunities for curvilinear forms and violently contorted ornament; it was, after all, a material poured into moulds. This was a temptation which Perret resisted. Sometimes, indeed, his work was almost dour. Certainly there was more in him of Mackintosh than of Gaudi; also a good deal that was Greek or even reminiscent of John Soane.

Perret was at his peak just about the time (1908) when Le Corbusier first served in his studio. He had already built a most remarkable apartment house at 22 bis Rue Franklin. This building was an elegant but very stark structure. It consisted of a reinforced concrete frame, exposed and undecorated. This frame or grille could in theory be filled wholly with glass. Indeed, Perret was doing here, in concrete, something akin to what Mies van der Rohe would be doing in steel half a century later, and something which Le Corbusier from then on would be doing for the rest of his life, with infinite variations upon the theme. At 22 bis Rue Franklin, an apartment house some nine storeys high, the grid of columns and beams is frankly exposed and expressed externally—something almost unknown at that date. These columns and beams, moreover, are the *only* structural elements in the building; everything else is flexible, little more than furnishing and partitioning.

When Le Corbusier worked for Auguste Perret, the studio was itself the ground floor of the Rue Franklin building. Le Corbusier, therefore, worked every day in what we should now call 'an open plan', with nothing around him but glass and a few slender columns. Today the building may appear rather timid, as if it hardly dared to follow such radical construction to a logical conclusion. At the time, however, it left Le Corbusier amazed. Through him its ultimate effect was shattering. It was one of those seminal buildings which appear timid or embryonic only when we compare them with what followed in the next twenty or fifty years with the architecture of a later generation, with, say, Frank Lloyd Wright's General Office at the Racine Wax Office (1936–9), where the slender columns are each like a sonnet; or with Mies van der Rohe's Farnsworth House (1950) or his Seagram Building in New York (1956), where the starkness now has a kind of pure perfectionism, like a Ming pot; or with Le Corbusier's own Villa Savoie of 1929 or the Carpenter Arts Center at Harvard, thirty years later, which all show quite clearly that Le Corbusier's architectural life began in the Rue Franklin, in Auguste Perret's studio.

In 1908, apart from Perret's elegant effort in Paris, the frame building, whether of concrete or steel, was being honestly and courageously tackled only in Chicago and Buffalo by 'the Chicago School'—men such as Adler and Sullivan. Even they made great concessions to the past—arches (where a steel beam should have served), classical cornices, friezes and other ornament—although, as has been said, Sullivan did produce some marvellous *Art Nouveau* ornament for those steel-frame buildings which otherwise tended to compromise with a history they should have left behind. Auguste Perret, on the other hand, regarded ornament as something other men used to hide their mistakes. This, although Perret cannot have realized it, was really an early definition of functionalism. Now Le Corbusier's work was always full of grace—those curving external staircases; full of colour—the murals and the panels of primary colour at Marseilles; full of symbolism as at Ronchamp or La Tourette; touched with the occasional *jeu d'esprit* as in the 'roof-scape' at Marseilles; based always upon a sophisticated system of proportions. It is difficult to recall anywhere a single piece of ornament.

This exposed and completely unadorned frame was not, how-ever the only original or even significant aspect of Perret's work at that time. Reinforced concrete is an amazing material. Concrete alone, as the Romans used it in massive walling, is very strong in compression (you can pile weight on it) but very weak in tension. The insertion into the concrete, however, of rods and strands of steel, while it is being poured into the moulds, does give it very great tensional strength. This also enables the mass to be drastically reduced. The design of the moulds, or 'shutter-ing', and the scientific arrangement of the steel reinforcement give us a virtually new material of amazing toughness, great flexibility or plasticity, and also of great lightness. Its merits are equally evident whether one is building, say, a multi-cell apart-ment house or a vault over a great hall. It enables the architect to become master of space.

Perret realized this only slowly. According to all the most venerable traditions of architecture the base of a building tends to be wider than the upper part—a spreading of the weight by means of a plinth or some sort of platform upon which the building can stand. The extreme prototypes are the Greek temple upon its stylobate or steps, and of course the Pyramid. By 1902, however, in the Rue Franklin, Perret was actually recessing the lower storey. Structurally there was now no reason, given a reinforced concrete frame, why he should not do this. It was simply that it had never been done before.* We are now so accustomed to it—as, for instance, in Bunshaft's Lever Building in New York, or in a hundred buildings where the shop is recessed below the upper storeys—that we can afford to take it for granted, and to make the most of it. For Perret, however, thus to levitate his building ten feet above the ground was a genuine act of courage, indeed of 'heroism'.

Inherently also in this whole structural system was the reali-zation that almost always the function of the ground floor is different from that of the upper floor: shops below offices, hotel public rooms below bedrooms, foyers below auditorium, domestic living-rooms at foliage level with car ports below, and so on. It follows from this that inherent in the stark frame is the use of slender columns on the ground-floor—the *piloti*. From the very

---

* *Except in timber buildings where frame construction allows, on a small scale, the same sort of overhang of upper storeys, as, for instance in 'half-timber' houses.*

delicate white pillars of the Villa Savoie in 1929 to the gargantuan pylons of the big Marseilles building in 1952, this 'putting the building on legs'—*piloti*—is sometimes seen almost as Le Corbusier's trade-mark. It is nothing of the kind; it was something functionally desirable which, in this new century, had suddenly become structurally possible.

In spite of the seminal significance of Perret's early work, and the even more significant fact that Le Corbusier, with his alert mind, worked for fifteen months in the Rue Franklin studio, the fact remained that significant architecture and fashionable architecture—or, to put it differently, *avant garde* architecture and academic architecture—were still worlds apart. For the entire European and American bourgeoisie even *Art Nouveau*, although rejected as sterile by honest architects such as Behrens and Le Corbusier, was still thought to be 'advanced' and even dangerously so, at best decadent, at worst obscene.

But 'significant structure'—who had ever heard of that? And if one had heard of it, then what on earth had it got to do with real architecture? Architecture was a 'Fine Art'. Significant structure, if it mattered at all, was surely something that had come about by accident as it were: engineering, suspension bridges, the English Crystal Palace and the French Eiffel Tower. True, the Railway Age was crammed with it, but what had grimy stations to do with the mistress art? So for a long time even the élite, Peter Behrens for instance, had been almost compelled to think that significant structure must be found mainly in the field of industrialism. It was for Frank Lloyd Wright, as early as 1904, to build the Larkin Building in Buffalo. It was for Walter Gropius to eulogize American silos and to build the Fagus Factory. It was for Behrens, in his Berlin Turbine House of 1909 and in his Voltstrasse Factory of 1911, to suggest where the future of architecture must be sought.

Le Corbusier, as we have seen, had already admired Behrens. The Turbine House brought his enthusiasm to a high pitch. His debt to Perret was incalculable; indeed Perret would hardly be remembered apart from what he taught Le Corbusier. Perret lives as Le Corbusier's master, but in fifteen months Le Corbusier had learnt all that there was to be learnt in the Rue Franklin: the significance of structure and the nature of concrete. It was time to move on.

Le Corbusier now spent five months in the studio of Peter

Behrens. Behrens (1868–1940) was an interesting figure in the architectural world of his day—even though the Turbine House alone is now remembered—having at different times a foot in three camps. He began his career as a painter and craftsman; almost inevitably, therefore, as a disciple of *Art Nouveau*. This fashion or style, unlike Hoffmann, he soon repudiated for something more realistic. Behrens could also play the classical game, and play it very well, if asked to do so. His Art Building in the Oldenburg Exhibition (1905) has a most Hellenic severity, with a series of cubic pavilions arranged upon a raised stylobate; his German Embassy in Petersburg (1913), although later than his best modern work, is all that one expects an embassy to be. It was in his third phase, as architect to the great German electric firm, A.E.G., that Behrens became an architect of the first importance, imposing a consistency of design not only upon the buildings but upon every product of the firm, their furniture, typography and so on, a thing almost unknown at that date.

It was with the help of a special grant from his old art school at Chaux-de-Fonds that Le Corbusier was able to leave the Perret studio, travel to Berlin, introduce himself to Behrens and start working for him.

Le Corbusier's life is chequered with frustrations and disappointments, littered with great unbuilt projects; but he owed much to two extraordinary coincidences of his youth. The first was not merely that he worked for Perret but that he did so in the Rue Franklin studio, actually experiencing modern structure every morning. The second coincidence was that he worked in Behrens's studio side by side with two young men: Mies van der Rohe and Walter Gropius. Le Corbusier was now twenty-three, Mies twenty-four and Gropius twenty-seven. Apart from Frank Lloyd Wright, already in his forties, we may say that the Modern Movement in architecture was, for those few months, virtually concentrated in that one Berlin studio.

That youthful triumvirate would one day lead a 'movement', but more important is the fact that each separately, and each in a different way, represented a particular facet of that movement. Each had found a starting point in the Studio Behrens. First and foremost they were there because, thinking as they did quite radically about their art, they knew that the doors of 'polite' architecture must remain closed to them. Industrial buildings and an industrial technology, whether they liked it or not, must be their medium, or so it seemed at that date. Hence their allegiance to Behrens.

Mies, the perfectionist, who would one day design a building as if it were a Chinese vase or a Savile Row suit, and would handle the steel frame as an Athenian would have dealt with marble, was very ready to learn from Behrens's occasional essays in classicism. In the German Pavilion at the Barcelona Exhibition (1929) we find this Miesian marriage of modern structure and Hellenic purity already consummated.

Walter Gropius, again, saw a different side of Behrens. He saw the beginnings of 'product design'. Not only were the A.E.G. buildings, light-fittings, furniture, notepaper conceived as a series of items in a single whole; the idea, as Gropius realized, had a much wider application. He could envisage the whole design process as a single thing, as something giving unity to a whole society. He saw that that had been true of any great historical epoch: the mediaeval manuscript and the cathedral are clearly part of the same unified scheme of life; so also are Greek vases and Greek temples; and so on all through history until the chaos of the nineteenth century. The corollary, as Gropius saw it, was that craftsmen of all kinds must be trained together, as in the past, except that the basic tool would now be the machine. Certain principles of design, however, no matter what was the technology, would be equally valid in every work-shop and every craft. By 1919 this whole concept, born in Behrens's work for A.E.G., was embodied in the first Bauhaus.

As for Le Corbusier, he discovered many things, mainly a whole new world of form, not necessarily geometrical but certainly vivid and functional. It was the world which Picasso was already painting and which Le Corbusier was now determined to build. He knew already that he was an urban creature and had decided that nature had little to offer him. One must of course, as with Frank Lloyd Wright's 'organic architecture', marry the building to the site, make it grow from the site. In that sense, it goes without saying, Nature governs all. And indeed, to hear Le Corbusier, forty years later, dilating upon his great Marseilles building, and upon how its form had been dictated by the sun and the Provençal mountains, was a remarkable experience. All that, however, did not mean that one need, as in *Art Nouveau*, create a new style from effete lilies and distorted leaves, nor that one need, like Frank Lloyd Wright at Taliesin, sleep beneath the desert stars. Le Corbusier decided very early in his life that he was an urban man, urban in the great French tradition. He knew also that spiritually he was a man of the Mediterranean, repudiating all past styles but prepared, with new methods and new materials, to recapture the scale and the energy of Greece and Rome—always those volumes set in the sunlight. In short, when Le Corbusier left Behrens in 1910 his apprenticeship was over. He knew his mind. He was ready to build.

Two

l'esprit nouveau

'A great epoch has begun.
There exists a new spirit.'
Le Corbusier

He was quite unmistakable: that white face deeply carved, in a concave manner, like some Easter Island deity, and the heavy, black-rimmed spectacles. In his earlier days, as Mr Peter Blake has told us, as he cycled around Paris in a dark Homburg hat, Fernand Léger thought that he looked like an English clergyman. That was in 1921. In later years, with the boldly chequered shirts, the clerical illusion vanished and he appeared like nothing on earth except the man whom all the world knew as Le Corbusier. With such men as, say, Picasso or Freud, he became indubitably one of the prophets of the twentieth century, each standing in his own way for eternal values. With Gide and Einstein he even became, in 1950, the subject of a brilliant film, *La Vie Commence Demain*.

He was forbidding, suspicious and sarcastic. Like most great architects he had more than his share of arrogance. The reason is easily found. If a painter does not sell a painting, that is that; every architect is a cathedral-builder *manqué*; rightly or wrongly he knows that he could have done so much more; his lot is eternal frustration—more true of Le Corbusier than of any great architect who ever lived. He suffered badly therefore, although not quite so badly as Frank Lloyd Wright, from a *prima donna* complex, a state of mind encouraged by thousands of students all over the world who worshipped at his shrine. Those disciples, like all disciples, worshipped too uncritically but were dismissed by Lewis Mumford rather too easily as 'all the little Corbs'.

Many may not have understood too well what their 'master' was up to, but they flattered him—their bare existence was flattery—and flattery was always acceptable. He was vain. He might loathe the Establishment everywhere—he had good reason to—but was probably the only man in the world who had the Légion d'Honneur ribbon both on his jacket and on his overcoat. When in 1953 the Royal Institute of British Architects, in deference to the wishes of the Palace, engraved his gold medal with his legal name of Charles-Édouard Jeanneret, he was enraged. As if it mattered! What mattered was the inconsistency and folly of ever accepting the award. This was one of the few moments when he betrayed himself; perhaps he redeemed himself the same night by hanging the medal round his wife's neck.

There was another side to him. He is known to have spent hours hunting through a town in search of a couple of stone-masons who had worked at Ronchamp—to pass the time of day with them. He once drove a little green Fiat, but on the whole he preferred the Metro. He certainly had no use for the paraphernalia of the 'successful' man. In the studio in the Rue de Sèvres he worked serenely with a minimum of typists, telephones, dictaphones, etc.—what he called 'civilized simplicity'. His own private office off the large studio, which had once been a cloister, was smaller than the average bathroom. His rectitude was absolute, and if he lacked all semblance of outward humility he nevertheless counted his failings every morning, to make himself humble; we have his word for it.

He had the architect's usual unwillingness to admit that other architects existed. This might be dismissed as being just part of the *prima donna* complex, but in his case there were excuses. There was every excuse. At a time, for instance, when he had been writing books and publishing articles he was refused admittance to Taliesin on the grounds that Frank Lloyd Wright never received journalists—something for which Wright's most fervent admirers have never forgiven him.

A lifetime of frustration, the perpetual erosion of one's creative ability against the futility, pomposity and jealousy of mandarins and *petits fonctionnaires*, does not make for human charity. The history of architecture is crammed with great unbuilt buildings; Le Corbusier had far, far more than his share, including the Palace of the Soviets and the League of Nations Building in

Geneva. He became bitter—that is undeniable—and yet, when the sun broke through the clouds, when he was sure of you, sure that you were on the right side, and the smile came at last, he could be the kindest man on earth, the wittiest and, oddly enough, the humblest. Not surprisingly there have been no half judgments; his own colleagues either shunned him as being an altogether impossible creature, certainly impossible to work with, or else they proclaimed him with conviction and sincerity as the Leonardo and Michelangelo of our time.

La Chaux-de-Fonds is three thousand feet up in the mountains, on the last westward slope of the Jura, two miles from the French frontier at Franche-Comté. For centuries it was a refuge for the politically and religiously persecuted, thus becoming the home of a stern but simple liberalism. The mountainside, dotted with homesteads, was peopled by a free and independent Swiss peasantry. To these must be added the townsfolk, mainly artisans in the watch and clock trade. Charles-Édouard Jeanneret's first Diploma of Honour, at the age of fifteen, was for a watch chased in silver, steel, copper and gold, which he showed in the Decorative Art Exhibition at Turin in 1902. There were many branches of the Jeanneret family; Le Corbusier's branch was Jeanneret-Gris. His father had an enamelling shop. His mother was a good musician. When she died, in the little house he had built for her on Lac Léman, the Jeanneret maxim from Rabelais was printed on her funeral card—'*Ce que tu fais, fais-le*'. 'Whatever you do, see that you do it'.

At the Art School, from the age of thirteen to seventeen, Le Corbusier always had the tool of the watch-case engraver in his hand or, like some Renaissance artist, the goldsmith's hammer. It was his master, L'Eplattinier, who, seeing that he was destined for something bigger, sent him off to serve the apprenticeship already described: Hoffmann in Vienna, Perret in Paris and Behrens in Berlin. Obviously that period of apprenticeship had allowed him to get around a little: Budapest and Munich in 1907, and Munich again in 1910. Nearly all of it, however, had taken him to Central Europe—historically the world of Baroque, modernistically the world of *Art Nouveau*. The older, classical Europe, except as it revealed itself in Paris or Provence, he had hardly seen. But now, in 1911, with the maturity necessary to a fuller understanding, he went eastwards with a knapsack. He went to Prague and then down the Danube to Serbia, Bulgaria,

Turkey and Asia Minor.* He spent three weeks on Mount Athos looking at the landscape and at Byzantine painting, and then six more weeks on the Acropolis. He came back with crammed sketchbooks, mainly very rapid scrawls of Pisa, Pompeii, Athens, Venice—some of them incomprehensible, some of them very beautiful, and every one of them, presumably, done only to make a point. Forty years later he wrote of those weeks in Athens. Like Louis Sullivan in his *Autobiography of an Idea*, he speaks of his younger self in the third person, as a half-forgotten being from some other world. A lifetime of struggle and disappointment, however, has never shaken his faith in the enthusiasm and idealism of this young man in Athens—this other Corbu.

> 'The columns of the North façade and the architrave of the Parthenon were still lying on the ground. Touching them with his fingers, caressing them, he grasps the proportions of the design. Amazement: reality has nothing in common with the textbooks. Here everything was a cry of inspiration, a dance in the sunlight . . . and a final and supreme warning: do not believe until you have seen with your own eyes, measured . . . and touched with your own fingers.'[2]

In 1914 he went back to his native land. He was Swiss and this war was not his affair. Back in Switzerland he studied and he painted. He helped L'Eplattinier in the Art School. He even browsed through Owen Jones's *Grammar of Ornament* (1868). That seems incredible now, but after all, as he wrote: 'ornament pure and simple—a process of putting together—is a thing of significance; it is a synthesis . . . it is decoration that is debatable'.[3] That—from a man who never in his life used any ornament.

He annotated his sketch-books. To a very rough sketch of the Walls of Byzantium and of the Grand Seraglio he put this caption: 'Come, you town builders, note it down in your files—Silhouettes!'[4] To a sketch of Turkish wooden houses—Théophile Gautier's 'hen coops'—he put simply, 'beautiful and inspiring'.

In Rome and Athens he had been concerned mainly with discovering that lofty, mystical beauty which is so very far above those symmetrical patterns which the academies had always held to be the essence of classicism, always missing the point.

* *More than one person, viewing his little white pilgrim church on the hillside at Ronchamp (1950–5), has felt vaguely but strongly the Byzantine spirit of some church on an Aegean island or on a Balkan mountain.*

Of the Acropolis, for instance, he wrote: 'What price Vignola and the Prix de Rome? Where now are those axes radiating from star-shaped figures? Here are the true dimensions . . . very small . . . proportion is what counts.'[5] To see is everything—of the landscape of Ithaca, between a Greece bathed in limpid sunlight and a dramatic vision of the Peloponnese, he wrote simply: '*Others* stood indifferent—but you *saw*'.

Pisa moved him more deeply, it would seem, than almost anywhere. The Pisa sketches are bold, black and very rapid. He noted: 'When you draw the Tower of Pisa and show how sharply it slopes in relation to the Cathedral and the Baptistery, you will realize that this astounding phenomenon contains the very stuff of poetry.'[6] 'Even in drawing scenes of the Campo Santo in Pisa, you will have expressed the torments of hell: you will have witnessed crimes.'[7] One wonders what he is getting at, what it is that is moving him so very deeply. One looks again at Pisa, at that serene city plan—buildings and spaces so perfectly related —and from a distant future there comes an echo of other buildings and spaces, no less serene, no less beautifully related: St Dié and Chandigarh.

In Rome he wrote of 'the obscene Punch and Judy show of pediments, columns and radiating axes'.[8] And yet, in the end, Rome meant more to him than any other city except Paris. He insisted, however, that it must be seen 'as a compound of horizontals and prisms, cylindrical and polygonal'. Much later, in *La Ville Radieuse* (1933), he was saying much the same thing. 'Rome is a simple word; it is a sign expressing a precise concept: the idea is there . . . the Rome that sets one's heart beating is ancient Rome. Rome is geometrical! Here are the fundamental forms of architecture.'[9] And then he sketches, very roughly indeed, a few curves of vaults, domes and arches. 'The Latin spirit is a spirit of orderliness.' Rome always held more for the engineer than for the architect, and most of all for the designer of cities.

Then, quite suddenly, he came down to earth and invented the Maison Domino. In 1914, outside the cosy world of the English garden city, or of such cottage-like building in northern Europe —Germany, Holland and Scandinavia—as was derived from Muthesius's *Das Englische Haus* (1905), nobody had ever really thought of 'housing' as distinct from houses. Today, after half a century of prefabricated housing of every kind, the Maison Domino looks simple enough, even commonplace. In 1914 it was unique; its concrete structure could have been conceived only by a pupil of Auguste Perret. The whole concept was unique in that for thousands of years men had built houses in only one way—by piling up bricks or stones or mud or sticks. Now here was a house, or the core of a house, ingeniously cast *in situ* with extreme rapidity: two floors, a roof and a stair. Anything beyond that was partitioning, furnishing, equipment. The structural core was standardized and economic. The house, as it finally emerged, was extremely flexible. In the whole idea of the concrete frame and the absence of walls, with spaces to be filled in as one pleased with either slabs or glass, there was certainly a ghost of the Rue Franklin.

After the First World War, after 1919, such houses could have been built quickly and economically by the thousand. It was cocky of Le Corbusier to say forty years later that the Maison Domino had never been used, that it was still too new. The basic idea had been used again and again. A more legitimate boast would have been that in 1914 it was he alone, Le Corbusier, who felt that housing was now destined to become both a social service and an industrial process; also a world problem.

For the time being, however, the Maison Domino remained on the drawing-board, Le Corbusier's first single-handed flight into modern architecture. Then at last, in 1917, he left La Chaux-de-Fonds for ever. He became a Parisian once and for all: 'Paris, the city that can never be wrong . . . Paris, a monster of the most primitive kind.' He set himself up in 'a beastly little street' in the Faubourg Prisonnière, in a servant's room on the seventh floor. This 'studio' at 20 Rue Jacob he occupied for seventeen years.

It was Auguste Perret who introduced him, about this time, to Amédée Ozenfant. This partnership lasted until 1925, a long time as Le Corbusier's partnerships went. It was Ozenfant who said 'nothing will be built for forty years'.[10] He exaggerated, but he did not exaggerate wildly. It is difficult to believe now that when Le Corbusier published *Vers une Architecture* in 1923, at the age of forty-six, he had built almost nothing. In fact, to all outward appearances, the Corbu-Ozenfant studio was just one more of those curious Parisian affairs where nobody makes any money, but where everyone is rather passionately but vaguely concerned with 'Art', whatever 'Art' may happen to be from day to day—painting, architecture, journalism, propaganda or typography.

'A great epoch has begun! There exists a new spirit, *L'Esprit Nouveau*'—those were not only the opening words of *Vers une Architecture*, they were also the title of the review which, for some years, had emerged regularly from the attic in the Rue Jacob. *Vers une Architecture*, the most important architectural book of the century, was mainly an edited collection of such essays or statements upon architecture as had appeared from time to time in *L'Esprit Nouveau*. This unfortunately makes one wonder to what extent Ozenfant was in reality part-author of *Vers une Architecture*; at any rate its publication, without mention of Ozenfant, marks the beginning of the end of the partnership.* It was also the first occasion upon which Le Corbusier completely abandoned the name of Charles-Édouard Jeanneret to become 'the crow'. Vanity, self-dramatization, *réclame* or just a symbol of a fresh start?

Meanwhile, from 1917 to 1923, the publication of *L'Esprit Nouveau*—important, lively and influential—was the background to life at the Rue Jacob studio. Le Corbusier, writing in his *Le Modulor*, nearly thirty years later, said:

> '*L'Esprit Nouveau* had appointed itself the exponent of cubism, a word which covers one of the most creative and revolutionary moments in the history of thought. It was not a technical invention causing an upheaval of the social and economic spheres, but a liberation and a flowering of the spirit. It was a beginning: the way ahead . . . a time of radical reform in the plastic arts. At the moment of which I speak, this reform penetrated into architecture.'[11]

Few Left Bank magazines lasted as long as *L'Esprit Nouveau*. It is perhaps worth noting, lest *L'Esprit Nouveau* should be thought of as no more than just another ephemeral journal of the Paris art world, that the complete set of twenty-eight issues was for sale in London in 1970 for £118. It was concerned with the plastic arts, above all with *l'esthétique de la vie moderne*. Why did the journal last so long? For one thing, since no one during those years ever invited either Le Corbusier or Ozenfant to design a big building, there was nothing for them to do except to write or paint, which, nevertheless, they did to some purpose.

---

* *Paul Dermée, the poet, also had a hand in founding the magazine, but to mention Dermée while ignoring Ozenfant, as does Boesiger in* Le Corbusier 1910–60, *is extremely questionable.*

That is the difference. Any English or German architect lacking a patron would work for another architect. Not so Le Corbusier. That would have been too much like going back to his apprenticeship. He was now an artist, *tout court*, and if he couldn't build, well, he might carve or, as actually happened, paint.

If Le Corbusier had never been an architect—and it was a narrow shave—would he have been a great painter? Probably. From the lobby of the *Pavillon Suisse*, for which he painted a mural in 1932, to the big painted tapestries in the Courts of Justice at Chandigarh almost thirty years later, many of the walls within his buildings were made expressive, more effective, by the brush of the architect. The Library mural in the *Pavillon Suisse*, which he painted in 1940, has been compared to Picasso's 'Guernica'. As painters both Le Corbusier and Ozenfant—at least in the honeymoon period of the partnership—probably considered themselves as being post-Cubist.

Although a painter almost before he was an architect, Le Corbusier always saw his buildings primarily in technological terms, and of course three dimensionally. The aesthetic starting point of any building was the structure, from which the design grew. Neither the *Pavillon Suisse* in Paris nor the *Unité d'Habitation* building in Marseilles could ever have been conceived at all if the main theme, the great supporting pylons, had not, thanks to reinforced concrete, already been an economic and technical possibility. Le Corbusier, therefore, while always fascinated by new developments in structure, was directly concerned with them only if they were also a spur to an aesthetic inspiration and to the solution of a human or functional problem. So also in painting: it was pure forms—cylinders, cubes, spheres, etc.— the forms of what was then called 'machine art', that were his inspiration. The actual objects painted or depicted were always heavily played down, sometimes deliberately destroyed under strong chiaroscuro, colour or counter-pattern, and were themselves invariably quite plain objects such as bowls, fiddles or bottles, objects carefully chosen as lacking any romantic content. The real theme of the painting must always be a violent explosion of form and colour to which any literary image, any 'subject', must always be strictly subordinate. It is the explosion of form and colour that must strike the beholder; that is the life of the painting, the reason for its existence.

All this, of course, was really no more than what Picasso was doing already. It was Cubism. However, thought Le Corbusier, Cubism was not enough: Cubism was degenerating already, as *Art Nouveau* had done, into a merely decorative movement. Le Corbusier and Ozenfant issued a manifesto advocating a revival of a truly geometric Cubism. They called this 'Purism'; it might equally well have been called 'back to Picasso'. It was on the basis of this manifesto, in 1918, that they held a joint exhibition of their painting at the Gallery Thomas. This was a sensational exhibition. It was the real beginning of the short-lived but not unfruitful partnership. It also leaves one wondering whether Le Corbusier might not have been happier with the brush than with the T-square. As a painter he would have been spared many disappointments and frustrations. But of course it was not to be: in spite of all the bitterness, the urge to build—to set those great masses in the sunlight—was irrepressible. It was his destiny.

Cubism had a great influence upon Le Corbusier, not only as a painter but also as an architect. In Cubism there already existed that peculiar fourth dimension, that eternal unattained goal of painters and architects. In Cubist painting, in Picasso or Braque, this dimension is movement; the object or figure is conceived almost as if in motion, seen from different angles and, like some phantom of itself, in different places as it moves across the canvas. The equivalent fourth dimension in architecture is transparency. Glass on a large scale has, one must remember, ranked with concrete and steel as a revolutionary factor in modern building. One sees, or feels that one sees, through the building from one space to another, or into the building from outside; the whole thing is an affair of cube within cube, of related volumes. (This is something made possible, incidentally, by yet another technical advance—heating.) Every great modern architect, Mies van der Rohe even more than Le Corbusier, has used this 'transparency' theme in a big way. In a large building, as one glimpses space beyond space, the occupants and furniture and colours of, say, foyers or lobbies or staircases or galleries emphasize perspective and provide movement; they thereby define space and give life to a building. If Picasso and Braque painted the interpenetration of space by form, then it was Le Corbusier who built it. 'Façade' was now dead, a building was something that you saw through and moved through.

By 1923 Le Corbusier had decided that he was destined to be an architect. True, for the rest of his life he painted—it was his greatest resource during the German Occupation—and in his painting departed very little from his Cubist doctrine. Many of his buildings, as has been said, would be much poorer without his murals, but now the final decision was made—to be an architect —and he sealed it with the writing of *Vers une Architecture*. It is there that we find that famous definition already quoted: '*L'Architecture est le jeu savant, correct et magnifique des volumes assemblés sous la lumière*', together with the startling *aperçu*: 'Passion can create drama out of inert stone.' *Vers une Architecture* inevitably displayed such things as docks, silos and suspension bridges, as well as cars and liners, as being the real architecture or best design of our time—*l'esthétique de la vie moderne*; but it also made very clear the fact that 'passion' not 'functionalism'—not at least in the popular sense of that word —was the key to great design. This is important: thanks largely to that phrase—'a house is a machine for living in'—having been torn from its context, Le Corbusier is often thought of as the great prophet of 'functionalism' in the most arid sense. Nothing could be farther from the truth; he designed with humanity and with passion.

In architecture, as in painting, it is the basically simple volumes, such as the sphere, cylinder and cube, which the eye and mind can grasp instantly and which therefore are a first ingredient of beauty. Le Corbusier's definition suggests, almost, that Picasso had become an architect. All this in turn involved a relationship, a proportional relationship, between these geo-metric forms. Each form, each simple cube or cylinder, may be beautiful in itself, but each has to relate to the others; they can be seen only collectively. Only if there is some relationship between them can they become vivid to the eye and mind, and thus achieve unity. Le Corbusier's attempt to arrive at some rule or system in this matter—some harmonious progression with its analogy in music—whereby masses of different shape and size should be aesthetically related, involved him in one of the major enterprises of his career. That, however, was still in the future—the famous system which he called The Modulor. That system was not worked out in full detail until the time of the German Occupation, when it became a solace in dark hours. We shall see later, therefore, how he found himself going back to Vitruvius, to Leonardo, to Alberti and even to mediaeval systems of proportion. With none of these was he entirely happy, although to all of them he owed something. It was to be another thirty years before he was able to use his own Modulor system—progressive dimensions related to the human body and carried on a tape measure in the pocket—in the building first of *L'Unité d'Habitation* at Marseilles, and then in the pilgrim chapel at Ronchamp, the monastery at La Tourette and the city of Chandigarh.

Meanwhile the outstanding fact which emerged from *Vers une Architecture*—the book's proclamation as it were—was that this new architecture, this *esthétique de la vie moderne*, must be both an art born of romantic passion—passion for form and space—and at the same time an art of great mathematical precision. To a man who sees that 'God is a mathematician' some such combination is inevitable. As Bertrand Russell said, 'Mathematics possesses not only truth, but supreme beauty—a beauty cold and austere, like that of sculpture'.

That was not all. When Le Corbusier came upon the scene it might have been said that for a hundred years no city had been designed; a few 'civic centres' and other pieces of pompous futility, yes, but no city like Rome, Venice, Paris, Siena, Bath, Nancy, fit for men to live in. As a social thing, a setting for life, as well as an architectural thing, the time had come for the city to be born again; above all for the city to be brought back within the province of the architect. What use, after all, were a few good buildings if they had to be built in the streets of our ghastly or worn-out towns. It was to be another ten years before Le Corbusier would publish *La Ville Radieuse*, his second great written work; but by then his concept of the city already existed. By 1925 it had been seen in two projects. These were no more than plans on paper and models, but they were the start of an urban revolution which, in one form or another, is still with us. The first of these projects, the *Ville Contemporaine*, a 'City for Three Million Inhabitants', was shown at The Salon d'Automne in 1922; the second was shown in his *Pavillon de L'Esprit Nouveau* at the Paris Exhibition of Decorative Arts in 1925. This was the sensational *Plan Voisin* (1925), an admitted fantasy, for the rebuilding of a portion of Paris, which led to some very stupid accusations that Le Corbusier wished to destroy the city that he loved most in the world.

In these projects we can find the germs of at least two ideas to which Le Corbusier remained faithful throughout his life. They will, as we shall see, run like a golden thread through the tapestry of almost all that he did. The first of these ideas is to be found in *La Ville Contemporaine*, where he demonstrated that the traditional house, conceived as two or three layers of rooms all of the same height, each room a little box, was architectural nonsense. Logically, large rooms should be higher than small rooms, and modern construction had made that easy. This whole theme of varying room heights—hanging gardens, balconies looking down into living-rooms, living-rooms into gardens, and so on—ran through all Le Corbusier's earlier houses, and came into its own in the *Unité d'Habitation* at Marseilles only after the Second World War, when he achieved fifteen-feet-high living-rooms, each with its balcony, in artisans' flats.

The second concept contained within those early projects in town design, fifty years ago, was the theme of the tall building within the town; the Corbu concept that has left its mark, more than anything else he did, upon the world's cities, and has also been more misunderstood than anything else he did. The concept in itself is quite explicit. Le Corbusier's use of the tall building, and the only use he had for it, is the very opposite of the American use. In New York the skyscrapers are put as close to one another as the law permits—which is a lot closer than is humane or desirable—solely to exploit the Manhattan land values. With Le Corbusier, on the contrary, the tall building must at all costs be a liberating thing. To build high is, for him, to release land for other purposes: recreation, foliage, lakes, schools, crèches, theatres, restaurants, highways and so on. These things, taken together, constitute the 'carpet' from which Le Corbusier's buildings should rise like tall pencils above the trees, with light all round. That at least was the concept, already made clear in those projects of the early twenties. How often it was completely realized is quite another matter. The blocks he built at Marseilles and Nantes are complete in themselves, each a *Unité d'Habitation* with its shops, restaurant, etc., as well as its apartments. But one block does not make a *Ville Radieuse*. They were marvellous buildings in their own right, but were not a realization of the entire concept; at Marseilles, for instance, eight blocks were planned with all the adjuncts in the surrounding space. Porte Maillot, Algiers, St Dié and others were planned to have been true Le Corbusier cities. Not one was built.

At the International Exhibition of Decorative Arts in 1925, Le Corbusier's pavilion, *Le Pavillon de L'Esprit Nouveau*, caused

1   Pavillon de l'Esprit Nouveau,
Exhibition of Decorative Arts,
Paris. 1925

Villa Stein at Garches. 1927

2   north façade

3   south façade

7, 8, 9, 10   Pavillon Suisse, Paris. 1930–32

a sensation (Pl. 1). It was deceptively simple, a mere realization in concrete of one of the two-storey superimposed apartment blocks of *La Ville Contemporaine,* to show at least that the thing could be built. It was the first real manifestation of the cube within the cube, Cubism in building form, the hollow court with the two-storey apartment inside it, and a two-storey living-room within that; a network of geometric relationships within that. The *Pavillon de L'Esprit Nouveau* was then no more than a full-scale model of one such double-cube apartment, and yet this simple building must rank with Mies van der Rohe's German Pavilion at Barcelona (1929) as being one of the smaller seminal buildings of its time. It was small and economical, and yet in a flash it established a mode, almost a new architecture, certainly a new approach to architecture. It made clear that 'façade', in the old sense of a careful and two-dimensional arrangement of windows on a wall, was dead. For 'façade' in that sense there was now substituted a new three-dimensional architecture, an attempt, if no more, to design on the basis of an interpenetration of volumes, of solids and of voids.

If the result was shattering, the reaction was more so. Opposition and hostility were positively vitriolic. Le Corbusier had already been given the worst site in the Exhibition. A fence was now put round his building so that nobody could see it properly. This fortunately advertised the building far better than any of Le Corbusier's own strange staccato journalism. Moreover not everyone was as dense as the Exhibition authorities. In spite of the fence an international jury would have awarded Le Corbusier's Pavilion the first prize; unfortunately the French held a right of veto, and this was used by a French academician to disqualify the building on the grounds that 'it was not architecture'.

All this hostility may well have had another cause. The nominal theme of the whole Exhibition was that of the Decorative Arts. The wider consequences of this were manifested in the modish but mercifully short-lived *Art-deco,* mainly an affair of peach-coloured glass sand-blasted with pseudo-cubist designs, with touches of futurism, of gold-backed murals and tapestry panels. This was limited mainly to Paris, the Riviera and Mayfair restaurants. Le Corbusier's whole object was to reject all such decorative art as something separate, as something 'applied' to architecture, and through his design to affirm that architecture itself extends from the smallest furnishing to the house, to the street, to the city and beyond; to what now, fifty years later, is called 'total environment'. In this total environment the house was the practical and habitable unit, as functional as it was beautiful, and at least as carefully considered and meticulously designed as the automobile or the car—'a machine for living in'—which was the occasion of that notorious phrase which has been thrown in Le Corbusier's face ever since.

There must, however, have been a few people who knew what he was getting at. Between 1922 and 1930 Le Corbusier actually acquired patrons and was, at long last, putting up buildings, if mainly rather modest houses. He was thirty-eight, and it was high time to build. He was now established in the Rue de Sèvres, in that white and tranquil studio that was once a cloister, well hidden behind the houses of the busy street. It was here, with an absolute minimum of the paraphernalia of the modern office, that he worked for the rest of his life, with assistants drawn from half the countries of the world.

Among the smaller houses built or designed at that time were three—all, as it happens, in 1922. The project for the so-called Citrohan House demonstrates in simple form a number of themes that actually recur through all Le Corbusier's work. The Citrohan House was, first of all, raised up on columns or *piloti*. It was a simple cube but contained the basic idea of the 'two to one' internal space, i.e. a living-room of double height with a correspondingly high window. It has a roof-garden, virtually a two-storey garden terrace. The whole thing was apparently very simple—certainly in its basic form, the model of which could be made from half-a-dozen bits of cardboard—but was in fact an extremely sophisticated piece of work. One has the feeling that the Citrohan House could equally well be a 'living-unit' in a city, an apartment extracted, as it were, from an apartment block. Almost every feature, highly developed, is still recognizable thirty years later in the *Unité d'Habitation* at Marseilles. The work of most successful architects, at any rate during the last hundred years, has consisted of a series of separate and detached 'masterpieces', each a stylistic essay, either more or less good, but with no underlying theme or architectural philosophy. Le Corbusier's career is highly consistent, a continuous development through forty years of a number of architectural features, each in accordance with a philosophy of life. That, whether one a cepts the philosophy or not, is a fact.

The studio in the house in Paris which Le Corbusier built for Ozenfant, while the *L'Esprit Nouveau* partnership was still flourishing, is a very simple but impressive arrangement of levels, of light, of voids and of solid geometry; above all, with a great feeling of space and coolness. Cool rather than cosy; but then this was a studio, not a study.

The Maison La Roche was one of a pair of houses, one for M. Raoul La Roche and one for the architect's brother, Albert Jeanneret. The two houses had to be fitted together on a very 'tight' urban site in Paris. Vastly different though it may be, one cannot but recall Peruzzi's famous Palazzo Massimi in Rome (1515), where a similar problem had to be solved. The ingenuity with which the two houses are fitted together caused Le Corbusier to describe his plan as 'belaboured'. Nevertheless it really is ingenious, and a tall double-height hall with a big window and a spacious gallery-landing combine to make a fine setting for the famous La Roche collection of Cubist paintings.

In 1925 Le Corbusier built a modest but very charming little villa for his mother. Traditional Swiss furniture, textiles and pottery look astonishingly well in their modern setting, and the house is unassumingly arranged—low and long—on the shores of Lac Léman. When it was finished the Municipality said that 'this house is a crime against nature; it must never happen again'.[12]

To summarize the work of the years that followed—his first really serious commissions, although still almost wholly domestic —is to list a series of houses not perhaps very important in themselves, at any rate not shattering, but all of which incorporated structural and aesthetic features which were fundamental, and which were to become part of the language of modern architecture. Le Corbusier tabulated these features, rather grandiloquently as it must have seemed at the time, as 'The Five Points of a New Architecture'.[13] They are further summarized here:

1. The Columns: ... the house on columns! The house used to be sunk in the ground: dark and often damp rooms. Reinforced concrete offers us the columns. The house is now in the air, above the ground; the garden passes under the house, the garden is also the house, on the roof.

2. The roof-garden: For centuries the traditional roof-top has usually supported the winter layer of snow, while the

house has been heated with stoves. From the moment central heating is installed, the traditional roof-top is no longer necessary. The roof should no longer be convex but should be concave, with the rainwater flowing towards the interior rather than towards the exterior. A truth allowing of no exceptions: cold climates demand the suppression of the sloping roof-top, and demand concave roof-terraces with water draining towards the interior of the house. Reinforced concrete is the means for realizing such a homogeneous roof. Reinforced concrete undergoes much expansion and contraction. This can cause cracks in the structure. Instead of trying to drain the rainwater away quickly, one should maintain a constant humidity for the concrete of the roof-terrace, and thereby assure a regulated temperature for the concrete. An especially good protection is sand covered by thick cement slabs laid with staggered joints, the joints being seeded with grass. The sand and roots allow a slow filtration of the water. The garden terraces become rich with flowers, shrubs, trees and grass. Thus we are led to build roof-terraces for technical reasons, for economic reasons, as well as for comfort and beauty.

3. The free plan: Until now load-bearing walls have risen right up from the basement, upon which they are superimposed, right up to the roof. The plan has been a slave of these load-bearing walls. Reinforced concrete in the house brings about the free-plan! The floors no longer superimpose rooms of the same size one above the other. They are free. A great economy of constructed volume follows, also a rigorous use of every inch. A great economy. The easy rationalization of the new free plan.

4. The long window: The window is one of the essentials of the house. Progress has brought about a liberation. Reinforced concrete has brought about a revolution in the history of the window. Windows can now run from one edge of the façade to the other. The window is the repetitive element of the house: for all our town houses, all our villas, all our workers' houses, all our apartment houses.

5. The free façade: The columns are now set back from the façades, while the floor extends outwards as a cantilever. The façades are now only light membranes of insulating or

window elements. The façade is free; the windows, without being interrupted, can run from one edge of the façade to the other (Pl. 4).

These, then, were the 'five points' which, with journalistic emphasis, Le Corbusier suggested as being the basis of his new architecture. True, they were all incorporated, in some form or other, in the houses which he built during the twenties. There were, however, additional (and perhaps more important) elements in building which he achieved as an architect, but which, as a journalist, he may have found impossible to communicate: the nature of light, proportion, space, variation in heights, and that marriage of geometric volumes and transparency which he had derived from the Cubists, and so on. Moreover one must remember that although Le Corbusier's 'five points' have long since become part and parcel of modern architecture—and been debased a thousand times in the process—they were not, to start with, fully understood even by his *avant garde* disciples. Handled by other poeple they can still be seen, terribly dated, in all the suburbs.

If the medium-sized, suburban family dwelling is an acid test of architecture, then the Cook House, built at Boulogne-sur-Seine in 1926, is a modest triumph. It has a frontage to the road of only twenty-five feet. Le Corbusier's 'five points' are all there. By traditional standards this is an 'upside-down' house. The ground-floor is almost entirely open to the garden—a kind of undercroft—and contains only a car-port and a small entrance-hall giving access to the stairs; for the rest, around the *piloti* which support the upper floors, this area is paved and planted—in effect a kind of loggia. The first floor contains the bedrooms. The second floor, virtually the top, is the living-room, with its wide views of the Bois de Boulogne and in itself a justification for the whole design. Almost half this living area breaks up, as it were, through the flat roof terrace to form a room of double height; only the dining area and the kitchen being of single-room height. The windows form a continuous band right across the façade.

Within the Cook House, therefore, the *piloti* or columns, the flat roof and the long windows, are not merely incorporated as novel architectural features in an otherwise ordinary house;

they are basic to the design and arise from its structure. Also to be noted is the first floor—divided into bedrooms and bathrooms —where Le Corbusier has made full play with the curving and free handling of these partitions. Glorying, perhaps overmuch, in the fact that these partitions are independent of the *piloti* and that load-bearing walls are non-existent, Le Corbusier plays all manner of tricks with them. He lets the *piloti* stand free. He curves the partitions as the whim takes him; sometimes it follows the curve of a grand-piano, or the form of a lozenge-shaped bath, and so on. Here once again, in the Cook House, is a whole series of themes which, in various forms, were to run through the whole life-work of Le Corbusier. One also remembers how, in those days, the curved partition so often crept timidly into the design of otherwise commonplace houses.

When Le Corbusier built the *Pavillon de L'Esprit Nouveau* in 1925 his French confrères, as has been said, saw to it that he should be given the worst site in the Exhibition. In 1927, in the housing section or 'colony' of the Weissenhof Exhibition at Stuttgart, a young architect, Mies van der Rohe, was in charge; with memories of the Hoffmann studio in Vienna twenty years earlier, he invited Le Corbusier to choose his own site. 'Naturally,' said Mies, 'he chose the best.'

On that site Le Corbusier now built the famous Weissenhof houses. He was working from the Rue de Sèvres; his cousin, Pierre Jeanneret, assisted him, together with those innumerable young men who were now flocking to the studio from all over the world.* The Weissenhof houses were launched with a kind of manifesto written in Le Corbusier's emphatic journalistic style: 'This is by no means an aesthetic fantasy or a search for fashionable effects; we are dealing with architectural facts which call for an absolutely new way of building.' As so often, and with some reason, he was meeting criticism in advance. In that manifesto he also tabulated his 'five points': *piloti*, roof-garden, free plan, long windows and free façade. One should really add a sixth, in fact a very important one: internal variation in height. One should also emphasize again that these points, all six of

---

* *Pierre Jeanneret had a kind of working partnership with his cousin until 1940, and then again at Chandigarh in 1950. As for the young men in the studio, it must be admitted that 'the master' exploited them disgracefully on the grounds that to be able to say 'I once worked for Corbu' would be a lifelong asset.*

them, derive from structure, made possible through the application of reinforced concrete to domestic architecture and 'by no means an aesthetic fantasy'. In the two houses of the Weissenhof Exhibition this architectural *credo* was, therefore, both accentuated and committed to a formal statement in terms of real building. Those two houses still stand outside Stuttgart; Hitler condemned them as 'manifestations of Bolshevism'.[14] In 1958, having somehow escaped, they were scheduled as 'historic monuments' and Le Corbusier, whatever he might usually think of Establishment decisions, was duly delighted.

The smaller of the two Weissenhof houses was a very finely proportioned white cube set on *piloti*. The living-room, as in the Cook House, was on the top floor with the more important part taken up to double height. Considering its date—some thirty years before Mies van der Rohe's famous Farnsworth House—the glass box—outside Chicago—this Weissenhof House has a very large area of glass. These big windows were a very positive functional part of the house, a contribution to its beauty and to its general happiness. Aesthetically and externally they were also a foil to smaller apertures. One can no longer really speak of 'windows'. One area of the wall is opaque, another area is transparent; that is all. The whole thing is an elegant Cubist essay, voids and solids carefully composed to create a tranquil unity.

The second of the two Weissenhof houses was really a slice of a town: two houses which could be multiplied indefinitely to form a whole terrace of housing. When viewed externally the building appears to be a three-storey structure, but in actual fact has only one living area. This living area is sandwiched between the 'undercroft'—i.e. the car-port, servants' rooms, etc., planned between the *piloti*—and the roof-garden which, being partly covered and enclosed, appears when seen from outside to be a third storey. It is fully justified by its splendid views over Stuttgart. The whole of the middle storey, the big living area, has mobile partitions and can be thrown into one, only the kitchen and bathroom being permanently enclosed. For the rest, this large single living area can be divided, when required, into bedrooms by means of the mobile partitions. These partitions, together with the beds and wardrobes, vanish during the day; an ingenious piece of planning, and moreover the sort of thing that no one had thought of at that date. Practicality apart, these fitted wardrobes and sliding beds—things that have since become so commonplace—are still regarded in this house as connoisseur's examples of modern furniture design. At night the bedrooms are approached by a very narrow corridor. This gave rise to violent criticism; Le Corbusier's defence was that the corridor was the same width as that of an international sleeping-car. Perhaps he just forgot that one does not live permanently in a sleeping-car. Illness and children's bedtime were also forgotten; to partition off bedroom space for either of these would subtract a large area from the living-room. These are severe criticisms. Nevertheless the whole thing disarms criticism because it is so beautifully designed, and because the whole concept was an attempt—perhaps admittedly experimental—to take farther the idea already inherent in the curved partitions of the Cook House and in the other Weissenhof House—to achieve a maximum of flexibility. The design actually went beyond the 'free plan' as we know it today; it was a brilliant *tour-de-force* appropriate to an exhibition house or as a stimulus to thought, not perhaps part of a genuine architectural revolution.

In 1927 also came the Villa Stein at Garches (Pls. 2, 3). Le Corbusier had a wonderful patron in Gertrude Stein's brother, the man who had built the San Francisco street-car system and had been the first to buy a Matisse painting. The Villa Stein was described by the architect as showing 'the modern aesthetic at its sparkling best'. That, at the time, was possibly true. At any rate the house at Garches has always, in more ways than one, been regarded as a kind of landmark in Le Corbusier's career. It was based throughout, for instance, upon a system of proportions. This system was not yet Le Corbusier's famous *Modulor*, it was the application of the well-known 'Golden Section' to the façade; but it was the beginning of the idea that some such system there must be in order to create a unified and harmonious whole. The villa at Garches not only incorporated the 'five points', already used in the Weissenhof houses, but also developed them aesthetically. There were also such things as the elegant and sculptural stair, a kind of three-dimensional poem, standing clear of the house and seeming, somehow, to be almost part of a great liner. This, even from a practical point of view, was a vast improvement upon the narrow and rather dark stair which, as at Stuttgart and the Cook House, had led up from the 'undercroft' to the main first floor living level. The external stair, moreover, was not only a delightful thing in itself, it could be so placed that one now entered the house at an appropriate point in the plan. Hitherto it has needed careful and even tortuous planning to avoid bringing up the staircase on the first floor right into the living-room, or at least where it was not wanted.

The structure of the Villa Stein at Garches was also further refined. It was not only a hollow cube lifted up on *piloti*. The *piloti* themselves are now planned on a grid 15 ft 3 in. by 7 ft 8 in. without regard to the planning of the floor above. If these *piloti* were collected together as it were into a tight bundle they would form a single pier 3 ft 4 in. by 2 ft 5 in. supporting the whole house, like an open hand carrying a loaded tray. This pregnant fact—and the *Pavillon Suisse* (1932) was indeed carried on a single central line of gargantuan *piloti* as opposed to a lot of columns—so appealed to Le Corbusier that he actually wanted to decorate the hall of the Villa Stein with a mosaic of just that size. His patron declined, preferring not to know how delicately poised above the earth was his whole house: 'I want to sleep at night.'[15] The other notable and even seminal thing about Garches is the arrangement of all the windows on the two long walls, keeping the end walls quite blank; a theme which was to run through Le Corbusier's work almost to the end of his life, almost as if he felt that every building—or at any rate every house and apartment block—was some kind of experiment for a unit intended to be part of a city. The great towns that Le Corbusier never built were never far from his mind. At Garches, moreover, we see the whole Le Corbusier vocabulary waiting, as it were, to be deployed on a larger scale and in a bigger world.

By 1931 Le Corbusier had completed the Villa Savoie (Pls. 5, 6). It stands on the hills above Poissy, overlooking the valley of the Seine. This house, for nearly thirty years now, has been a rather tragic ruin, crumbling and derelict. Madame Savoie has banned all sightseers, perhaps merely because she does not want them to see the accumulated junk, the peeling paint and the boarded-up windows—for that is the state of the house since the German and American occupation. The gates are fastened with barbed wire. Only occasionally, perhaps, when there is a glimpse of sunlight and the imagination is at work, can one sense the lost beauty of the Villa Savoie, a pristine beauty too delicate to triumph over the present squalor. All this is perhaps a good thing. So uncompromising a piece of modern elegance should be seen new, furnished and in use, or not at all. It was not until after the war that M. André Malraux, in response to hundreds of telegrams, saved the house from complete demolition. It still awaits restoration and habitation.

Seen among the meadows and orchards of Poissy, the Villa Savoie was always a very pure white box. The purity and simplicity, however, like the purity and simplicity of a Greek temple in fields of asphodel, concealed great elaboration. Basically this house may be one of the series we have already examined, all built in the twenties and all incorporating the 'five points' of the Weissenhof manifesto; but it was certainly large and more luxurious than the others, and architecturally more sophisticated. Although the Villa Savoie seems to be, and is, the culmination of this series of houses—and nothing Corbu ever designed but was part of a series, in some ways a lifelong series— it is also said to be based upon an earlier and unrealized project for the Villa Meyer, near Paris, now known to us only through a beautiful set of drawings.

Basically the plan and structure are as we would expect. There are three levels: first, at ground level is the usual 'undercroft' planned around the *piloti*; second, the main living-area lifted up by the *piloti* to what one might call foliage level; and third, the roof-garden with its solarium.

The whole house is supported upon some twenty-six very slender columns—the *piloti*. The slenderness of these supports and the mass of the house above is, of course, a deliberate piece of piquancy. Among the *piloti* Le Corbusier had fitted in at ground level a variety of useful accommodation: at least four servants' rooms, a garage for four cars, other store rooms, and so on. In addition we here find ourselves at the foot of a charmingly sculptural stair, as well as a ramp giving access to the main floor above. This main floor was, at the time when it was built, the most elaborate thing that Le Corbusier had done. The windows, each a single sheet of glass in an incredibly thin steel frame, takes us almost into the Miesian age of American architecture, the United States in the fifties, the era of the Farnsworth House. At the Villa Savoie the living-room itself was a splendid room, over forty feet long, with one whole side looking out over the valley, while part of another side opened onto a spacious terrace contained, as it were, within the cube of the house. This terrace is at living-room level, one floor up, but as one looks down upon it from the roof garden it seems to be more like a courtyard surrounded by the main rooms of the house. It is this realization of the vista as being a vertical as well as a horizontal thing that is here so important: important to look down upon as well as through. For the rest, the main floor, with its big living-room, games room, four bedrooms, three bathrooms and large kitchen, is unusually large and spacious and light. No sleeping-car corridors here! At this level the house is entirely surrounded by a long sliding window band, a Corbusier-Jeanneret patent.

The ruinous state of the Villa Savoie is not due entirely to war. It must be admitted—and it is important—that Le Corbusier's contemporaries such as Frank Lloyd Wright in America or Edwin Lutyens in England were traditionalist and romantic; they worked almost always with what they would call 'natural' materials—granite, pine, handmade bricks, stone and oak. These men, according to their lights, understood their craft; their buildings have weathered well and gained in beauty with the passage of time. Not so with Le Corbusier. He was obviously an urban and sophisticated creature if ever there was one, as sophisticated as, say, Proust in literature. He tended, at least in his earlier work, to see architecture not only as part of an intellectual movement, part of the *avant garde* world, but also as a thing of its own time: one must take every advantage of modern science, one must build in the materials and according to the technology of one's own day. Wright and Lutyens were the dead-end kids of architecture. This use, always, of the latest materials or techniques had its dangers. Le Corbusier's clients were more liable than those of most architects to be the subject of an experiment. To the Villa Savoie, and also to the Villa Stein, he gave an exterior of smooth stucco and of glass, an appropriate and extremely elegant finish for a building of the Machine Age and for any product of *L'Esprit Nouveau*. It looked marvellous when it was new and fresh and pristine. Alas, very quickly the cracks began to appear and the surface to be streaked with rain.

This state of affairs was, in its earlier years, destined to be the curse of the modern movement, especially in the northern climates, and was a gift to the movement's critics. It was in

England that Berchtold Lubetkin, building a film laboratory at Denham, first used metal filings in the aggregate of his concrete. Le Corbusier, on the other hand, gradually admitted defeat and after the Second World War, as at Marseilles for instance, his buildings were left with the rough natural surface of the concrete, untouched and as it emerged from the shuttering. This would have hardly done for these lush and expensive villas, but in the larger work of Le Corbusier's later years—Marseilles, Ronchamp, Chandigarh, etc.—it was extremely effective. He had made a great virtue out of a necessity.

The total form of the building itself also tends in the later work to be as it were a crystal rather than a cube, designed not as an essay in smooth solid geometry, but in depth: recessed balconies and so on—an actual avoidance of very large unbroken areas. The pure, smooth forms of the Villa Savoie or the Villa Stein, seen against a blue sky, were, for the generation who knew them, a dream of beauty; but clearly such smooth perfection would have been more possible, more practical, in, say, Pentelic marble than in Parisian cement.

In 1935, however, Le Corbusier did make one foray, if only on a small scale, into natural materials. This was an entire house built with walls of stone rubble, as rough as possible. He had already used rubble, as in the *Pavillon Suisse*, but only as a decorative thing in a non-structural wall. In 1935, at Mathes, he used it structurally, he built with it. Madame de Mandrot de la Sarraz had been a good friend to modern architecture, helping Le Corbusier, together with a group of men such as Siegfried Gideon and Maxwell Fry, in 1928, to found the *Congrès International d'Architecture Moderne*, the famous CIAM of so many international gatherings around the world. For the first meeting she offered the hospitality of her château at Sarraz. Then, a few years later, she commissioned Le Corbusier to design this little house at Mathes, a charming, simple cottage on the dunes. It had to be built so economically that it was not possible even for the architect to visit the site. However, he supplied an honest village builder with every detail drawn to a large scale, and then let the man get on with it, building it in rubble, a material he understood. It was a little house which, as the architect said, is without fault. This was the nearest thing that Le Corbusier ever came to designing in the vernacular; a vernacular design for a vernacular material. Rubble was as logical in Mathes as reinforced concrete in Paris. Working with a village builder he used the man's own material and own methods.

It was at this stage of his career that Le Corbusier produced some very beautiful furniture. It was surprising that he had not done so sooner. To the end of his days he naturally insisted that the 'total environment'—furniture, building, town—must be a single entity. He had learnt this almost twenty years earlier in Berlin from Peter Behrens, who, as will be remembered, was imposing a unity of design upon all the products of A.E.G. Le Corbusier proclaimed that doctrine again and again. It was implicit in all his projects for ideal towns; it was explicit in the Exhibition of Decorative Arts in 1925 when, in his own *Pavillon de l'Esprit Nouveau*, he refused to separate architecture from the other arts. His Pavilion was not a place for displaying objects; the Pavilion and everything in it was a single thing, to be seen as a whole.

In 1928 Le Corbusier was remodelling an old house at Ville-d'Avray, and was there able to design his first chairs, tables and shelving. This was just before the great influx of furniture, ceramics and textiles from the Scandinavian countries with their long craft traditions; before the big influx of such things as Finmar furniture and Orrefors glass. It was also before the 'discovery' of the anthropometric chair, the design of a chair in accordance with precise anatomical shapes and dimensions, the logical conclusion of functionalism.

Le Corbusier's chairs at Ville-d'Avray were therefore almost without precedent apart from Marcel Breuer's work at the Bauhaus, to which Le Corbusier always acknowledged his debt. The three main types of Ville-d'Avray chair were: one for reclining, one for normal reading, conversation, etc., and one heavily upholstered. Each chair was framed in tubular steel, either chromium or coloured, and upholstered in leather.

The chairs themselves were almost sensationally novel although tubular steel in itself was not, of course, an innovation. Marcel Breuer who, more than anyone else in the world, had excelled in the design of modern furniture under Bauhaus inspiration, had already designed steel-framed chairs, and Thonet had manufactured them. Breuer's chairs, in accordance with German theories of functionalism, were very practical in use—almost anthropometric—as well as being easy to make, as were most Bauhaus products. They were also good to look at. Le Corbusier's chairs were a little less functional, a little less easy to make, but so far from being merely good to look at, they were quite ravishingly beautiful.

The most beautiful of all was, for some unknown reason, called the 'British officer's chair'. This is slightly funny. The chair is not in the least like a Frenchman's idea of a chair in a London club; and surely the last person in the world to use a Corbu chair, to live in a Corbu house, or even to have heard of Corbu, is a British officer!

Such eminent architects as Eero Saarinen, working for General Motors, Mies van der Rohe, whenever he was given a chance to design the furniture of his buildings, and even some Danish designers such as Arne Jacobsen, have followed Le Corbusier's lead. The last is all the more surprising in view of Denmark's own high standing in the world of furniture design. Younger men, as one would expect, have also followed Le Corbusier's lead—there are thousands of pseudo-Corbu chairs in the world— but have not really improved upon the original. Le Corbusier's chairs and tables, as well as much of his fitted furniture, some of which he had made in Sweden, have fixed a standard by which other men's work is now judged.

The essence of his furniture was the clear distinction between materials performing different functions. That at least is the logic one would expect from an architect. The most obvious example is the distinction between, say, the metal tubes which carry weight, and the upholstery which is to be sat upon. The English club chair is, absurdly enough, leather all the way. In Le Corbusier's chairs, however, the differentiation is not only there, it is often the essence, almost the starting point, of the design. For example, in one of his table designs, a tubular metal frame supports a marble top; in fact the marble rests, almost floats, on tiny steel pins on top of the frame. The supporting frame and the marble top are, almost literally, separated from each other; they barely touch. Their separate function is turned into physical separation and thereby becomes also a visual delight.

One thing is certain: if modern architecture is part of an architectural revolution, then furniture, an extension of the building, must also be part of that revolution. You cannot reasonably—except as a kind of foil to the design or as a kind of exhibit—put the old sort of furniture into the new architecture. Another thing is certain: so far as modern architecture is concerned, the architects, not least Le Corbusier, have proved better designers than the cabinet makers; they know the principles upon which their buildings rest, and that the furniture must do likewise. This is really good, suggesting that once again, as in the historic epochs, furniture and architecture are one thing. This becomes more and more obvious as Le Corbusier's career moves on. The kitchen and wardrobe fittings of a great apartment block such as Marseilles must surely be the province of the architect, while later still, as in the Chandigarh Courts of Justice or the La Tourette Refectory, it is clear that only Le Corbusier could have been allowed to design the furniture. In the sublime altars of Ronchamp or the church at La Tourette all distinction between the two arts has vanished.

Three

the master
builder

'The defeats of these past years
represent so many victories . . .
the day will come when these
plans will force a change.'
Le Corbusier

Prior to 1930 Le Corbusier had studied a good deal, travelled a
good deal, written much and painted much. He had also, as we
have seen, designed some excellent furniture and built half a
dozen houses. These houses are of the greatest significance, if
only as landmarks in the development of Le Corbusier's architectural philosophy and vocabulary. On their own merits they
have also passed into history. The Villa Savoie was a rich man's
house, but when all is said and done, these houses were really
rather modest affairs, mainly suburban. The time had now come,
however, after the years of apprenticeship and the years of experiment, for Le Corbusier to build and, moreover, to build big. The
decade prior to the outbreak of the Second World War is filled
with opportunities and filled with disappointments. That decade
offers us a list of some of Le Corbusier's greatest projects, most
of them ill-starred. In 1927–8 we have the plans for the League
of Nations Building at Geneva; in 1929–33, the Centrosoyus
Building in Moscow; in 1931, the Palace of the Soviets in
Moscow; in 1932–3, the *Cité de Refuge* (Salvation Army Building)
in Paris; in 1930–2, the *Pavillon Suisse* in the Cité Universitaire
in Paris; in 1933, the Rentenanstalt Building in Zürich and an
apartment house in Algiers; in 1938, the Cartesian Skyscraper;
in 1938–42, the Skyscraper in the Quartier-de-la-Marine in Algiers;
in 1936–45, the Ministry of Education and of Public Health in
Rio de Janeiro.

Some of these splendid and highly original large-scale projects

L'Unité d'Habitation, Marseilles.

L'Unité d'Habitation, Marseilles.
15 The restaurant terrace

16 The big *piloti* which carry the
entire weight of the building

L'Unité d'Habitation, Marseilles.
17 The 'roofscape'

18, 19 Carpenter Center for Visual
        Arts: Harvard University.
        The ramped approach to
        lecture hall and studio block

Carpenter Center for Visual Arts: Harvard University.
20 The lecture hall and studio windows

21 A studio or workshop

remained, alas, only as projects, designs that never left the drawing-board. The Centrosoyus Building in Moscow, the Salvation Army Building and the *Pavillon Suisse*, both in Paris, and the Ministry of Education Building in Rio were the only ones actually built; and they were spread over a good many years. Every project, however, left behind it, if only on paper, some revolutionary idea, some significant piece of design, some brilliant handling of a difficult site, or at least some creative spark from a romantic and innovating mind. Eero Saarinen, Walter Gropius, Mies van der Rohe, Oscar Niemeyer, Denys Lasdun, Jane Drew and Maxwell Fry have all paid tribute, during those years, to this 'giver of form'.

Le Corbusier, perhaps more than any other artist who ever lived, paid the price of original thought. He paid that price in terms of disappointment and frustration. He tried to be philosophical about the inevitable status of the pioneer, saying that disappointments were inevitable; but it was undoubtedly this decade that, for all his occasional gaiety and perpetual buoyancy, left him an embittered man, a man not easy to know or to work with. If we have a finer sort of architecture here and there in the world—not much of it—than we had fifty years ago, then it is mainly due to Le Corbusier. Indubitably it would be finer still, intrinsically and in fact, if his League of Nations Building at Geneva and his Palace of the Soviets had been built. The latter particularly might have been one of the great buildings of this century; its rejection remains a symbol of the collapse of Soviet culture.

In 1927 an architectural competition was held for the League of Nations Building. Eight miles of plans were submitted by 377 architects. The competition was doomed from the start, doomed by sheer protocol. If St Peter's in Rome suffered from being built by fourteen architects, the League of Nations competition suffered from having six assessors from six countries. H. P. Berlage from Holland was a 'safe' modernist in nice Dutch brick; Josef Hoffmann from Vienna had already had Le Corbusier in his studio, Le Corbusier ultimately fleeing from Hoffmann's *Art Nouveau* 'doilies'; Karl Moser from Switzerland was an exponent of that odd school of design (seen at its worst in Britain's Wembley Exhibition of 1924) which inexplicably thinks of modern architecture as a thing of mass, power and weight, whereas its glory is its potentiality for lightness and delicacy; Victor Horta from Belgium was the most extreme *Art Nouveau* architect of the century, his Brussels apartment houses being well covered with swirling, swooning lines; M. Lemaresquier of France was a dyed-in-the-wool École des Beaux Arts traditionalist and savant, while John Burnet of Britain was the architect of Selfridges. What on earth the Secretariat of the League expected or hoped to get out of that lot, Heaven alone knows. In fact, the Secretariat got what it deserved.

The composition of that jury would seem to be the perfect recipe for indecision, if not for violent disagreement or, worse still, hopeless compromise. It was, needless to say, M. Lemaresquier who made history by demanding that Le Corbusier's scheme should be instantly disqualified as having been drawn in Indian instead of Chinese ink and thereby having broken one of the rules of the competition. At one moment, however, there would seem to have been a chance that Berlage, Hoffmann and Moser would vote for Le Corbusier. The decisive vote would have been Horta's, but after innumerable sessions of the jury he cast it with the two traditionalists, the Frenchman and the Englishman. The result, therefore, was a tie, and although nine prizes were awarded, including one to Le Corbusier, the League of Nations was still left looking for a building and an architect.

For two years there was agitation, propaganda, lobbying and general bitterness, all in a setting of high comedy compounded of architectural ignorance and general confusion of thought. *Le Figaro*, for instance, had a series of articles by Camille Mauclair, culminating in 1933 in Mauclair's book, *L'Architecture, va-t-elle mourir?* Le Corbusier's reply is historic: 'It is far from dying— it is just being born!'

The League, through its politicians and not through its professional advisers, now chose four traditionalists from among the nine prize winners, and knocked their heads together in the hope of getting them to agree between themselves upon a single design for a building upon what was now, after two years, a different site. The result was surprising. The League of Nations Building was utterly inadequate from the day it was built; nor was that remarkable. What was unexpected was that the new design managed to be both vaguely neo-classical but also 'modernistic', not of course technically modern or revolutionary in plan, but nevertheless what many people would call 'modern in its outward 'style'. Did the designers fear lest the League, when faced by a totally reactionary design, might turn back after all to Le Corbusier? There is evidence that this was so. Anyway, Le Corbusier and Pierre Jeanneret, the original design having been submitted in their joint names, now sued the League of Nations on the grounds that their plans had been pirated.

All this, of course, came to nothing. The League 'could not deal with private persons'. The only lesson to be learnt from the whole sad story is an architectural one. One may compare Le Corbusier's design with the other prize-winning schemes or with the League of Nations Building still surviving at Geneva. The lesson is that what is desirable according to protocol, what is correct, diplomatic, tactful, respectable or hallowed by time, has nothing whatever to do with great art.

Le Corbusier's League of Nations Building would have been open, free, asymmetrical but beautifully balanced, with fine vistas down avenues or across spacious foyers. It would have been full of glimpses of foliage or water, and full of light. The large auditorium for 2,600, properly designed both visually and acoustically, would have stood almost clear of the other buildings, such as the secretariat and the library. Clarity was all, and the whole thing, although actually very complex, would have had unity, and would have been easy to find one's way in, to work in. It would have been perfectly related to the road and to the shore of the lake. It would have been both practical and romantic. It would have had great dignity, a quality having nothing to do with either respectability or pomp.

The other schemes, almost without exception, would have been congested, urban and conventional—mainly with inner courtyards, when in fact every room could have been made to look over the lake or the mountains—and their façades surmounted by masses of classical or monumental architecture. Such designs might once have looked appropriate had they been used, say, to close the axis at the end of one of Baron Haussmann's boulevards, but hardly by a Swiss lake. They would also have been extremely expensive and not at all practical. The name of the architect of the League of Nations Building is fortunately, like the League itself, almost forgotten. Le Corbusier's plans were purchased, as a work of art, by the University of

Zürich where they may be seen, and where they will be preserved in perpetuity.

The fiasco of the League of Nations Building—the fiasco of what was built as well as the fiasco of what was not built—was not quite a dead loss. It did not quite put modern architecture on the map; it put the *issue* of modern architecture on the map. To people generally it probably made clear that architecture was not just an *avant garde* movement, not just an ephemeral fashion as *Art Nouveau* had been, but rather a most significant element in twentieth-century culture or, as Le Corbusier himself put it: 'Architecture is not an ostrich feather stuck with or without grace in a hat by the diligence of a modiste. Architecture is the spirit of truth.' There were still battles to be fought before such an architecture could be universally accepted as our generation's way of building, but after the League of Nations fiasco things were never quite the same again. For one thing, the rejection of Le Corbusier's plans—not least the shabby manner of their rejection—led to the formation of CIAM (*Congrès International d'Architecture Moderne*), which has already been mentioned. This was a banding together of architects of all countries, both to protect and to inform each other, to influence architecture through their work and through the schools—CIAM always had strong support from students, if necessary in defiance of their instructors—and to keep before the public the basic principles of architectural integrity in both structure and design. For over thirty years CIAM was an invaluable organization. Its annual conferences, its propaganda, its exhibitions and—even during the war and in collaboration with Le Corbusier in the Pyrenees— its research work, all helped to win the battle. Throughout those thirty years the central figure of CIAM was Le Corbusier, and it was in CIAM meetings, among his colleagues, that both his arrogance and his bitterness vanished. One of CIAM's best gatherings was held on the roof of Le Corbusier's *L'Unité d'Habitation* at Marseilles, the occasion when Walter Gropius, looking around him, said: 'Any architect who does not find this building beautiful had better lay down his pencil.' But CIAM was neither a mutual admiration society nor a Le Corbusier Society. In such things as the *Charte d'Athène* and the *Charte d'Habitat* it did much hard and fruitful work into housing standards and matters of that kind. When, after thirty years, it saw that the battle for modern architecture had been won, that

54

modern architecture was not yet good but that it was accepted everywhere as the way to build, then CIAM had the wisdom to disband itself rather than to become a club for elderly men. Something like CIAM had been bound to occur in those years; as it happened the tragedy of Le Corbusier's plans for the League of Nations Building was the start of it all.

Among the large-scale pre-war projects which Le Corbusier did actually build was the Centrosoyus (Co-operative) Building in Moscow. Work on this big scheme went on all through 1928. In 1929 these plans were sent to Moscow where a complete schedule of building operations had already been prepared. It was, however, the epoch of the First Five-Year Plan and there was some delay owing to a shortage of building materials.

The programme for the Centrosoyus Building was for modern offices for 3,500 workers with, in addition, restaurant, club, theatre, gymnasium, small lecture halls and one very large auditorium or assembly hall. All these very diverse elements were linked together through the vast foyer by a system of sweeping ramps. The perspective and the vistas across the foyer, between the delicate columns, are impressive and spacious, with the business of hurrying figures to emphasize the long, low proportions and the multiplicity of converging lines. The very open plan, with long blocks of offices strung along endless corridors, and the almost detached, acoustical fan-shaped assembly hall, was at the time very advanced. Forty years later it is still good and, though it rather dates in Western eyes, still the only good modern building in Moscow. The construction was of reinforced concrete with an infilling of red tuff-stone from the Caucasus. Le Corbusier intended this to be a hermetically sealed building with complete air-conditioning, *respiration exacte*. In spite of a series of careful experiments with ducts and 'neutralizing walls' in the laboratories at St Gobain, *respiration exacte* was still just a little too advanced for the Soviet Union. It was laughed at. Le Corbusier was not there, in Moscow, to supervise and so ultimately an orthodox system of radiator heating was installed, which dealt with the Moscow winter but not with the hot Moscow summer. In this respect the building was a disappointment to the architect; after all, air-conditioning was at that time a fascinating innovation. But the building was otherwise an outstanding example of good modern design.

It is, however, important to remember that the omission of the air-conditioning was not a mere technical disappointment or a mere reduction in the building's standard of comfort; it was an architectural failure, although no fault of the architect. Such technological triumphs as air-conditioning are an integral part of design, and the building cannot be judged without them. That vast foyer, for example, must always have been designed to have its whole volume of air raised uniformly to a very precise temperature. There could be no better instance of the fact that in modern architecture technology and planning are a single operation—or should be.

The open plan of the Centrosoyus Building—with light and air and foliage on every side, and garden courts between the blocks—was as much part of Le Corbusier's philosophy, his feeling for Man and Nature, as were his towers of some ideal Radiant City. It is something that has now become the commonplace of any modern school almost anywhere in the world. In Moscow, in 1929, for an office block it was something virtually new. Of this Centrosoyus plan Le Corbusier himself wrote:

> 'This plan and the Pavillon Suisse which followed, as well as the Villa Savoie . . . opened the way for the flexible, open plan of today, the full-flowering of reinforced concrete. It possesses unique powers of architectural expression, an almost infinite richness. It has nothing in common with what has gone before, with the classical period (a room = four walls). Its ancestors, however, include Gothic. Gothic however, was rigidly restricted by its plan and section and the technical limitations of stone construction; freedom came seven centuries later with the use of concrete.'[16]

This is only Le Corbusier's way of emphasizing the nature of reinforced concrete—that plasticity which enables one to mould it to almost any shape, and that peculiar strength—when reinforced with steel mesh—which enables one to build over almost any span.

The Salvation Army Building in Paris—*La Cité de Refuge*—is an interesting building although not one upon which Le Corbusier's reputation will finally rest. It was commissioned in 1929, but because of delays caused by the slump was not finished until 1933. There were also great foundation difficulties, the piles having to be driven down some forty-five feet to the underground waters of the Seine.

In this building Le Corbusier at least did what he had wanted to do in the Centrosoyus Building in Moscow. The *Cité de Refuge* was hermetically sealed for *respiration exacte*, for air-conditioning. This had to be done with great economy, but of the 'forced air' plant Le Corbusier was able to say: 'The results were sufficient to permit the best hopes for the future use of the system.' The architectural result of this hermetic sealing of the building— what Le Corbusier called the 'neutralizing walls'—was a very glassy façade with the concrete columns set well back behind the main window surface and therefore almost invisible. The suspended and rolling trolleys for the window cleaners were forerunners of those used on the Lever Building in New York twenty years later. The planning of the library, dining-room and dormitories is altogether fantastic, both cars and pedestrians being provided with sweeping ramps which link the whole thing together; something derived perhaps from the Centrosoyus foyer while also foreshadowing the Carpenter Building at Harvard.

In front of the long, flat and smooth glass façade the entrance, with its steps, canted canopy and glass brick screen is effective but also a gallimaufry of modernistic clichés. During the war the Salvation Army Building was occupied by the enemy; Le Corbusier, however, spoke of it as having been completely ruined *after* the evacuation of the German troops from Paris, by the architectural incompetence of the staff of the *Cité de Refuge*. 'The building,' he said, 'can no longer be thought of as architecture.'[17]

Another project to be summarily rejected—perhaps the greatest building never built—was that for a new Palace of the Soviets in Moscow. This was in 1931. On paper the design probably incorporated more important elements, then novel but today accepted, than any other example of Le Corbusier's work. To take only one instance, there was the enormous parabolic arch from which was suspended the roof of the Great Hall. Such construction had for some time been possible in reinforced concrete but had been restricted almost wholly to the work of engineers, to the fine Swiss bridges of Maillart, for example. Of course, if one could suspend a motor road from a parabolic arch there was no earthly reason why one should not similarly suspend an auditorium roof

—except that no one had thought of doing so. Its main functional justification is twofold: it is economical, and it clears the auditorium floor of all supporting columns or thick walls. In the Palace of the Soviets it would have been used with tremendous architectural effect; neither by architects nor by engineers had it ever been used on such a large scale.

The programme for the Palace of the Soviets was a vast one, involving not only a most elaborate complex of halls, offices, libraries, restaurants, etc., but above all, and dominating all, an auditorium for 15,000 spectators and a stage for 1,500 performers. The backstage accommodation would have been technically advanced, while the auditorium itself would have had foyers, lounges, restaurants and so on, as well as the very big cloakrooms essential in a snowy country where furs, overshoes, etc., have to be disposed of and dried. (The whole space beneath the auditorium would in fact have been one large cloakroom—a very common arrangement in Sweden, as for instance in Ivar Tengbom's famous Stockholm Concert Hall of 1926.) There would also have been unique and luxurious accommodation both for the Diplomatic Corps and for the Press.

Most important of all was the fact—by no means universally accepted as a *sine qua non* in 1931, and positively non-existent in some of the world's most famous opera houses—that every spectator would have enjoyed perfect sight-lines and perfect acoustics. By hanging a light roof from the big parabolic arch and, of course, casting it in light reinforced concrete, it would have been possible to shape the roof with great precision so as to form a perfect acoustic shell.

The entire Palace of the Soviets was planned to be surrounded by an 'automobile circuit' giving access to all parts of the building, while also completely separating pedestrians from cars. No such total approach to traffic segregation can be found until the planning of Brasilia nearly twenty-five years later, Oscar Niemeyer's and Lucio Costa's great 'fiat city' on a virgin site.

Le Corbusier's claim that the grouping of the main masses of the Palace of the Soviets was based upon a thumbnail sketch, made from the train, of the cathedral group at Pisa must surely be taken with a grain of salt; only in the very broadest sense is there a rough correspondence of one mass against the other. On the other hand it must be admitted that it is in such moments that ideas are born. The studio in the Rue de Sèvres prepared a very remarkable model of the building, showing the interiors as well as the exterior. This model was shown at the Museum of Modern Art in New York in 1935; it then toured several American cities. As Le Corbusier remarked, 'it never came back'. Where it is now?

The scheme had aroused enormous interest in Moscow; immediate construction was envisaged. Then, quite suddenly, it was announced that the Palace of the Soviets would be built in the style of the Italian Renaissance. The architect allowed himself one of his rare moments of real bitterness. He commented: 'Out of considerations which I must recognize, the jury of this competition decided that the Palace of the Soviets should be in the style of the Italian Renaissance. It must be admitted,' he added, 'that a Palace which in form as well as technique should be an expression of the new age, can only be the result of a social development that has reached a high point—and not a social development which is at the beginning.'

For an idealistic and, perhaps, starry-eyed generation who were still looking to the Soviet Union for the building of a new world, not only politically and economically but also culturally, the 1931 rejection of Le Corbusier's design was the end of a dream. This went far beyond architecture. For the communist intellectual the Marxist honeymoon was over. This was an episode which, however important or unimportant in itself, became a symbol of the Soviet Union's abdication from a modern culture; it cast its shadow over the next half century.

The *Pavillon Suisse* of the Cité Universitaire in Paris, completed in 1932, has always been considered a landmark both in the history of modern architecture and in the development of Le Corbusier as an architect. It brought to fruition many of the ideas which he had been using tentatively. It is one of several claimants to the title of 'the first modern buildings' (Pls. 7–10).

The Cité Universitaire, as is well known, contains a number of buildings which are in fact hostels for students of different nationalities. There is no attempt at planning or unity of any kind. The buildings are chaotically arranged, and chaos is worse confounded because each nation has been allowed to build its own hostel in its own way, often in some ludicrous parody of its own national vernacular. The British Pavilion, for instance, looks like some small but outlandish slice of Girton. When it was decided to build a Swiss hostel it was also decided that a decent

architecture should be attempted. The commission was immediately offered to Le Corbusier. He was, after all, a Swiss. He
declined. The conduct of the Swiss authorities and the attitude
of the Swiss people in the League of Nations affair still rankled;
it had been neither forgotten, which was hardly possible, nor
forgiven. Under pressure from the combined universities of
Switzerland, however, Le Corbusier eventually gave way and
took the *Pavillon Suisse* to completion at a cost of three million
francs—a sum which the President of the Cité Universitaire
thought should be doubled. Certainly the building shows every
sign of a rigid economy.

Le Corbusier himself has described this building as 'a veritable
laboratory of modern architecture'. He probably had in mind
such things as dry-wall construction, acoustic separation (i.e.
insulation) or internal plumbing; but in reality the building is a
landmark because all those elements of modern architecture
which we have already seen in, say, the Villa Savoie or the
Palace of the Soviets are now found in a single building. These
elements might have declined into being mere clichés of the
style, mere gimmicks, but in this single building they are fused
into a single architectural unity of great strength, into a single
concept free from every superfluity—a thing rare indeed in
architecture. All through the thirties, until the outbreak of war,
this building—not large but deceptive in its simplicity—was
continuously visited, almost haunted, by the architectural
students of the world. It is still a very svelte pavilion, although
not extraordinary at first glance; in those days it became almost
the banner of a cause.

The *Pavillon Suisse* is a five-storey slab block. It is mounted
upon *piloti* which leave the 'undercroft' entirely free as a covered
but outdoor recreation area. Also on the ground floor, almost
detached from the main building, is an interesting structure
containing the entrance lobby and staircase, the library or
common-room and the warden's flat. This structure has a very
free form which serves to emphasize its near-detachment from
the main block. One wall even is subtly curved and is of random
rubble, again emphasizing its non-structural nature, its detach-
ment. Rubble walling of this decorative kind, often only a panel
of rubble, was used more than once by Le Corbusier, and far too
often by his disciples, by 'all the little Corbs . . .'.

The curved wall of the common-room is echoed in the curved

form of the staircase tower above it. Internally this curved, non-structural, common-room wall was clearly a very proper place for a mural or decoration of some kind. 'For two days,' says Le Corbusier, 'there was deadly warfare.' Pictures of mountain scenery were produced and tried out. It was then agreed that you could not hang pictures on a curved wall; this is something with which the curator of Frank Lloyd Wright's Guggenheim Museum in New York would wholeheartedly agree! Le Corbusier then thought up the inexpensive idea of a 'photo-mural' or collage, the first of its kind. He used enlarged photographs of minerals, crystals and micro-biology. The *Gazette de Lausanne* immediately proclaimed a scandal, accusing Le Corbusier of the corruption of youth! The wall was empty again! Another photo-mural was erected. Fortunately Hitler, in due course, used the roof of the *Pavillon Suisse* for anti-aircraft guns. The structure stood up well to the colossal vibration, but the Germans for some unknown and unimaginable reason removed the second photo-mural. Professor Fueter, the initiator in 1931 of the whole idea of a Swiss Pavilion, commissioned Le Corbusier immediately after the Liberation to fill the wall with a real mural; no nonsense about a collage this time. This became one of the finest examples of Le Corbusier's Cubism, in the tradition of the earlier Picasso. He has since called it 'the painting of silence, since silence envelops it and envelops it still'.[18]

The main block of the *Pavillon Suisse* is a single slab. This five-storey rectangle, absolutely unbroken in outline, stands strong, clear and precise, a prism cantilevered out from its *piloti*, lifted above all the irrelevant excrescences of the earth; all pure geometry with piquant contrasts between plain walls (the end walls being quite blank) and the carefully proportioned panels of the glass infilling on the long side. The proportions are so careful as to foreshadow the 'Hellenic' work of Mies van der Rohe. The *piloti* themselves are no longer the forest of slender columns that we saw in those earlier houses; they now have all their strength and mass gathered together, concentrated as it were, into half a dozen carefully shaped piers, forerunners of the cyclopean pylons of the Marseilles Building fifteen years later. This 'gathering together' of the strength of several slender columns into a single mass was an idea which struck Le Corbusier, as we have seen, upon the completion of the Villa Stein in 1927, when he wanted to represent the area of that single mass by means of a mosaic in the hall of the house. The whole grouping of all these elements of the *Pavillon Suisse*—the slab block itself, the *piloti*, and the detached entrance block with its rubble wall —is a very successful and also a highly unified piece of design.

The internal plan of each floor is really the prototype for most hostels and many apartment buildings erected since. The living space of each student's room is, as it were, pushed forward to the light, giving it a maximum window width, while all the utilities— lavatory, shower, wardrobe, etc.—are at the back of the room where light is least. This prevents the room itself from being disproportionately deep and also provides a sound barrier—the fitments and pipe ducts—between the room and the corridor. On a much larger scale this idea, at least basically, will be found again in the big apartment building at Marseilles: living-rooms with fifteen-foot-high windows, but with kitchens, bathrooms, etc., forming a barrier between the big living-room and the public corridor.

Apart from its prototype plan—prototype for hostels, nurses' homes and so on all over the world—the whole building was something of a prototype for the best slab blocks that have since been built, such as the United Nations Building and the Ministry of Education in Rio, to mention two by Le Corbusier, as well as scores of others by his disciples. These all incorporate the long glass façade, the blank end walls, the *piloti* and the free form of an entrance block at ground level. The *Pavillon Suisse* does in fact incorporate many features and ideas which can be traced from embryo to maturity through all Le Corbusier's work up to that date. Marseilles may be seen as a continuation of that process, the 'blowing up' of the *Pavillon Suisse* into a vast apartment building, both buildings in the same line of descent. Those who, over thirty years ago, saw in the *Pavillon Suisse* both a culmination of Le Corbusier's work and a significant moment in architecture were enthusiastic and were not entirely wrong.

Not everyone, however, saw the building in that way. We may allow Le Corbusier the last word. 'The inauguration ceremony was like a funeral. Professor Fueter of Zürich University, a mathematician of international reputation who had promoted the scheme in the first place, declared in his speech: "This is the finest modern building." Silence followed. The fanfare of the trumpets was the only cheerful response.'[19]

. . . . .

In many of the world's cities today one may look up at a variety of tall high-rise office buildings. The layman may well be a little puzzled to note that more than one of these slick towers is, on plan, somewhat lozenge shaped—thickened at the centre, or like a tubby boat with square bow and stern. Among the more famous of these lozenge-shaped blocks are Gio Ponti's Pirelli Building in Milan (1959) and the Pan-Am Building over Grand Central Station in New York, begun in the same year. The first building to be thus designed on paper, however, had come twenty-six years earlier—the Rentenanstalt Building, a competition project by Le Corbusier for insurance offices by the lakeside in Zürich.

Now this 'lozenge' or thickening of the skyscraper at its centre is a perfectly logical rationalization of the fact that lavatories, archives, stairs, lifts and lift lobbies should be placed at the centre of the building; they should (a) form a core at that point where they are easily and centrally accessible, and (b) occupy that part of the building where daylight is at its minimum. This core, however, must not encroach upon the office area, which in effect forms a broad band of well-lit rooms around the perimeter of the block. The lozenge shape, which need not be unpleasing aesthetically, is nothing more or less than a product of functionalism in planning.

Really, Le Corbusier should never have expected to win competitions. It was asking for trouble. The history of architectural competitions is thick with cautious and safe 'firsts' and brilliant 'seconds'. Le Corbusier's 'failed' plans are usually milestones on the highway of history, but are almost always, by implication, an attack upon the low intelligence of the promoters of the competition and of the jury of assessors. The Rentenanstalt Building, for instance, was conceived by the promoters in advance —in which case why have a competition at all?—as a relatively low building planned around a courtyard. The site was quite inadequate for such a spreading plan, as it must be if justice was to be done to it. And why have a building with internal court-yards when it was perfectly possible to design a building with every room having a view of the lake or the mountains? Le Corbusier designed, therefore, not what he was asked to design but what he thought should be built. He not only substituted a tower for the courtyard, but also pointed out that the large office block is something new in architecture—as is also its services or equipment—and that it must, therefore, have its own organic being, its own biology (*la biologie architecturale*). Different as the end product may be, this phrase does remind one forcibly of Frank Lloyd Wright's 'organic architecture'. Indeed the two ideas have much in common, the response of a building, in its total design, to all the complex conditions of its being. The Rentenanstalt, for instance, in its design takes full account not only of its site, but also of modern techniques such as built-in services, air-conditioning, etc., not merely as useful things added to a design but rather as factors dictating its form.

Although not shown on the photograph of the model, the Rentenanstalt would have been equipped on its south side with the first of Le Corbusier's *brise-soleil*. Often misused by Le Corbusier's admirers, the *brise-soleil* is really a marvellous invention, a fascinating substitute for the Venetian blind or the *jalousie*. Large concrete fins are attached to the outside of the building, running its height or fitted separately to each storey. These fins are mechanically operated, opened or closed or set at an angle, so as to shade the windows according to the season or the elevation of the sun. Le Corbusier's design for the Rentenanstalt Building having been rejected by the jury, this idea of the *brise-soleil* had to wait until the completion of the office block for the Ministry of Education in Rio de Janeiro in 1936–45, where at last it was both possible and desirable to use it on a large scale.

One popular, if highly erroneous, estimate of Le Corbusier may well be that he is the man responsible for filling our cities with 'skyscrapers'. If the seventeen-storey building at Marseilles really counts as a skyscraper, and if we drag in Le Corbusier's one-tenth share in the design of the United Nations Building in New York, then it may just be said that he has built three skyscrapers, the only real one being the beautiful Ministry of Education Building in Rio. It is an absurd word anyway— skyscraper, *gratte-ciel*, *wolkenkratzer*, high-rise building. The country that really builds them never uses the word. What, in any case, does it mean? A slab? A pencil tower? Seven storeys, which is certainly a skyscraper in the middle of an English village? Or seventy, which is good going in Manhattan? Architecturally there is no such thing as a high building. The height of a building is relative—relative to other buildings, relative to the scale of a whole city, relative above all to the space around it. The absolute perfection of, say, the church tower at Lavenham in Suffolk, set in the cornfields, or the Campanile at Siena, set in the Piazza Publico, has nothing whatever to do with height as such, but only with height in a particular setting.

By 1935, however, if only on paper, Le Corbusier had admittedly designed the best high-rise building in the world. Infinitely more important, he had in this Rentenanstalt and his *Ville Contemporaine* projects established the conditions under which a high building is not only permissible but actually advantageous. The main condition is that the surrounding space—'the carpet' of the *Ville Contemporaine* or of the *Ville Radieuse*—shall be proportionate to the height of the buildings, and also available for the use of the occupants. High buildings must give land back to the people, not take it from them, and must not spoil it. It cannot be too strongly stated that this is of course the absolute reverse of the American concept. In New York or Chicago they build high to exploit land values, and darken the streets and buildings in the process. Le Corbusier would have built high to give people light, prospect and air. The Rentenanstalt would have looked across the lake in Zürich, while twenty years later every apartment in the Marseilles building really did look either to the sea or to the mountains. The whole point is emphasized by the fact that the saving grace of New York—and it is by chance rather than design—is that a few buildings do in fact have space around them—the space of the East River, of the Hudson and Central Park—and that these buildings thereby acquire a marvellous skyline denied to the rest of Manhattan.

Not, however, until 1935 did Le Corbusier actually see a skyscraper. In that year there was an exhibition of his work, mainly of the *L'Esprit Nouveau* period, at the Museum of Modern Art. Le Corbusier, like so many before him, crossed the Atlantic to lecture. He beheld New York.

He was shattered but not fooled. As he said, a building one thousand feet high is after all, by any standards, 'an event in architectural history'. The Americans, however, as Le Corbusier made clear to them, had no idea how to use their skyscrapers. They had invented the damned thing—Louis Sullivan had invented it in Chicago in the nineties—and it was now ruining their cities, one city after another. Without a city plan, without a town design in which masses are related to spaces, the skyscraper had become nothing less than a menace. Unfortunately the average American regarded, and still regards, planning as little less than a communist assault upon his liberty. So the skyscraper remained as the most dangerous weapon in the armoury of the real estate man. It had also defeated itself. It had turned streets into canyons. It had concentrated rather than relieved traffic, while each skyscraper was the enemy of its neighbour, cutting off its view, its air and its light. Above all, in places like Manhattan or Lake Shore Drive in Chicago, a childish prestige had become attached to height as a thing in itself. Le Corbusier was able to make this quite clear; it did not make him more popular. Years later when he came back to build the United Nations Headquarters, it was remembered against him. More than thirty years ago in *The American Architect* he wrote this:

'The New York skyscraper is only negative. It has destroyed the street and brought traffic to a standstill. It consumes the very life of the population and eats up whole districts around itself, emptying them and bringing ruin. Build the skyscraper bigger and make it really useful—place it in a park and it will reclaim a vast amount of land, will compensate for depreciated properties, will provide a perfect system of circulation, and will bring trees and open spaces into the city. The pedestrians will have the freedom of the parks over the whole ground area and cars will travel from skyscraper to skyscraper at a hundred miles an hour on elevated roadways at a distance from each other. Notice how the big hotels and apartment houses around Central Park have naturally come to be built there so as to have the advantage of looking onto space. But Central Park is too big; it is an island in a sea of buildings. Crossing it is like traversing no-man's land. The trees, grass and space of Central Park ought to be multiplied and spread over the whole of Manhattan.'[20]

Le Corbusier, before at last building his own high-rise building in Rio de Janeiro, was to experiment on paper with a variety of tall structures. Outstanding among these was an apartment house (*maison locative*) for Algiers in 1933, and then in 1938 the tall building for the Algiers Quartier-de-la-Marine, a building pregnant with ideas for the future. In the same year he designed the famous 'Cartesian Skyscraper'. All these buildings, abortive projects though they were, might have found a place in one or other of Le Corbusier's town-planning schemes—to be considered later—such as Anvers, Barcelona, Buenos Aires, Manhattan or Algiers. These designs for tall buildings were in fact probably 'try-outs' for those large-scale city plans.

The Algiers apartment house of 1933 was a very peculiar affair, but by no means unimaginative. Conceived as being on a steep cliff, all the apartments look out to sea. About two-thirds of these apartments are in a tower rising above the cliff-top level; the remaining third are below cliff-top level, the tower in effect being continued down the stepped face of the cliff. At cliff-top level itself a whole storey is, as it were, omitted. Only the slender *piloti* connect the lower and upper parts of the tower. Outwards, therefore, one looks out through the building to the sea, or one can walk right through it to look over the edge to the shore below. In other words, in that warm climate, the whole ground floor of the building has in effect become a big loggia open both to the land and to the sea. It is a remarkable and imaginative essay, an ingenious piece of geometry, but applicable of course only to a particular site.

The Quartier-de-la-Marine skyscraper of 1938 is, like the Rentenanstalt Building, a lozenge-shaped tower but very much higher. This project dates from 1938, but was eventually incorporated by Le Corbusier in his 1942 master-plan for Algiers. This remarkable building, which should have been part of a remarkable group, may look back for its basic lozenge-shaped plan to the Rentenanstalt, but it also looks forward to the United Nations Building and to *L'Unité d'Habitation* at Marseilles. Although destined never to be built it made use of forms which have passed into the ordinary vocabulary of modern architecture. It is, for one thing, not a mere piling up of one layer of offices upon another. It has an independent frame—a concrete grille designed to accord with a system of proportions—and an entire façade of glass with *brise-soleil* devices to let in all the sun or none, according to the season on that hot North African coast. As in the Palace of the Soviets, the proper segregation of pedestrians and cars throughout the whole Quartier-de-la-Marine would have been beautifully dealt with by curved ramps, an approach to traffic planning almost unknown at that time.

In the building itself, at three different levels marked by three solid horizontal bands on the façade, there is provision for archives and services, while on the roof are the free forms of hotel and restaurant. All this did much to destroy the monotony of the orthodox office block. Years later this system of bands, each one storey high, running right around a skyscraper façade, turns up more than once in many cities. In the United Nations Building each solid band marks a storey which contains the services and the air-conditioning plant. In the Marseilles Building the bands are not solid and do not represent service floors; they are formed by *brise-soleil* and a variation in the fenestration pattern, outward expression of the restaurant and shops which occupy a whole floor in order to serve the entire building. The gay roofscape at Marseilles—crèche, gymnasium and running track—also had its counterpart in this Algiers building, in the free shapes, already mentioned, of hotel and restaurant. Le Corbusier's career was nothing if not a life-long development, a progressive transformation of his own ideas. This curious consistency is to be found running through almost half a century; the exact opposite of the previous generation and indeed of the previous century, when each building was a separate 'masterpiece' asking to be judged as such without reference to its setting or to the life it was to serve.

The danger of monotony in the skyscraper is obvious. Between such variations as may be introduced at street level—the treatment of the ground-floor or 'podium'—and the potentialities of a gay skyline, there may well lie 600 feet of uniformity. What does one do with it? Art must always be definite. Compromise is fatal. One may exploit this uniformity or one may break it. Most architects have fallen between the two stools. Mies van der Rohe, however, did the first; Le Corbusier did the second. In Mies's Seagram Building nothing is allowed to break the sheer unabashed and svelte verticality: by pure artistry (and 'pure' is the *mot juste*) monotony is turned into serenity, even into drama. Le Corbusier did the opposite: he gave richness, even an encrusted richness, to his skyscrapers; the service floors, the *brise-soleil*, balconies and colour were all brought into use for this end.

The *Pavillon Suisse* in Paris (1930–2), the Ministry of Education Building in Rio (1936–45) and the United Nations Building in New York (1947) were all slab blocks raised on *piloti* with 'free form' structures—lobbies, foyers, shops, etc.—'slid' beneath the main building. All three have glass façades on the long sides and blank ends, as for that matter had the *Pavillon de L'Esprit*

Nouveau in 1925. For the *Pavillon Suisse* Le Corbusier was the sole architect. For the Ministry of Education Building in Rio there was some collaboration. This collaboration was with the two great Brazilian architects, Lucio Costa and Oscar Niemeyer, although they would acknowledge not only that the main concept was Le Corbusier's but also that that concept changed the whole direction of Brazilian architecture. For the United Nations Building there were at least ten architects. The story of that building is therefore somewhat complicated, to say the least; even so, it cannot be doubted that Le Corbusier dominated the situation and that the basic inspiration was his and his alone. These three slab blocks, then, not only have certain major elements in common, they also contain other elements and ideas which we can trace back to *L'Esprit Nouveau* days and forward to La Tourette and Chandigarh. It is that kind of consistency, compounded of his own originality and of the great Mediterranean tradition, that we may also find in the work of Michelangelo.

The Ministry of Education Building at Rio was, however, the first elegant urban office block to be actually designed and built by Le Corbusier. It has been an inspiration to architects all over the world. It has been debased and travestied a thousand times.

When Le Corbusier visited Rio de Janeiro in 1936 the greatest architect was Lucio Costa, grand old man of Brazilian architecture. At the Government's request Costa had already formed a group to design and build the new Ministry. He now invited Le Corbusier to join him. From then on Le Corbusier was bound to dominate the situation. Lucio Costa was fortunately modest and unambitious; he was quite content to surrender control of the design to Le Corbusier, while Le Corbusier was of course glad to have a reliable colleague to deputize for him in Rio. (Incidentally almost all Le Corbusier's foreign work was done with a minimum of travelling; he never even saw his Carpenter Center building in Harvard (Pls. 18–21).)

The group in Brazil now suddenly produced a young designer of great power and brilliance—Oscar Niemeyer. Today Niemeyer is famous for having worked so well with his former master, Lucio Costa, on the wonderful and indeed fantastic plan for the city of Brasilia, a plan, incidentally, owing much to the pioneering work of Le Corbusier, from the *Ville Contemporaine* onwards. It would not, in fact, be unfair to say that Brasilia is the final culmination of Le Corbusier's life work as a designer of cities, although he himself never had a hand in it. It does many of the things which Le Corbusier did on paper, and much that he so nearly did at St Dié and elsewhere. A new capital city, a 'fiat city' on a virgin site, is a rather rare thing in history—one thinks of Byzantium and of Washington—and one is thankful that in our own time there have been two, both memorable: Brasilia and Chandigarh. Le Corbusier strongly influenced the first, he designed the second.

It was therefore under Le Corbusier's influence that Oscar Niemeyer came to maturity.* It was this relationship—this happy link between the three men, Lucio Costa, Oscar Niemeyer and Le Corbusier—which so largely explains the great architectural renaissance of modern Brazil.

It was inevitable, therefore, that Oscar Niemeyer should play a large part in the design of the new Ministry Building. That it is sometimes attributed to him may be partly due to the absurd Brazilian law decreeing that no emolument shall ever be paid to a foreign architect. This situation was circumvented by placing Oscar Niemeyer in charge of the work and then paying Le Corbusier, the real designer, a swollen fee for lectures.

When looking at any photographs of the Rio building (Pls. 34, 35) it must be remembered that either the camera is necessarily too near, or the building itself appears cluttered up with irrelevant structures. Le Corbusier had started by choosing a better site, nearer to the sea. This was refused.

This building, while it has much in common with the *Pavillon Suisse*, such as the *piloti* and the blank end walls, is seventeen storeys high and in that respect more comparable with Marseilles or the United Nations Building. This is indeed the city office block *per excellence*, and also Le Corbusier's largest pre-war building. In the Brazilian climate the *brise-soleil* are no gimmick; either in this modern form of adjustable concrete fins, or as some kind of sun-blind they are a necessity. These fins, as in Bernasconi's Olivetti Building in Milan, can be the full width and height of the building, or, as at Rio, they can be designed separately for each window, almost like an external Venetian blind except that they are controlled by a switch. Either way the

---

* *As an amusing demonstration of the relative status of Le Corbusier and Niemeyer it has been pointed out by Le Corbusier himself that on the published perspective drawings of the Rio Ministry the numerous little figures—which give life to the drawings—are from the pencil of 'Oscar' but that the single big statue on the terrace, 'The Man of Brazil', was drawn by 'Corbu'.*

effect of this grille, as it were, laid on the main structure is both rich and scintillating.

The *piloti* at Rio are two storeys high and on a rather grand scale. They are not, as at Marseilles, a series of gargantuan pylons, but a very fine set of cylindrical columns. The whole entrance court, in fact, of which these columns form a part is a rather splendid affair. These *piloti*, the paving of the court, all site work and the blank end walls of the building itself are of a particularly beautiful pink Brazilian granite. Le Corbusier was shocked, as well he might be, when he discovered that most official buildings in Rio had in the past been constructed from stone brought from Burgundy as ballast in cargo ships! With the pink granite Le Corbusier used some blue and white faience from Lisbon. With the rich and glassy façades and the almost perpetual play of sun and shadow, this symphony of pink, white, blue and glitter makes a very brilliant building. This is rather unwonted for Le Corbusier who, in less brilliant climates, relied more often on the natural colour of concrete with the sparing addition of a few primary colours in paint.

The roof of an office block does not perhaps give the architect the same opportunities as the roof of an apartment block. At Rio one does rather yearn for, say, a roof-top restaurant or a penthouse of some kind. In the handling of his skyline—the usual tanks and lift machinery—Le Corbusier has not really been much more successful than many lesser men.

The aesthetic essence of a modern office block, with its panelled or grille-like façade, its separation from the ground on its *piloti*, together with its great height, is surely that one sees it as a whole, as a single concept or work of art, as opposed to the older kind of building where the architecture was either a series of windows punched in the wall in some more or less stylistic manner, or else carved ornament, such as classical pilasters. The difference is absolutely fundamental, but it has its corollary. As we have said in connection with all tall buildings and their place in the modern town, space and the long view are essential. They are part of the architecture, the total form of the building being the most important architectural thing about it. The long view, the surrounding space, is lacking at Rio. Le Corbusier had fought for a better site and had lost. At Marseilles, as we shall see, the space is there up to a point, while in New York one can at least behold the United Nations Building from across the East River.

In every other way the Rio building is almost the first and almost the best of these modern city blocks. Its influence throughout Latin America was profound, carrying the culture of that continent from the seventeenth century to the twentieth.

The years immediately before the Second World War were very full ones for Le Corbusier. They were crammed with numerous minor projects as well as with more ephemeral things such as exhibitions and exhibition buildings. These latter included a very remarkable tent of 17,000 square feet at the Paris World Fair of 1937—the first use of a translucent canvas supported only on cables, which assumed their natural catenary curve. The translucent linen roof in Frank Lloyd Wright's Taliesin West was not designed until the following year, but the general structural form—the canvas carried on cables—became common form throughout the United States, especially where the climate permitted, and has been used many times in California by the distinguished young architect Paul Rudolph. In other exhibition buildings Le Corbusier developed yet another universal lightweight structure—the space frame. In this field he quietly proved himself as ingenious as the ubiquitous Buckminster Fuller. At the same time, as always, he was necessarily occupied with many of those major projects which, alas, never got off the drawing-board. This, inevitably, is part of the life of every great architect; some day someone will make a study of buildings that were never built. It was only about the League of Nations Building and the Palace of the Soviets that Le Corbusier showed any permanent bitterness, and with some reason. Although his studio was now full of work, he had not altogether finished with writing. On his return from New York and Rio in 1936 he wrote *When the Cathedrals were White*, which has been described as a kind of love letter to America; it was also an appeal to be allowed to prove his love. In the end, in 1962, in the Carpenter Arts Building in Harvard, he was given the chance. It had been a long wait.

Meanwhile it is worth noting that the Paris World Fair of 1937—apart altogether from Le Corbusier's huge and remarkable tent or *Pavillon des Temps Nouveau*—was an interesting event in itself. Most big exhibitions, because of the greater freedom allowed in temporary buildings, acquire some sort of architectural significance for good or bad. The Crystal Palace (1851) or the Festival of Britain (1951) are merely among the best known. The significance of Paris in 1937 lay in the virtual disappearance both of stylistic imitation and of 'façade architecture'. Almost every pavilion was now conceived as a three-dimensional object, of aesthetic interest in itself, rather than as a carefully composed but flat façade, or as a plaster simulacrum of, say, an Egyptian temple, as at Wembley in 1924, or of a Baroque palace, as at the Chicago World Fair of 1892. The tentative advance made in Paris—and it was not more than that—was certainly due more to the influence of Le Corbusier's work and teaching than to anything else.

Up to the very outbreak of war Le Corbusier went on creating abortive projects of various kinds for Algeria and for French North Africa generally. He never built there, but he could never leave it alone. After all, even the Roman Mediterranean, the ancient world that somehow was always in this man's blood, had a southern as well as a northern shore. Almost, one could write Le Corbusier's biography in terms of a progress towards the tropical and the exotic, towards white buildings in blazing sun, towards hot sand, palms and the dark of a reflecting pool. Switzerland, Paris, Vienna, Rio, Marseilles, North Africa, Bombay, the Punjab . . . a deliberate progress or just chance?

Of these various projects two more at least must be mentioned: the Philippeville Museum and the Vaillant Couturier monument. For Philippeville in French North Africa, in the Constantine province of Algeria, he designed a museum which would have been the first break with the old orthodox system of planning galleries as a series of vast apartments *en suite* as in almost every great public art gallery and museum in the world; an irrelevant method of planning derived from the *piano nobile* in an Italian palace, where the paintings are incidental, the entertainment and movement of people essential. Breaking with this habit in museum design, Le Corbusier planned for Philippeville a building designed as a square snail. Nothing less. Or, to be more accurate it was, so to speak, a flat spiral around a square core, a form capable of almost infinite expansion. It needs no further explanation. He had sketched out some such idea, with ascending ramps, as early as 1929. In its circular form it is now familiar in Frank Lloyd Wright's Guggenheim Museum in New York, although that was not even on the drawing-board until 1943. Moreover, Le Corbusier was a painter and already, as in the common-room in the *Pavillon Suisse*, he had decided that you cannot really hang paintings on a curved wall. The Philippeville Museum was never built. This was not altogether a tragedy. Le Corbusier had to wait almost twenty years; then, in 1956 at Ahmedabad, in Bombay Province, he was commissioned to build a museum. This was the Philippeville museum come true; it had been maturing in Le Corbusier's mind through the years, through the dark years of the Occupation. At Philippeville this museum would have been interesting and original, a genuine innovation, but at Ahmedabad it became one of the most charming of the world's smaller galleries. It will be described in its place. It also led in the same year to the building of another 'spiral' museum; this was in Tokyo for the housing of the Matsukata Collection.

Le Corbusier was never a political activist. Culturally, of course, his whole life was one long battle waged against the forces of orthodoxy, against the Establishment. It would be absurd to suppose that this had not bitten deep, colouring his whole outlook. And yet, for all that, both the extreme left and the extreme right abused him, and also, needless to say, claimed him as one of themselves. 'Fascist Collaborator', 'Bourgeois Reactionary', 'Red', 'Commy'—he was at some time or other labelled with them all. Le Corbusier was a rebel, and, like any artist and humanist who would change the world, he was a Man of the Left. Beyond that he would not go. His bitterness over the Palace of the Soviets brought Communist wrath upon his head, and yet in 1942, when he was ready to present his master-plan for Algiers, the whole thing was vetoed by the Vichy Government —Le Corbusier was a Communist! More to the point was his impatience with politics, his complaint to the present writer about the intolerable delays at Marseilles. *L'Unité d'Habitation* was the joint responsibility of the national and the municipal governments.* But, said Le Corbusier, when the authorities in Paris were socialist, in Marseilles they were communist, and *vice versa*; his problem was to knock their heads together.

It was politics that involved him in one of the last but finest of his abortive designs. Le Corbusier, a Man of the Left in the noble sense of desiring passionately the progress and the happiness of the human race, may be said to have almost symbolized himself, as it were, in his sketch for the monument to Vaillant

* *Since there was a crèche on the roof, the Ministry of Education paid a precisely calculated proportion of the cost of the sewer, etc. etc.!*

Couturier. This was in 1938, not a good time for Communist projects in France. Vaillant Couturier was a veteran deputy and had been the first editor of *L'Humanité*. About 1938 he seemed to vanish from the scene. His monument was the subject of a competition. Le Corbusier submitted a dramatic and highly sculptural design. Its theme was the 'Open Hand': a giant palm open to the sky spelling out 'man against the world', and the giant head crying out against injustice. These naturalistic forms were set in a tremendously powerful composition of planes and slabs set at a big road junction so as to be lit by the moving and intermittent headlights of cars. It was a design which could have been produced only by a man who was equally architect, painter and sculptor. The design was rejected but was exhibited after the war in New York, as an inspiration to designers of war memorials! In America it was not understood. Many years later the 'Open Hand' rising from the 'Ditch of Consideration' was revived in the Punjab, to become the focal point of Le Corbusier's great city of Chandigarh.

achievement and frustration

'Any architect who does not
find this building beautiful
should lay down his pencil.'
Walter Gropius at Marseilles

One key to an understanding of Le Corbusier's character is that within him there were, one suspects, both poles of the European genius. He was the Swiss—all that is orderly, well organized, clean, puritan. This gave him the power to achieve so much, simply to get the work done. But he was also the Latin—everything that is imaginative, romantic and grand; those architectural masses set so boldly in the sun. Those two poles of genius: hence his place in history.

For one who was necessarily in revolt against every convention of his time, his own life was astonishingly well ordered. There was nothing, or very little, of the popular idea of the Bohemian, apart from his views on almost everything! For one thing, in spite of so many disappointments, he was fundamentally happy. He enjoyed the actual work of designing and drawing a project, even if, as so often happened, it was never built. Mme Le Corbusier, warm, humorous and simple, was the one thing in his life which was outside and above the polemics and sophistication of the world he lived in. For him she was the perfect wife. She died in 1957, when he was seventy, and none of us knew what a blow this was to him—the matter was a sealed book. In addition to domestic happiness he not only had, on the whole, excellent health, but also consciously aimed at the Greek or Renaissance ideal of 'the total man', as sound in body as in mind. Hence the regular swim —he died in the sea—and, after he was sixty, the amazing sight of the regular run every morning round the Bois de Boulogne.

It was yet another facet of his character that he should, without any of the mechanical apparatus of the modern office, be efficient. He achieved quantity as well as quality because, surprisingly, he worked by the clock. Incredibly, at least to those who knew him only by repute, his delivery dates were excellent. In spite of his enthusiasm for painting, for many years he painted only on Saturday afternoons and on Sundays. That was true until, with the outbreak of war in 1939, all building ceased; he then painted every day, with the world in ruins about him, until the pigments ran out.

With the fall of Paris and the Exodus he had gone south to the Pyrenees, where he painted, as has been said, until the paints and the canvases, and even the bits of plywood, no longer existed. It must be remembered that during the First World War Le Corbusier was still Swiss—it was not his war. In any case there was his sight; he had worn those huge glasses since he was a boy. By the end of the Second World War he was nearly sixty and unwell. As hostilities came to an end, however, like all starry-eyed architects he sniffed the years of reconstruction ahead. When the painting was finished he turned to the future and in the last months of war occupied himself with a number of projects. He did a great deal of work on basic housing: prefabricated housing, methods of dry construction and those studies in housing needs which were in reality the germ of the *Charte d'Athène* and the *Charte d'Habitat*, those great studies for which years later CIAM (*Congrès Internationale d'Architecture Moderne*) was to assume responsibility. Above all, he made very deep studies into those systems of proportion which had been used by the Greeks and by the architects of the Renaissance; all of which led him on to the development of the Modulor, his great system of harmonious progression in dimensions and of proportions. The Modulor will be described separately; it was first used on the Marseilles building and then became the basis of all Le Corbusier's later work.

As a specific contribution to reconstruction Le Corbusier prepared his master-plan for Algiers (1942). It came to nothing because it was ill-timed. Le Corbusier, like any decent man, disliked the Vichy government; but for the sake of post-war reconstruction, for the sake of the future—after all Laval and his gang would not be there for ever—he was prepared to meet them. He did not find them difficult; he found them impossible.

It was all so typical of those terrible days in France. Le Corbusier was accused of being a 'collaborationist' because he presented his plan at all, while Vichy rejected his plan because, having once worked for the Soviet Union, he must be a 'communist'.

The Algiers plan was a very fine one, the best of Le Corbusier's paper projects for town building, with the single exception of the even finer plan for St Dié. The Algiers plan was based upon very careful studies of the town at an earlier date and on a detailed knowledge of that lovely coastline. The Casbah, magnificent urban complex of Arab culture, would have regained its integrity with its mosques intact. The Quartier-de-la-Marine would have had three carefully spaced high blocks, one of which would have been the remarkable skyscraper already described (pages 67–8). Basically the new Algiers would have been a Le Corbusier town, a few high and elegant buildings set in a 'carpet' of open space and lower buildings. Nevertheless, these mature plans for Algiers and the later one for St Dié show that the earlier 'ideal' plans— *Ville Contemporaine, Plan Voisin,* etc.—were meant only to be diagrammatic, in spite of accusations at the time that Le Corbusier was plotting the destruction of Paris. At Algiers we can see how a highly flexible theory could have been used in the solution of a real problem without any loss to its validity. The 'typical' plan, the original *Ville Radieuse* concept, was, at Algiers, completely adapted to a particular culture (Muslim) and to a particular site (the Bay of Algiers)—two powerful forces.

The Liberation. . . . The roof-garden of Le Corbusier's Paris flat was overgrown with weeds, and there was no coal. Architect-soldiers, British and American, visited the master to discover whether or not he was still alive, and Mme Le Corbusier cooked for them. Le Corbusier had been ill, but now he was in Paris again, a liberated Paris. The details of the Modulor were in his portfolio, and the sun was shining . . . *la vie commence demain.*

The big Marseilles apartment block, *L'Unité d'Habitation,* begun in 1947 and actually built and taken to completion, was in a sense the culmination of a lifetime's work and thought. To bring such an enterprise to a conclusion involved great problems, but the worst of these proved to be human rather than archi-tectural. The real thinking had been done years ago. Every element in the design of *L'Unité* may be found in embryonic form somewhere or other in the architect's work, somewhere or other throughout the previous forty years.

Housing at the end of the war was Europe's most intractable problem, socially and architecturally. As four allied armies closed in upon Berlin the Republic of France asked Le Corbusier to put his experience in housing and planning at the service of the people. The consequence was *L'Unité*. The sparks have been flying ever since.

A few minutes by bus from the centre of Marseilles, half hidden by the plane trees of the Boulevard Michelet, stands this large building known to everyone in the city as *L'Unité d'Habitation Le Corbusier* (Pls. 13–17). Inevitably there were many—not least the advocates of the English garden city or of Frank Lloyd Wright's 'Broadacres'—who found this thing appalling. It was, all too clearly, a gesture of defiance towards a world already slowly dying. It was more than just housing, it was more even than just architecture: it proposed a way of life.

More than architecture? More, at any rate, than the dead stylistic architecture of the last two hundred years. It had something to do with life, hadn't it? Its faults, and there are many, are irrelevant to its rather uncompromising purpose. *L'Unité d'Habitation* knows, when it looks upon the smug prettiness of an English housing 'estate' or upon the emasculated compromise of a 'new town', not to mention the 'ranch houses' of American suburbia, that once again the time has come for an artist to build.

Le Corbusier's starting point was that a great architecture must not only express a manner of living—and that is the most important of all—but that it must also, since the artist is a poet and a visionary as well as a technician, inaugurate and propose one. That is one of the plain dialectical facts of history. For too many years it had been only in the realm of ideas that Le Corbusier had mattered. It was in that realm, despite one or two realities such as the *Pavillon Suisse*, that he had bewitched a whole generation of young architects who had looked in vain, in every country in the world, to their own teachers and universities for leadership.

He himself had called the building the child of forty years gestation. The human background was still destined to be one of vexation, misrepresentation, political spite and professional jealousy. But sooner or later this thing had been bound to happen. The old idea of the *Ville Radieuse* or the *Ville Contemporaine*, of the vertical city with compensating space and landscape, had been studied on paper in such a diversity of forms that by the end of the war it was, with all its social and romantic connotations, embedded in the consciousness and conscience of the progressive world. A quality of the inevitable, therefore, hung over the event when, in 1945, the Minister of Reconstruction, Eugène Claudius-Petit, invited Le Corbusier, magnificently and unconditionally, to rehouse the people of Marseilles.

The municipality of Marseilles considered three other sites before deciding upon the Boulevard Michelet. The Boulevard Michelet is the most beautiful of the three. Whether that is why it was chosen is another matter, but all this held up the plans until March 1947. This must be remembered against the complaints of delay. The Germans having blown up the Vieille Port the housing situation for the working people of Marseilles was desperate, but at least that delay gave Le Corbusier's team of young men in the Rue de Sèvres time to think. And only the young, he said, could work on this project. In 1945–6, therefore, in the Rue de Sèvres studio, Le Corbusier started work on the first plans of *L'Unité d'Habitation*. 'In a studio parallel to my own,' he said, 'engineers and architects were assembled, some clever and wily like foxes in the thicket of technique, others devoted and impassioned like true fighters for a cause—the cause of civilization.'

Le Corbusier had at least one gift of genius: he could evaluate things on different planes (the rhythm, say, of human life and the design of kitchen cupboards), relate them, draw a conclusion and then transmute it into a building. He started with cosmic values, remembering that man is a biological organism on a sunlit planet. To live, work, eat, to cultivate the body and spirit arc necessary to the diurnal rhythm; work, rest, sleep and then that larger rhythm of birth, childhood, manhood, maturity and old age. For the savage, the peasant and the privileged bourgeoisie these things could always happen—they had space—but in our worn-out cities they were so left to chance that even before the nineteenth century had run its course the point of genocide for urban man had been reached. Le Corbusier, of course, knew all this, but also remembered—it was his starting point—the primal needs of man as a biological organism. He listed them: air, light, sun, foliage, space, silence, liberty, intimacy, isolation and beauty. In his actual solution he remained the romantic architect; social philosopher first and architect second perhaps, but for that very reason the greater architect.

L'Unité d'Habitation is a single block, 420 feet long, 60 feet wide and 185 feet high. It is so orientated that the sun moves round the block during the day. It is never overshadowed and casts its own shadow only on its own lawns. Compared with the complexity of so much modern housing there is a ruthless simplicity about this one rectangular block, alone in a twelve-acre park. As its position—the interesting way in which it is canted to the line of the road, giving the three-quarter view as one approaches—is fixed by the sun, so is its height by insistence upon unbroken space. To give a comparison: Dolphin Square, London (fair example of speculative middle-class 'luxury' flats), has a density of 415 persons per acre, whereas *L'Unité* has only 139 to the acre and its space is a single green area, not dark courts or negligible little gardens.

The block is of course only a fragment of Le Corbusier's complete city. There should be six, ten, twenty such blocks spaced out over half a mile of parkland, each with its twelve acres. It is this spacing that invalidates all comparison with high building in the United States, where height is only a product of land value. Of course any man, as in England, may say that he prefers his cottage and a garden, but that is not the problem. The problem is numerical. The Welwyn Garden City motif spread over 200 square miles of London's suburbs would drive anyone mad, as would satellite towns coalescing into chaotic milky ways of bricks and mortar. On the other hand a mile of high towers *en echelon* among their own lawns and trees has only the horror of the unfamiliar. In England we almost have it—and it is acceptable—in the L.C.C. housing at Roehampton where, among the trees and mature but obsolete gardens of old Victorian villas, the towers form a panorama to Richmond Park—the whole thing a consciously inspired Le Corbusier scheme. Aesthetically the whole idea may also be seen as a kind of mediaeval romanticism—towers above the trees as when the castles were white.

To achieve the feeling that the entire site at Marseilles was one big single space, undivided by building, there came about *L'Unité*'s most striking feature: the avenue of big concrete *piloti* bearing the whole eighteen-storey mass some thirteen feet above the ground. The park, in the form of paved garden and play-ground, thus passes unimpeded below the building, the *piloti* being high enough to give this area a very real feeling of unbroken space, visual and physical, right through the building.

The *piloti* carry an extra first floor—that is between the top of the *piloti* and the lowest layer of apartments—thick enough to contain a walk-way or tunnel, what Le Corbusier called the building's 'artificial ground level'. Within this walk-way are contained with great ease and simplicity all the services: water, electricity, heat, sink-waste and sewage. Aesthetically this service floor also gives a very strong plain line between the massive *piloti* and the more grille-like façade of the building above.

This lifting of the lowest level to give a wider view, as well as giving space below the building, is classical in Le Corbusier's work. It is a far cry from these enormous *piloti* to the slender columns which supported his earlier villas in the twenties—at Garches and Poissy for instance—but their evolution through the *Pavillon Suisse* is clear enough. At Marseilles each of the thirty-four *piloti* carries 1,500 tons. They are on a heroic, a cyclopean scale. The whole of the building above is very human, both in fact and in scale, but down in this vast 'undercroft' one is back, almost, in Roman Provence. This piquant contrast between the massive lower storey and the sheer intricacy of the other seventeen storeys is of course the main aesthetic fact about *L'Unité d'Habitation*; it is one thing, one of many things, that distinguish it from a thousand other apartment buildings all over the world.

The crudity of the concrete, left as it is when the rough timber shuttering, or moulds, is removed—revealing even the marks between the planks—is here in complete accord with the design. That roughness has been criticized and maybe it is unpardonable in such details as stair and balcony rails, but by and large it is seen now as being an important element in Le Corbusier's work, one that he was to use again, at Ronchamp for instance, and also at Chandigarh. Surely it arose from the desire, common among great architects in the days of their maturity, to give their work some kind of primaeval quality. It is there, in other forms, in the work of Michelangelo and of Vanbrugh. It is also marvellously part and parcel of Le Corbusier's definition of architecture: great volumes massed in the sunlight. Perhaps, too, it is a gesture of defiance against all the smooth, slick, plastic and metal architecture created by the younger generation in America, even perhaps a gesture against the perfectionist Savile Row tailoring of Mies van der Rohe. There was also Frank Lloyd Wright. In spite of the bitter jealousy between the two men, this primaeval quality is something that Wright, with his pine and his granite and concrete, ought surely to have understood. Perhaps he did, but remained silent. Anyway, under the *piloti* at Marseilles there is no doubt that the whole thing can stand this ruggedness, and moreover needs it and carries it with an air. The *piloti* of Marseilles are one of the great things of modern architecture; they are part of history.

Above this gigantic undercroft are the remaining seventeen storeys with their flats for 1,600 people. These group themselves as follows: eighteen small flats, called *chambres d'hôtel*, for the guests of tenants; twenty-seven flats for single people or couples

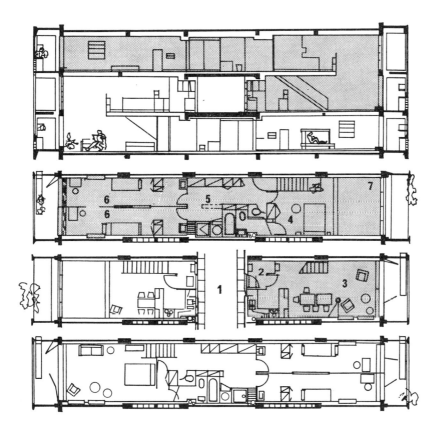

Figure 1 Section and plans of a pair of split-level apartments, for families with two to four children.

1 Main corridor ('Interior Street'); 2 Entrances; 3 Living-room with kitchen; 4 Parents' room and bathroom; 5 Cupboards, hanging fitments, ironing board; shower for children; 6 Children's rooms; 7 Space over living-room.

without children; forty-five flats for families with one or two children; 196 flats for families with from two to four children (Fig. 1); thirty-five flats for families with from four to eight children. A further analysis is given below in André Wogensky's account of the building.

It is really a misnomer to speak of eighteen storeys, or of seventeen if we discount the *piloti* 'undercroft'. The flats and roof-terrace are arranged on seventeen levels, but they have living-rooms of double height with windows fifteen feet high running through two storeys—yet another element to be traced back to those villas of the twenties. This big double-height window gets sun and air to the back of a room that might otherwise be too deep. Each flat is, in fact, a maisonette with a light internal stair from living-room to bedroom. The whole focus of the individual flat, its visual centre of gravity as it were, is this point of family life in front of the high window looking always either to the Provençal mountains or to the Mediterranean. The other rooms, however, such as children's bedrooms, also have their balconies, as well as space for freedom, isolation, reading, hobbies and so on. These children's rooms are rather reminiscent of the students' rooms in the *Pavillon Suisse*, with plumbing and wardrobes at the back of the room to reduce its depth, to occupy the space that would be least well lit, and to act as a sound barrier to the public corridor. With 1,600 people packed into a single block noise was a major problem. Each flat, therefore, is a box in itself, inserted into the main structure like a drawer into a huge chest, but insulated from that chest by pads of lead.

The flats are marvellously equipped with cupboards, kitchen fittings, etc., to a Swedish rather than a French standard, much of the joinery being actually made in Sweden. The larger flats have showers as well as bathrooms. The rooms have electric heating elements below the windows, with air driven through them from the plenum; but it is the view and the sunlight that make those tall windows the Mediterranean equivalent of the northern hearth, the focus of life. The Garchy system takes all refuse down a giant sink-plug to the walk-way above the *piloti*, and so to the destructor. One might think the flats over-equipped with cupboards, kitchen cupboards, wardrobes and so on. But all this is not only an immense saving in space, but also a reminder that Le Corbusier's original instructions were to build for those who had lost all their possessions when the Germans blew up the

Vieille Port. *L'Unité d'Habitation*, alas, became a political shuttle-cock, with the municipality determined to reduce all subsidies as far as possible. That not all the present tenants are the sort of humble working people for whom the building was originally designed is a lamentable fact, but no fault of the architect.

As one looks along the façade in perspective it is not the windows that one sees but the front of the balconies running across them. The side walls of the balconies project like fins, at right-angles to the building, and each is a square of bright, clear colour—red, green, yellow, blue, ochre. It is said that Le Corbusier made a kind of confetti of the colours he wanted and then stirred this round and round in a bowl until he liked the arrangement which he saw; this then became the basis of the apparently random system of coloured panels on *L'Unité*. Normal decoration would in any case be lost but for the fact that these gay squares of colour are so assertive; they also bring the eye back all the time to something small, thus contributing a great deal to the very human scale of a very big building. Everyone agrees that the building is an understatement; it never overwhelms.

These squares of clear colour also emphasize the network of proportions that overlies the whole building, every part mathematically related to every other part. The Modulor System is explained in greater detail in the next chapter, and in greater detail still in Le Corbusier's own book *The Modulor*. This method of arriving at related proportions, upon which Le Corbusier worked during the war, may yet prove to be his most enduring contribution. The point about the Modulor, which Le Corbusier has explained so fully and also patented, is that it is not just a proportion, as for instance $8:3$, nor is it a proportion arrived at in some special way as by forming a rectangle with the long side equal to the diagonal of the square of the short side, or some proportion of a similar kind. It is rather a series of dimensions, increasing and maintaining a constant ratio to each other —a kind of musical notation for lengths. The mystical mathematical ratios underlying the design of the Parthenon and the Doric Order are much nearer to the Modulor than any other system. Le Corbusier carried the whole system on a tape in his trouser pocket, and claimed that in the Marseilles Building there were only seventeen dimensions.

Why the name—*L'Unité d'Habitation*? Because it is a genuine unit for the whole of life. Most of the seventh and eighth floors are given up to social activities and to various forms of service. Here are the household shops, the barber and the laundry, the library, a magnificent restaurant and a club. The club is double-storey height and has a window 250 feet long. On the seventeenth floor are a health centre or clinic, and a crèche whence children can walk up an easy slope to the playground and paddling pool, both on the roof. Also on the roof is Le Corbusier's fascinating *jeu d'esprit*: the gymnasium, sunbathing platforms, running track and highly sculptural ventilation shafts, all 180 feet up with views all round unrivalled in Europe. All this is explained further in the following fairly comprehensive description of *L'Unité d'Habitation de Marseilles* written by André Wogensky,[21] Le Corbusier's assistant who virtually lived on the site during construction.

1 APARTMENTS

The first feature of the basic type of apartment is that there are two floors as in an ordinary family house.

The general living-room (or rather a considerable part of it) is two floors high, measuring 4·80 m. to the ceiling. This gives a spaciousness that allows the family to gather together without feeling cramped.

The other rooms are 2·26 m. high.

In the living-room, the lower part (one floor high) serves as a dining-room. It is only separated from the kitchen by a sort of low dresser which opens on both sides so that the crockery can be put away from the kitchen side after washing-up and taken out on the other side for laying the table.

The kitchen is a little labour-saving laboratory, everything being within easy reach.

The kitchen fittings are all built in. They include an electric cooker, a double sink (one part of which empties automatically into a refuse chute) and an ice chest. To save expense, the latter is not a refrigerator, so ice must be provided. This can be done directly from the 'indoor street' without entering the apartment or in any way disturbing the housewife. [To-day a refrigerator would certainly be provided; remember the date. R.F.J.]

The cooker, the sink and two sizeable metal-topped tables are all of the same height, making a uniform working level. [Common practice now, not then. R.F.J.]

To give maximum space at working level, cupboards for saucepans, vegetables, kitchen linen, etc., are either below it or a little above it.

The outer wall of the living-room (3·66 m. wide by 4·80 m. high) is completely glazed, allowing an abundance of light to reach the kitchen.

The tall window is divided into two parts. The lower part, 2·0 m. high, can be thrown open for the whole width onto a balcony which provides an open-air extension of the living-room.

The balcony is designed to form a sun-screen (*brise-soleil*). That is to say, it allows sunshine to stream right into the apartment in winter while providing shade in summer.

A staircase leads to the parents' bedroom, which is over the kitchen and the dining-room recess of the living-room. In other words it consists of a sort of gallery jutting out into the living-room.

This bedroom is provided with a large built-in wardrobe and a bathroom, the latter being fitted with bath, shower, wash-basin, w.c. and bidet.

Right in the centre of the apartment is a lobby with numerous cupboards to serve as box-room, linen cupboard, etc.

From the lobby two doors lead to the children's rooms, which are separated by a partition fitted with a sliding panel.

Each room has a corner for play or work (by the window), space for beds, cupboard (with hanging space), and a wash-basin.

In the case of very young children who sleep together, the sliding panel can be withdrawn to make a single room. Or it can be withdrawn during the day to make a common nursery or playroom, where children can romp about without disturbing the grown-ups.

A shower for the children is in close proximity to their rooms.

The two children's rooms are lit by windows which, like the living-room's, stretch across the apartment and open on to a balcony.

This apartment has been designed with a view to fostering close family life whilst allowing scope for independence to

each member of the family from the most tender age.
Housework is reduced to a minimum.

2   THE BLOCK

It consists of 337 apartments, there being twenty-three
different variants of the typical one described above, rang-
ing from the smallest, for childless couples, to large ones for
families with six to eight children.

The apartments are composed of three standard elements:
   (a) Kitchen, living-room.
   (b) Parents' bedroom, bathroom.
   (c) Children's rooms, showers, lobby with cupboards.

By combining these three elements in different ways a
large number of variations may be obtained, of which
twenty-three were selected for Marseilles.

These apartments not only resemble private houses by
virtue of being maisonettes, they are also *constructed*
independently. Complete in themselves, they are also so
to speak inserted into the reinforced concrete framework
without touching each other. Between their floors and the
concrete beams which carry them are lead pads which
absorb vibrations. The degree of insulation thus obtained
is very considerable indeed.

The apartments overlap. The spaces left between them
in the middle we call 'indoor streets'. That is what they
really are, interior streets for pedestrians one above the
other.

The whole building is 137 metres in length and 24·5 metres
in depth.

Most of the apartments have their windows in the two
long frontages. If the parents' bedroom and the living-room
face east, the children's rooms face west, and *vice versa.*

Another group of apartments faces south. In this case the
children's rooms are placed at the side of the other rooms
instead of in line with them.

So that each of these three frontages should have its fair
share of sun, the longitudinal axis of the building runs
north and south. The north frontage is blind, the building
thus turning its back on the *mistral.*

The block has eighteen floors, including the terrace roof
at a height of 56 metres from the ground.

The indoor streets are on floors 2, 5, 7, 8, 10, 13 and 16.

Four high-speed lifts of large capacity, grouped together, serve the indoor streets and the terrace roof, starting from an entrance hall at ground level, which is comparable to that of a big hotel.

A characteristic feature of the building is that the whole weight of the framework is carried by great reinforced concrete pylons. Between the pylons are open spaces. [These 'pylons' are of course the famous '*piloti*'. R.F.J.]

This has many advantages as regards traffic. Not only can pedestrians pass under the building but so can roads if desired. With these pylons the actual amount of ground occupied is reduced to zero, and besides the practical advantages they admit of an almost uninterrupted view of the whole terrain. As Le Corbusier has said, 'the pedestrian's eye passes under the house'. So does the air and the sunshine. If this principle was applied to a whole built-up area, towns would become practically uninterrupted areas of parkland. [Wogensky illustrates the point with a quite devastating plan showing the alarming acreage covered by ordinary small houses and roads to give the same population as *L'Unité*. R.F.J.]

Aesthetically the pylons have the effect of making the whole building seem lighter.

3 COMMUNAL SERVICES

Half the seventh and eighth floors are allocated to a big co-operative store and a few individual shops, so that the tenants can satisfy all their daily needs without leaving the block.

Also provided here are a small restaurant and a hotel of eighteen rooms, intended to take the place of spare rooms which economy denies to the apartments.

Communal services also include rooms equipped with the latest machines where the tenants can do their own washing.

4 EXTENSIONS OF THE HOME

The facilities provided under this head demonstrate Le Corbusier's anxiety to provide, within easy reach of the home, all that may be necessary to supplement it. Hence the title—*L'Unité d'Habitation*.

Chief among these are a crèche on the seventeenth floor and a kindergarten on the roof. From the crèche a ramp leads up on to the roof where there are a swimming bath and playgrounds, one of which is covered.

The remainder of the terrace roof provides amenities for adults, e.g. a covered and an open-air gymnasium, a 300-metre running track, and on a higher level a solarium with music and pastis.

The other structures above roof level are: lift shafts, water tank and two ventilation shafts.

Other 'extensions of the home' are situated on the ground, viz. garage, swimming bath, tennis courts, sports ground and playing field. To these should be added schools and other things which could not be provided with the funds available.

The Marseilles Block stands in grounds of $3\frac{1}{2}$ hectares (8·65 acres). It is a prototype. Similar buildings can be constructed to replace whole districts or even towns. Erected two or three hundred metres apart in grounds laid out as parks, they would be the realization of Le Corbusier's *Ville Radieuse*, for which he has been battling for the last thirty years. France is the first country in the world to have made it possible to carry out such an experiment.

Wogensky's reference to 'indoor streets' is of course to the public corridors serving the flats on each floor. As these run down the centre of the block they do not get any direct light. When the present author saw them in 1951 they were, in spite of their width and good proportions, somewhat gloomy. They are now said to be a feast of colour. One criticism of the building has been directed against the internal shops; does not the French housewife, it has been asked, prefer the visit to the street and the market? This is partly true but, obviously, the alternatives are open to her, while the population of *L'Unité* itself must provide much social life and gossip. Also, to walk to the shops in a Provençal August or in the *mistral* is no joke for any housewife.

Both because of *L'Unité d'Habitation*'s intrinsic qualities and because of its ruggedness, its escape from the slickness of so much modern architecture, this is a timeless building. Le Corbusier's disciples, trickling back into France after the war and remembering Garches and the *Pavillon Suisse*, were left gasping. This was in many ways the consummation of Le Corbusier's life work but also, at the same time, an architecture of an altogether different order. Le Corbusier had spent his whole life struggling for recognition, only to meet with one rebuff after another. Even while he had been building at Marseilles he was being snubbed in New York. And yet now, here in Marseilles was a man who belonged to the world and to history.

If Le Corbusier's Palace of the Soviets was the finest building never built, then almost certainly St Dié, in the Vosges, was the finest city never built. St Dié, together with *L'Unité d'Habitation*, are concepts of beauty and of courage. Tragically, only the latter was actually built. One local industrialist, it is said, vetoed the St Dié plan which had otherwise received universal approval. The Church, the factory owners, the Corporation, the trades unions and all the political parties welcomed Le Corbusier's scheme, and yet, somehow or other, could not save it from sabotage. If, as one may presume, it was 'killed' for economic reasons, then one need hardly point out that in 'tourism' alone the Municipality and citizens would long ago have recouped themselves. Who, now, would want to go to St Dié?

It is an industrial town in the Vosges. The Germans, retreating before the American army, evacuated some 10,000 inhabitants and then systematically, for three days and three nights, destroyed the place. In 1945 Le Corbusier was invited to rebuild it. His plan covered a square mile. This area was bounded to the south by the River Meurthe and to the north by the cathedral on the hill. To east and west, up the wide valley, run the main roads to Nancy and Strasbourg.

Le Corbusier planned all the factories to the south of the river, and the apartment blocks to the east of the main central area. This gave him—sandwiched between cathedral and river—a magnificent site for his town centre. It was this centre, this *place*, that was unique in the history of town design. It has served as a model for many urban projects of the last twenty years. It was abortive but its influence has been tremendous.

All through the St Dié scheme, as in all Le Corbusier's town plans since the *Ville Contemporaine* of 1922, there was a most careful segregation of traffic and pedestrians. The great *place* was reserved for pedestrians and all its dimensions were studied, not in terms of metres but in terms of how long it would take to walk from one point to another. Here, therefore, we might have had a very splendid piazza, as traffic-free as Venice itself. The main area would have been a kind of platform about 1,000 feet across, reached by ramps and bridges. This area would have been defined or demarcated by tall slabs—the apartment blocks—to the east; and then to the north a single tall office building, lozenge-shaped like the abortive tower at Algiers, would have dominated the town like some great campanile. To the south the whole *place* would have been open to the river. So far, so good: any brilliant planner might have arrived at some such arrangement. Then, however, came the touch of genius. All bleakness, all excess of space, was removed from this vast area without loss either to its open character or to its monumental scale. Lower structures, such as the restaurant, theatre, shops and a 'snail' museum, were very carefully placed and spaced, not like buildings but more as if they were huge pieces of sculpture. There is a reminiscence here of the 'carpet' of Le Corbusier's earlier theoretical cities. The whole thing was planned to be *walked* through: a series of vistas and dramatic perspectives, always changing as one moved and always designed to be seen from a man's eye-level. The result would have been both dynamic and serene; also, like Venice, curiously human in scale. It would have been 'classic' in the best sense of that word.

The present writer passed through St Dié on a winter night. Le Corbusier had already in fact built one factory there. He built it for M. Jean-Jacques Duval, a young industrialist interested in art and in ideas; in fact the true sponsor of St Dié. The factory was all Le Corbusier ever would build, but that night, under the arc lights, the last ruins of war were still being cleared away. Some of the seas of mud—destined to remain mud—were just beginning to assume a wonderful relationship, a wonderful proportion. That was about as far as they ever got, and that scene, half veiled in darkness, may well have been St Dié's best moment. Ironically it was the plan of St Dié that was exhibited throughout the United States as an example of good town-planning. It was exhibited to a nation that dislikes planning; it was a town that was never built and it was an example that was never followed.

The United Nations Headquarters, on its fine East River site in the heart of Manhattan, consists basically of three units. There is (1) the tall Secretariat Block; there is (2) the fan-shaped auditorium or Assembly Block, and then across the courtyard there is (3) the Delegations Building, virtually an apartment block carefully subordinated to the Secretariat and Assembly. This general allocation of the United Nations functions into these three more or less separate buildings, carefully grouped on a single site and carefully related both to Manhattan and to the East River, was almost certainly Le Corbusier's idea. In other words the basic sketch, the *esquisse*, the germ, was most certainly his. The United Nations Building, however much it went awry in the execution and in detail, whatever claims may have been made by others, was most emphatically Le Corbusier's concept. This would be violently denied by some of his colleagues upon the United Nations Board of Design, and also by the rather anonymous officials and delegates responsible for United Nations decisions. That these people found Le Corbusier difficult and, indeed, impossible to work with may be true. That is evidence neither one way nor the other; one must credit these officials with common integrity; one must believe that they would not deliberately belittle or discredit Le Corbusier. The thesis that he was responsible for the basic form and arrangement of the United Nations Building, which are good, but was not responsible for the decoration and detail, which are bad, must be justified.

The whole story is complicated and in parts obscure. Many people have had an interest in making it more obscure. In general terms it raises the apparently simple, but in fact often very difficult question of who was the real designer of a particular building. In most cases the answer is obvious and usually unimportant. In a few cases—some of them quite famous ones such as the British Houses of Parliament or St Peter's in Rome —the answer is by no means so obvious, and not seldom highly controversial. If often happens that so many persons are concerned, that so many decisions may or may not be taken by the nominal 'architect'. There were two in the case of the Houses of Parliament; there were fourteen in the case of St Peter's; there were ten in the case of the United Nations. That is usually a recipe for disaster. Moreover it still leaves the vital question unanswered: Who in fact conceived the basic form of the building? As between two men, or as among ten men, the genius will impose himself, impose his basic idea, and let the rest go hang. He may dislike being hated, but it cannot be helped; ten men cannot have one idea. That is certain. And, just possibly, at the end of the day each may, in all sincerity, think that the idea was his, while all he did was to accept it, enlarge upon it, talk about it, until he finally believed it to be his own child.

A very large building or a complex of buildings—in the case of the United Nations Building, as with the Capitol in Rome, three related buildings—may be built technically and economically by one man. If that man is the 'architect' then the architect of the United Nations Building was Wallace K. Harrison, a professional of the greatest integrity and experience, a man who, having built the Rockefeller Center, had an unparalleled knowledge of sky-scrapers. What he did—and even so he made mistakes, terrible mistakes of taste—probably had to be done by an American. New York, admittedly, is architecturally unique; the qualifica-tions required of an architect by New York State are the highest in the world; Wallace K. Harrison had those qualifications. Nevertheless, what he did, necessary as it was, was not archi-tecture; it was competent building.

Every great architectural concept is fertilized by an idea in a man's brain. To take an instance: whoever may have built and carved the Parthenon were great craftsmen; the great architect was the man who so placed it that it could never be seen except against the Aegean sky, and who so placed it that the horizontal rays of the morning sun would shine directly through the great doorway upon the shrine. That was archi-tecture, and it was genius. In the same way, when all the splendours and miseries of Baroque have been argued away, when the folly of Blenheim Palace—the use of a Roman style in the English Cotswolds—has been dismissed, the fact remains that that vainglorious pile was placed by John Vanbrugh neither on a plateau, nor in a valley, nor across the valley on the wooded slopes—all of which things might have been—but rather on the very edge of the plateau so that one broad plain façade should be seen sunlit across level lawns, while the other, a broken mass of towers and pinnacles, should be seen from below, from the lake, in thunderous shadow against a southern sky. That again is the stuff of genius; having done that, Vanbrugh could, if he liked, leave all the rest to Hawksmoor. So in the cities of northern Italy—Pisa, Florence, Siena, San Gimignano, Venice—some un-known genius, by the placing of a fountain or a tower, the closing or opening of a piazza, could make a city immortal. This is architecture. One man will spend laborious weeks at the drawing-board; the real architect is the man who comes along and, in a flash, turns the building back to front . . . and solves everything. That man is the architect; that was the role of Le Corbusier in New York.

It would no doubt have been more comfortable for everyone concerned if Le Corbusier had never been involved anywhere or at any time in this ridiculous business of producing architecture by committee. It was a waste of Le Corbusier, an agony for everyone else, immoral in that other people got credit for Le Corbusier's genius, and the end result inevitably was more or less disastrous. The complete fiasco of the League of Nations Building might well have been repeated; fortunately twenty years had passed, and however reluctant his confrères might be, it was hardly possible to deny Le Corbusier some say in such a great international project. That no other architect could even be considered as the representative of France shows how much water had flowed under the bridges. So, in the end and in the sense suggested here, the one man with the germ of the idea, the fundamental concept, turned out to be Le Corbusier. In that sense at least, whatever might go wrong with the building in its later stages, Le Corbusier, and no one else, was the architect of the United Nations Headquarters in New York.

Immediately after the Second World War Le Corbusier was invited to serve on the United Nations Headquarters Commission. This was only, so to speak, the first round. That Commission was not concerned with the building—not in the narrower architectural sense—but only with the choice of a site. Of course, to choose a site is in fact to cast the architectural die; it settles most things. Moreover, in this case, so far as the site was concerned there was very little choosing to do. The foolish decision to establish the United Nations upon the soil of a conqueror having been taken, and John D. Rockefeller, Jr, having presented the Commission with seventeen priceless acres of Manhattan, there was not much left to do.

Le Corbusier, writing of himself in the third person, as he often did, discussed this problem of choosing a site for the United Nations Building, envisaging the whole matter upon a higher plane than was possible for his more commonplace colleagues:

'On the United Nations Commission Le Corbusier found himself face to face with an enthralling but difficult problem—

how to create a town that should also be a headquarters, a dynamic inspiration to modern life—life which, in accordance with the *Charte d'Athène*, should allow one to live, to cultivate the body and mind and so expand one's being to its utmost. The problem is a single thing—first, a site must be chosen, but to do this one must be able to imagine the building that will occupy it. Indeed, in this choice of a site it was the birth of an organism, urban in character, that had to be foreseen. Le Corbusier's own notebook, with a text of sixty pages and some twenty sketches, makes absolutely clear the conditions which must be fulfilled if this urban organism was to be created.'[22]

Even if the United Nations did have to be in the United States there was no particular reason why, *ipso facto*, it should be in a city. It was, however, left solely to Frank Lloyd Wright to point this out. 'Grass the ground where the proposed U.N. skyscraper would stand. Buy a befitting tract of land, say a thousand acres or more, not too easy to reach. Sequester the United Nations. Why does it not itself ask for good ground where nature speaks and the beauty of organic order shows more clearly the true pattern of all peace whatsoever?'[23] This, of course, was pure Walt Whitman, or perhaps almost pure Ruskin. It never stood a chance. The sort of men who run the United Nations are apt to be, at best, statesmen; much more probably they are just politicians, civil servants and careerists. They are urban men, not in the sophisticated Latin and Roman sense, but in the modern materialist sense. However, the decision in favour of an urban site, although in fact an assumption rather than a decision, did at least one thing: it effectively ruled out Frank Lloyd Wright as architect to the United Nations. To contemplate what he might possibly have built in an Arizona landscape of his own choosing, must remain a pleasant fireside fantasy. But of the two giants of the Modern Movement, the great American had eliminated himself at the start.

This left Le Corbusier, at least in the eyes of the progressive world, as the only possible candidate; certainly the only candidate if the United Nations Building was to be designed by a single architect. And that is the only way to get a great building and fine architecture. Those in power, however, were interested neither in great buildings nor in fine architecture. They were interested, one must assume, in respectable architecture. Primarily, however, they were far more interested in three other and quite different things: (1) diplomatic niceties or protocol, which means offending nobody at the cost of pleasing nobody; (2) covering themselves if the building should turn out to be a failure; (3) keeping effective control in American hands. These points, being political rather than architectural, were most skilfully handled. The diplomatic niceties were disposed of very smartly: an 'International Board of Design' was formed, a typical but non-sensical U.N. formula; no one could say exactly how a Board designs, nor did anyone dare to ask. This Board was composed of ten architects from ten countries: France, Brazil, Sweden, U.S.S.R., Belgium, Great Britain, Australia, Uruguay, the Island of Taiwan and, of course, the United States. A very pretty distribution according to power blocks and geography! Le Corbusier from France, Oscar Niemeyer from Brazil and Sven Markelius from Sweden were architects of great distinction, the remainder were mediocrities. In spite of the mediocrities the formation of the Board was also a covering operation: if the building was a failure, at least the right men had been undeniably appointed since each country had nominated its own man. All this, of course, had nothing whatever to do with architecture; it also revealed the weakness of the United Nations almost before it was founded—the absence of a collective mind and the inability to be a great patron.

As for the control remaining in American hands, this was handled very firmly indeed, so much so that it is quite clear that the International Board never was intended to be more than a device. The whole idea that it was difficult, even impossible, for an architect to build in a foreign country was exploited to the full. In fact the idea is absurd and contrary to experience. Frank Lloyd Wright had already built in Tokyo and Venice; Lutyens had built in Delhi and Washington; Basil Spence would build in Rome; Le Corbusier would build in Berlin, Tokyo, the Punjab and Massachusetts; Saarinen in London. Of course local advice must be taken, local supervision of the building operations arranged; that is elementary. If Le Corbusier had been appointed sole architect of the United Nations Building, a well-recognized process would have been put into operation—that is all. It is possible, even probable, that Le Corbusier would have entered into some sort of amicable partnership with Wallace K. Harrison.

The status of the two men would have been perfectly clear; it would have been that of architect and agent. This was the relationship in which the late F. R. S. Yorke stood to Eero Saarinen during the building of the United States Embassy in London. Wallace K. Harrison could, without dispute or difficulty, have executed Le Corbusier's plans. In the event, however, the very most was made of the peculiar difficulties of building in Manhattan—as if every climate, every soil and every city did not always have their own peculiar difficulties—and they would keep on talking about the American 'know-how'. Wallace K. Harrison should have been technical adviser—that is not in dispute—first to the Board and then, at a later stage, to Le Corbusier. In fact he was immediately made the Board's Chairman, and then, when the Board dispersed, executive architect to the Building. For this he had every qualification except that of being a great artist.

After the Board had agreed upon what it chose to consider as its own basic design—in fact Le Corbusier's *esquisse*—it broke up, leaving Harrison in charge. He set up his own 'United Nations Headquarters Planning Office' for the development of that 'basic design' and for the erection of the Building, and officially neither the Board nor Le Corbusier were ever heard of again. The deliberations of the Board having ceased, Le Corbusier—technically just one of the ten members of that Board—lost all control of the project and a situation already tense became explosive. Fortunately Le Corbusier had kept his own diary of the Board's meetings, illustrated by his own sketches, a document now destined to be famous.

When the Board abandoned its functions to Wallace K. Harrison, Le Corbusier, had he been just another mediocrity, could have increased his self-esteem by the usual resort to what is known as 'dignity and restraint'—the usual pose of the pompous martyr, the usual euphemism for the sulks. Le Corbusier was not like that. He was furious. He bubbled with hostility. He had regarded the United Nations Building as his right. He had been robbed years ago, and for reasons little less than scandalous, of both the Palace of the Soviets and of the League of Nations Building at Geneva. That was acknowledged. And now—even more infuriating—his brilliant sketch for the United Nations Building was to be used, was to be spoilt, and the credit given to ten men. It was to be built by a commonplace though quite capable American architect.

It must be freely admitted that Le Corbusier, with every excuse, behaved badly. He claimed that his illustrated diary of the Board's deliberations had mysteriously vanished in 1948, when Wallace K. Harrison began work, and reappeared only in 1950. This seems unlikely. Le Corbusier's love-hate of the United States went back to 1935 and to his *When the Cathedrals were White*; a love-hate felt by thousands of cultured Europeans, who combine a loathing for American institutions with a craving to be American, to belong to a world that is being born rather than to a world that is dying. This feeling within Le Corbusier's breast now found an outlet in a personal, unjust and quite vituperative dislike of Wallace K. Harrison. Possibly Harrison should have declined to be the executive architect; he certainly had not sought the appointment. He was a man of integrity and skill, although not a genius. Le Corbusier now referred to him as a 'gangster'—all Americans in his eyes were gangsters—and accused him of having got his job by marrying into the Rockefeller family. It was now twenty years since Le Corbusier had had his first brush with the Rockefellers, when they declined to put up more money for his Exhibition in the Museum of Modern Art. This was something that he had neither forgiven nor forgotten. Le Corbusier never forgave or forgot. Harrison's 'gangsterism', therefore, would seem to have lain, first, in stealing Le Corbusier's design, and, second, in social climbing. It was all rather absurd and spiteful. It was not, however, complete nonsense. Le Corbusier's design had not been actually stolen by Harrison, but credit for it was in effect stolen by the Board collectively. The most that can be said against Harrison is that he should have acknowledged more fully Le Corbusier's authorship of the basic plan, and that through his Rockefeller connection he took what came to him—the Rockefeller Center and the United Nations Building. He did not seek these things.

Nevertheless, the one great unhappy fact remains that what is good about the United Nations Building is to be found in Le Corbusier's famous 'Diary', whereas what is bad was the work of others, mainly of Harrison and the team of young architects he gathered round him.

The United Nations Building as it stands today on the East River is therefore a great idea gone wrong (Pls. 11, 12). The basic form, the Corbu concept which was claimed by the Board as its own, was absolutely right. There, with its broad façade

99

to the river, is the tall Secretariat Block from which any document, or for that matter any official, can descend at a moment's
notice to the Assembly. That was the functional theme of the
design. The aesthetic theme lay in the fact that the tall, elegant
Secretariat acted as a foil to the low, widespread and fan-shaped
Assembly. Around these two major units, in spite of the relatively
small Delegations Building across the courtyard, there remains
sufficient space to have justified Le Corbusier in considering
these seventeen acres as a tiny slice, so to speak, of *La Ville
Contemporaine*, Algiers, St Dié, as the 'carpet' between the great
blocks. He even did a diagram of New York—as twenty years
earlier in the *Plan Voisin* he had done a diagram for Paris—
to show how all Manhattan should become a genuine *Ville
Radieuse*, to show just how skyscrapers should be used. And if
anyone thinks that mad, let them remember that Buckminster
Fuller would have put all New York under one big plastic dome.
. . . And still his disciples kiss his hand.

In *Le Modulor*, Le Corbusier wrote:
    'March 1947, New York.
    'Planning for the United Nations Headquarters on the
East River in Manhattan . . . the plans are drawn up, introducing the "radiant city" into the tragic hedgehog that is
New York. . . .
    'This great rhythmic swing of the buildings might have
come into being, a "passion of glass" sparkling in the
Manhattan sky; and the fabric of the interiors, the glazed
bays and the solid walls, the brise-soleils, and the stems of
the steel and concrete columns that are seen everywhere,
so like the slender ankles of the chamois carrying a robust
body—the texture of the tremendous whole—might have
been as one, fountainhead of unity; tumult in the whole (the
great rhythm of the buildings), but uniformity and *unity* in
the details. No longer mere "shapes assembled under the
light", but rather an internal fabric, firm like the flesh of
good fruit, governing all things by the law of harmonies. . . .
    'All this manifests the striving towards a *molecular
organization of things built*, on a harmonious measure to
the scale of man.'[24]

This rather chaotic piece of prose—as chaotic in French as in
English—is typically Corbu; it also gives an impression of how

differently from ordinary men he saw the United Nations Building; how he saw it given unity by means of the Modulor, and how he saw it as part of a resurrected New York.

As things worked out, those two units, Secretariat and Assembly, so right in their essential form and placing, gained nothing in execution. Mr Peter Blake, in his study of Le Corbusier, says of the tall Secretariat Block:

> 'The glass curtain wall, with its clumsy grilles along floors
> devoted to mechanical equipment, looks like a tinny carica-
> ture of Corbu's majestic façades. The lobby of the Secretariat,
> with its black and white marble squares and great lighting
> boxes, looks like a giant bathroom. The stairs and ramps—
> those sculptural counterpoints Corbu has always turned
> into such lovely flights of poetry—are hardly more sensitive
> in design than those leading to Gimbel's basement. And the
> office spaces in the Secretariat are so undistinguished that
> their best feature, in all likelihood, is that nobody seems
> to have designed them at all—a blessing when one considers
> some of the "creative design" that has been employed to
> "jazz up" several of the more public spaces in the Head-
> quarters.'[25]

Mr Blake also describes how the General Assembly block was originally to have had two fan-shaped auditories arranged back to back, so that the plan somewhat resembled an hour-glass. At a later stage it was decided that one of these auditories should be omitted. This change was so radical that according to an agreed protocol the Board of Design should have been recalled. Harrison, however, was having none of that. . . . Bring Le Corbusier back to New York! At all costs he was not going to face Le Corbusier again; perhaps his conscience would not allow it. At any rate he set to work upon the absurd task of fitting a single assembly hall within a shape originally designed for two. It was not only absurd; it was—for all Harrison's integrity—architecturally dubious. Again to quote Mr Blake: 'it proved to be about as easy as trying to fit a mermaid into a pair of pants, and about as successful'.

Paul Rudolph, now head of the School of Architecture at Yale, and probably the most subtle and sensitive designer in America, was uncompromising. In *The Architectural Forum* he wrote a pretty tart comment:

'The interiors of the U.N. Assembly Building bring the so-called International Style close to bankruptcy. Of course the building is not really a product of the International Style at all but rather a background for a Grade "B" movie about "One World" with Rita Hayworth dancing up the main ramp. . . . Le Corbusier's diagram unfortunately did not indicate the way for the Interior of the U.N. Assembly Building.'[26]

Paul Rudolph was absolutely right. Of course Le Corbusier had not shown the way to the design of the interior. He was not allowed to do that. The Board of Design never reached that detail; perhaps they thought it would have been beneath their dignity to do such detailed and 'merely' decorative work. More probably most of them wanted to get back to their own countries and their own offices anyway, while to have allowed Le Corbusier to stay on alone in New York designing interiors and other details—and generally getting in everyone's way—would not have been possible without making him the sole architect. And this, as we have seen, was unthinkable; it was something that neither the United Nations authorities nor the Board of Design itself, neither Wallace K. Harrison nor John D. Rockefeller, Jr, were ever prepared to contemplate. The building, on those terms, would have passed out of American control, and in America all hell would have been let loose. So in effect, after a single sketch for the massing had been agreed upon, Le Corbusier was sacked. . . . And that was that. The main form of the United Nations Building, as we see it today, is a monument to the genius of Le Corbusier, but it is a monument to the frustration of that genius rather than to its consummation.

To the United Nations Building there was a single postscript, another episode of bitterness and frustration in Le Corbusier's life. This was the UNESCO Headquarters in Paris. UNESCO, although originally spawned by the United Nations, had become an independent organization, and Paris was clearly the best place for it—better, at any rate, than New York. Now admittedly there had always been something to be said on behalf of Wallace K. Harrison. To give the design and execution of a New York building to the architect of the Rockefeller Center was quite unnecessary and was architecturally disastrous, but it was not entirely daft. In Paris, however, there was no reason why Le

Corbusier, an experienced Parisian architect, should not have been given full control of the UNESCO Building. It was not to be. From any orthodox or obscurantist point of view he had long since acquired the reputation of being a difficult man, the *enfant terrible* of architecture. The United Nations fiasco had not only done nothing to mitigate this reputation, it had greatly magnified it. There were also plenty of people in New York and elsewhere very ready to make sure that the U.N. story, when it came to be told in Paris, should lose nothing in the telling. Le Corbusier was 'impossible'. That he also happened to be the greatest architect of the twentieth century—even, as has been said, the Leonardo of our epoch—was neither here nor there. He must, at all costs, be prevented from building the UNESCO Headquarters. This was done by a neat trick.

The U.S. State Department concerned with UNESCO established a 'Board'—the old dodge—to choose architects for the UNESCO Headquarters. Le Corbusier was immediately made a member of that Board and was thus excluded from any chance of being appointed as executive architect. He should have refused to serve; although in the long run refusal might have made little or no difference, it just might have led to his appointment, for the Board which might have appointed him, had he not been a member of it, was more enlightened than the bunch of ten architects from ten countries who had met in New York. To describe the UNESCO Building in detail, since it was not designed by Le Corbusier, is irrelevant to our purpose. The architects chosen were Marcel Breuer, a Hungarian-born American and a Bauhaus personality, Pier Luigi Nervi, a brilliant Italian engineer, master of concrete, and Bernard Zehrfuss representing the younger generation of French architects. They were all excellent designers. This makes the omission of Le Corbusier more tragic, since it shows that the Board, unlike the reactionaries in New York, were probably quite capable of appointing Le Corbusier as executive architect, had he not in effect disqualified himself by himself being a member of that Board.

As it turned out the UNESCO Building is an interesting structure. The façade is delicate, metallic, febrile; quite different from Le Corbusier's chunky and Cyclopean concrete, but not inappropriate to the richly adorned Baroque scale of its surroundings. In fact the UNESCO Building shows what many had deemed impossible—that modern architecture can reconcile itself even to the formal and classical planning of central Paris. The building has interesting contributions by Picasso and by Henry Moore, and just here and there the details reveal the fact that Le Corbusier was used as a consultant. Had he not attempted so continuously to muscle in on this building, Breuer, Nervi and Zehrfuss might well have made even greater use of him. The UNESCO Headquarters in Paris is a fairly good example of modern architecture. It remains, however, an architectural Hamlet without the Prince of Denmark.

In spite of these sad stories of St Dié, New York and Paris, one must also remember that the post-war decade had been dominated by achievement—by *L'Unité d'Habitation* in Marseilles and by the Ministry of Education in Rio. These buildings, more than any others, were at that date a culmination of Le Corbusier's life-work, a development and summation of all his teaching and his theories through the years. In August 1946 Clive Entwistle, one of Le Corbusier's English translators, wrote from London:

> 'I take this opportunity to thank you on behalf of all young people here, for your latest gift to architecture: the *brise-soleil*, a splendid element, the key to infinite combinations. Now architecture is ready to take its place in life. You have given it a skeleton (independent structure), vital organs (the communal organs of the building), a fresh shining skin (the curtain wall); you have stood it upon its legs (the piloti). And now you have given it magnificent clothes adaptable to all climates! Naturally you must be a little proud. . . .'[27]

The present writer, for over thirty years in close touch with architectural students everywhere, can confirm that Entwistle's statement was a fair reflection of the attitude of youth towards Le Corbusier: in their eyes he has stood through the years with Einstein, Picasso, Bertrand Russell, Gandhi, Martin Luther King, Mao, Guevara. For the architectural student—and there is no other student who sees so many dreams destroyed—back in the thirties, Le Corbusier was already a hero; he at least had never compromised with his ideals. That was why the *Pavillon Suisse* —perhaps altogether beyond its intrinsic merits—became a symbol. After that Le Corbusier stood the test of time and of war. By the fifties the symbol, the banner, was the Marseilles building, while in the sixties Ronchamp and La Tourette were yet to come. As Le Corbusier himself has described in *Le Modulor*: 'The young who bring us the support of their enthusiasm and that unawareness of responsibility which is the strength and weakness of their age.'

On 4th February 1960 he lectured at the Sorbonne, a rare event. It was a far cry from the ostracism of Viollet-le-Duc a hundred years ago. It did not much matter whether one liked his buildings, whether he talked about architecture, painting, mathematics, music, philosophy or what you will. He was an honest man. 'Four thousand five hundred people thronged in front of the Sorbonne. Only three thousand could get into the large amphitheatre. Fifteen hundred filled the Rue des Écoles right up to the Boulevard St Michel.'[28]

Since the world thinks of Le Corbusier as a man of arrogance it is necessary to say that he was also, paradoxically, a very humble man. He devoted some minutes every morning to the consideration of yesterday's failings and shortcomings. Also, for all his faults and arrogance—the failing of every *prima donna*—he was at least innocent of that self-sufficient pride, the besetting sin of every don, against which youth—pathetic, foolish, inarticulate youth—is so justly angry.

Five

the modulor

'The Modulor makes the bad
difficult and the good easy;
this weapon shoots straight.'
Einstein

The visitor, walking out of Marseilles along the Boulevard
Michelet, is aware that he is approaching Le Corbusier's famous
L'Unité d'Habitation. He expects to find himself confronted by
some vast block of flats, more skilfully designed perhaps than
most of those in the world, but not very different in kind. In
fact the richly textured, richly coloured building, eventually
seen through the trees, is a vast understatement. It impresses by
its apparent smallness, not by its real size. On a nearer approach
this apparent smallness—smallness both of scale and of parts—
is seen to be not only a desirable and human thing in itself, but
also a great foil to the gargantuan *piloti*. These *piloti* carry the
entire building, seeming to hold it up in the air—as if it were a
feather-weight—lifting it clear of the ground. That, however, is
not the only object of this smallness of scale: *L'Unité d'Habitation*,
although very big, is never overwhelming. It is restrained in its
good landscape. Above all, it is extremely human; it is welcoming.

How was it done? *L'Unité* is a big building humanized by its
good scale. This, incidentally, takes much of the sting out of the
standing criticism of modern architecture—vast blocks and slabs
destroying our cities. A few years later the pilgrim chapel at
Ronchamp, although a small building, might have seemed coarse
with its sweeping curves and enormous eaves; in fact Ronchamp
is a building of refinement and charm. Marseilles is a big building
but is never overwhelming; Ronchamp is a small building which

might have seemed clumsy. In both cases the scale of the whole and of the parts relatively to the whole is under absolute control. This is almost entirely due to the correct use of the Modulor.

In both buildings all the parts are disciplined within a single system of dimensions; they are related to each other by being, all of them, based upon a single harmonious progression of dimensions. The whole of *L'Unité*, so Le Corbusier always claimed, could be built from seventeen measurements. Certain portions of Ronchamp, the little side-chapels for instance, were, according to Le Corbusier, quite ridiculously small, but because of their harmonious relationship to the rest of the building did not seen so. When he built the Carpenter Arts Building at Harvard he sent over drawings without a scale on them; when this was pointed out to him by cable, he replied simply: 'You have the Modulor!' For him at any rate the Modulor was the absolute and final working tool, the answer to everything.

Again, how was it done? True, it was the Modulor. . . . But what was the Modulor? For one thing it was that peculiar plastic tape measure, in its little tin box, which Le Corbusier always carried in his trouser pocket. After Marseilles everything he designed—the plans, façades, details, spaces of Ronchamp, La Tourette, Chandigarh, Harvard—was designed from its very inception upon the basis of the Modulor.

Basically the idea of a series of dimensions, each proportionately larger than the previous one, so as to form a harmonious progression, is fairly simple. It exists in almost every plant. To arrive at the harmonious part of this progression, however, and to be sure that any one of those dimensions could be used in juxtaposition with any other one so as to give a well-proportioned rectangle or series of rectangles—just look at the Refectory windows at La Tourette—was much more difficult. It involved historical research, much debate and experiment, and some rather complicated mathematics The account given here has been made as simple as possible; the reader who wants the mathematics of it—the diagrams and the calculations—should consult Le Corbusier's own treatise, *Le Modulor*, which is the source of all quotations in this chapter.

The whole idea, the inspiration of the thing, was Le Corbusier's, but during the German Occupation a great many people worked upon the Modulor; they worked simultaneously but were often separated for months. This work was a solace to the mind and it filled the hours. It was, one would think, as harmless a way as any of passing the time. This was not so. Mlle Elise Maillart of the Musée Cluny, author of *Du Nombre d'Or*—a treatise on an allied subject—together with the student Hanning who had worked assiduously on the problem for three years and had secretly crossed the Savoy frontier line to see Le Corbusier, and of course Le Corbusier himself, could meet only at their peril. Did the Vichy Government still ponder upon Le Corbusier's professional visits to Moscow—so long ago—in connection with the ill-fated Palace of the Soviets? Probably. With the Occupation he had had to register as an architect for the second time in his life, and Vichy had ignored his application for fourteen months. . . . Until the British guns could be heard in Versailles in the summer of 1944. Only then did Vichy no longer matter. Once again these dedicated people could meet and could work. They met in the old Studio in the Rue de Sèvres, without heat and by the light of candles.

In spite of difficulties, it was during those years of the Occupation that Le Corbusier not only painted while working upon the Modulor, but also managed to found the organization which he called ASCORAL (*Assemblée de Constructeurs pour une Renovation Architecturale*). ASCORAL was concerned with scientific research into architecture and into structure, with a view to solving some of the myriad problems of post-war reconstruction. Meeting twice a month 'in a spot well away from prying eyes' it managed to produce a vast amount of material, 'enough to fill a dozen books' on housing, prefabrication, standardization, industrial processes and city planning. In effect the Modulor thus became a section of the work of ASCORAL, if only because of its possible application to industry. In any case the Modulor was always intended to be more than an aesthetic device. Its uses as an aid to tooling up, standardization and the international movement of mechanized goods is seldom realized; these uses, which might transform industry, have been overshadowed by the use of the Modulor in Le Corbusier's architecture.*

The work of ASCORAL, however, made it obvious that the post-war world would need a system of measurement which (a) should be international, (b) should be based upon a reality such

---

* *There is a British Modulor Society, but in spite of many attempts to internationalize measurements and to apply the Modulor to spare parts of machines and so on, Le Corbusier's Modulor is still confined almost wholly to architecture.*

as the human body, and (c) should have real aesthetic value. Neither a standard measure created by surveyors and engineers, nor a purely arbitrary measure such as the metre, would fit the case, even if it was internationally accepted. On the basis of these ASCORAL conclusions Le Corbusier decided that a system of *increasing* dimensions—increasing proportionately as one goes up the Modulor Scale and harmoniously related to each other—was not only possible but could also be the basis of a standardization as valid in the factory as in the studio. One might also discover a system of proportions such as architects had been groping for through millennia. . . . And so it proved.

First and foremost, therefore, Le Corbusier was convinced that any new system should be based not upon a single unit such as the foot or metre—both arbitrary—but upon a scale of differing but mathematically related dimensions, any one of which could be used in conjunction with any other one; very roughly and simply like this:

■   ■   ■   ▪   ■ ■ ■ and so on . . .

It is then possible, from this scale—which can be taken to infinity in either direction—to make a rectangle of which the two sides may be, say, ab, ac or df, etc. This is a highly simplified explanation of what the Modulor is all about. In fact Le Corbusier produced more than one 'harmonic scale' of dimensions which should be mathematically related to each other. He and Hanning and Mlle Maillart also worked on a series of rectangles which could be based upon the scale while being also ideally proportioned in themselves. Clearly by extending the Modulor scale to the left you arrive at dimensions of infinite bigness, while by extending it to the right you arrive at the microscopic. Extension either way does not invalidate the harmonious relationship of one dimension to another. The key to the harmony, in actual use on a building, is that any rectangle—a whole façade, a plan or a window pane—in the design is made up from the dimensions on the scale but from no others. The whole series—up to and down to a reasonable size—is on Le Corbusier's pocket tape-measure. Heights, widths, volumes, can be infinitely varied in size, but, being within the discipline of the system, not infinitely varied in proportion. Size is unlimited, proportion is controlled; you have variety but not chaos.

Le Corbusier soon realized that centuries ago mankind had arrived at some such system *in musical notation, but not in linear notation.* The harmonious and progressive increase in a series of lengths might surely be pleasurable to the sensitive eye as a series of notes to the sensitive ear. The lengths, like the notes, could then be combined in an infinite number of ways. Some such thought was the starting point of the Modulor.

In the opening paragraphs of *Le Modulor* he explained this analogy between a harmonious progression of sounds and a harmonious progression of lengths. Perhaps, as he said, the only astonishing thing was that it had taken so many centuries to get there. Greece and the Renaissance had wanted some such tool as this but had never found it. The Modulor will not make a bad architect into a good one—there are other things in architecture besides proportions—but in Einstein's famous words, the Modulor makes the bad difficult and the good easy. Le Corbusier's own explanation, the opening paragraphs of *Le Modulor*, gives the whole genesis of the Modulor system.

'Past decisions—customs—habits—all these stay with us through the most overwhelming events, disturbing, constricting, wantonly interfering with the free play of the mind. We pay no attention to hindrances of this kind; yet a simple adjustment at the root of the trouble might change everything, opening the doors of the mind to the free flow of the imagination. Customs turn into habits, some modest, some all-powerful; and no one, in the midst of the exhausting conflicts of life, will realize that a simple decision can sweep away the obstacle, clearing the path for life. Yes, quite simply, for life.

'Sound is a continuous phenomenon, an uninterrupted transition from low to high. The voice can produce and modulate it; certain instruments can do the same, the fiddle for example, or the trumpet; but others are incapable of it because they are based on an order of artificial intervals invented by men: the piano, the flute, etc.

'For thousands of years men used sound to sing, or play, or dance. That was the first music, transmitted by the voice, no more.

'But one day—six centuries before Christ—someone first thought of making music permanently transmissible in another way than from mouth to ear: that is, to write it down. No method or tool was available for this. Sound had to be registered at certain determined points, its perfect continuity being destroyed in the process. It was necessary to represent sound by elements which could be grasped, breaking up a continuous whole in accordance with a certain convention and making from it a series of progressions. These progressions would then constitute the rungs of a scale—an artificial scale—of sound.

'How to divide into sections the continuous phenomenon of sound? How to cut up sound in accordance with a rule acceptable to all, but above all efficient, that is, flexible, adaptable, allowing for a wealth of nuances and yet simple, manageable and easy to understand?

'Pythagoras solved the problem by taking two points of support capable of giving both certainty and diversity: on the one hand, the human ear, the hearing of human beings (as opposed to the hearing of wolves, lions or dogs); on the other, numbers, that is to say mathematics in all its forms: Mathematica, herself the daughter of the Universe.

'Thus the first musical script was created, capable of encompassing sound compositions and transmitting them through time and space: the Doric and Ionic modes, which later became of source of Gregorian music, and so also of the practice of the Christian cult for all nations and languages. Apart from a somewhat unsuccessful attempt during the Renaissance, this practice was continued until the XVIIth century. Then the Bach family, and especially Johann Sebastian himself, created a new system of musical notation: the "tempered scale", a new and more perfect tool, which gave a tremendous fresh impulse to musical composition. The tool has been in use for three centuries, and it has proved itself able to express that subtlest of things—musical thought, the thought of Johann Sebastian, of Mozart and Beethoven, of Debussy and Stravinsky, of Satie and Ravel, of the atonal composers of our own day.

'It may well be—and I take it upon myself to predict it—that the apotheosis of the machine age will demand a subtler tool, capable of setting down arrangements of sounds hitherto neglected or unheard, not sensed or not liked. . . . One thing remains: in the course of thousands of years, the white civilization has evolved only two tools for working in sound: sound being a continuous thing that cannot be transmitted in writing unless it is first divided into sections and *measured*.

'That brings me to the theme of this work: how many of us know that in the visual sphere—in the matter of *lengths* —our civilizations have not yet come to the stage they have reached in music? Nothing that is built, constructed, divided into lengths, widths or volumes, has yet enjoyed the advantage of a measure equivalent to that possessed by music, a working tool in the service of musical thought.

'Has this absence of a tool made the spirit of man any the poorer? It does not seem so, for the Parthenon and the Indian temples, the cathedrals, and all the refinements of recent human achievement, the incredible triumphs of the last hundred years, are there to mark man's progress along the path of time.

'If a tool of linear or optical measures, similar to musical script, were placed within our reach, would it help in the process of construction? That is the question I am going to discuss here, first of all by telling the story of an enterprise which sought, and attained, such an object; then by describing the nature of the invention; then by contemplating it in its present-day setting and trying to see what position it occupies. Lastly, leaving all doors open, I will throw out an appeal for help: for the ground is open to all comers, the doors are opened wide, and anyone may have the power to blaze a surer, straighter trail than mine. I shall conclude with a simple affirmation: in our modern mechanized society, whose working tools are being perfected day by day to supply mankind with new sources of well-being, a scale of visual measures has its place because the first effect of this new tool would be to unite, co-ordinate, bring into harmony the work which is at present divided and disjointed by reason of the existence of two virtually incompatible systems: the foot-and-inch system of the Anglo-Saxon world, and the metric system on the other side.'[29]

Le Corbusier's highly imaginative conception of a Modulor scheme whereby lengths and volumes could be written down and kept in tune through the use of a notational system, comparable with that used in music, was certainly new and inspiring and—if not quite so world-shaking as he thought—of inestimable advantage to the man who knew how to use it. What more than that can you say of musical notation? The Modulor would not have made a Michelangelo, any more than musical notation made a Beethoven. Nevertheless, that notational aspect of the Modulor, based upon the idea of dimensions increasing in harmonious progression, was Le Corbusier's contribution. The idea that great architecture might owe something to *some* sort of proportional system was of course not new at all. From time to time throughout history the architect has tried to design each part of his building in some mathematical or proportional relationship to every other part; he has subordinated the parts to a system or a discipline; he has laid imaginary diagonal lines across the masses or the voids to assure himself that they all had a common proportion. Le Corbusier knew that in this respect his Modulor was not new; he said so quite clearly.

'... the Parthenon, the Indian temples, and the cathedrals were all built according to precise measures which constituted a code, a coherent system: a system which proclaimed an essential unity. Primitive men at all times and in all places, as also the bearers of high civilizations, Egyptian, Chaldean, Greek, all these have built and, by that token, measured. What were the tools they used? They were eternal and enduring, precious because they were linked to the human person. The names of these tools were: elbow (cubit), finger (digit), thumb (inch), foot, pace, and so forth. . . . Let us say it at once: they formed an integral part of the human body, and for that reason they were fit to serve as measures for the huts, the houses and the temples that had to be built.

'More than that: they were infinitely rich and subtle because they formed part of the mathematics of the human body, gracious, elegant and firm, the source of the harmony which moves us: beauty (appreciated, let it be understood, by the human eye in accordance with a well-understood human concept; there cannot and could never be another criterion).

'The elbow, the pace, the foot and the thumb were and still are both the prehistoric and the modern tool of man.

'The Parthenon, the Indian temples and the cathedrals,

the huts and the houses, were all built in certain particular places: Greece, Asia, Europe, and so forth. There was no need for any unification of measures. As the Viking is taller than the Phoenician, so the Nordic foot and inch had no need to be adapted to the build of the Phoenician, or vice versa.

'One day, however, secular thought, in its turn, set out to conquer the world. The French Revolution was a struggle of profoundly human causes. A bid for progress was made, deliverance was at hand—or at least the promise of it: doors were opening upon tomorrow: science and mathematics were entering upon new and limitless paths.

'Do we understand clearly enough what is meant when, one fine day, the zero—key to the decimal system—was created? Calculation is a practical impossibility without the zero. The French Revolution did away with the foot-and-inch system with all its slow and complicated processes. That being done, a new system had to be invented. The *savants* of the Convention adopted a concrete measure so devoid of personality and passion that it became an abstraction, a symbol: the metre, forty-millionth part of the meridian of the earth. The metre was adopted by a society steeped in innovation. One and a half centuries later, when factory-made goods are circulating all over the globe, the world is divided into two halves: the foot-and-inch camp and the metre camp. The foot-and-inch, steadfast in its attachment to the human body, but atrociously difficult to handle: the metre, indifferent to the stature of man, divisible into half metres and quarter metres, decimetres, centimetres, millimetres, any number of measures, but all indifferent to the stature of man, for there is no such thing as a one-metre man or a two-metre man.'[30]

Clearly, therefore, Le Corbusier, like the architects of the Age of Humanism, was convinced that any ultimate system of proportion or of harmonious measurement *must* be derived in some way from the human body rather than from any other product of nature, let alone from some highly theoretical subdivision of the earth's circumference.

As early as the third millennium B.C., Imhotep, the first architect in the world, had most carefully considered this problem

The Chapel at Ronchamp.
22   Nave looking east, showing the
     small coloured windows, the
     cross and the altar

The Chapel at Ronchamp.

23 The outdoor pulpit, lectern and altar

24 The smaller towers above the side chapels, and the campanile

25 The steel and enamelled door for the great processions

The Chapel at Ronchamp.
26 Note the sweeping curve of the
    roof—like a crab shell—and
    the small windows in the south
    wall

Monastery of La Tourette.
27 The two upper floors are
    friars' cells, the larger and
    taller windows give light to the
    libraries, refectory, etc.

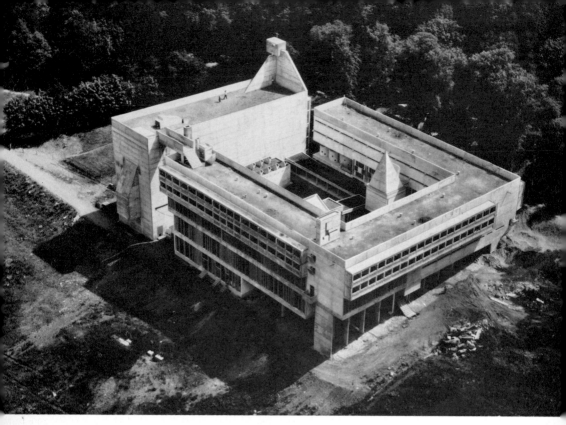

Monastery of La Tourette.

28 Air view showing the church on the left. The small pyramid within the cloister is the roof of the oratory for private prayer

29 The main Church with the Chapel of the Blessed Sacrament to the left of the altar

30 The Parlatorium. The litt kiosks near the entrance a places where friars may converse with relatives an friends

31 The refectory

Monastery of La Tourette.
32 The Lower Church where each
     friar may say privately his own
     Mass; top lit by telescopic
     windows

when designing the Stepped Pyramid at Saqqara, with its great windless courts of marble and its subterranean chapels. The Parthenon, in the fifth century B.C., was an incredibly complicated essay in mathematics—mathematics considered as a divine or mystical thing rather than as something utilitarian— mathematics as an end, not as a means. There were not only the famous and very subtle curves—correctives to optical illusions —which gave grace to a building which already had strength. The Parthenon would also seem to have had all its parts carefully related to each other by making them all multiples or subdivisions of a common module. This module—which has been most minutely calculated by modern archaeologists—was certainly not the human body or any particular division of it. Approximately it was the diameter of the column of the Doric Order, and the Roman Orders—Doric, Ionic, Corinthian, Composite and Tuscan —as we have been given them by Vitruvius are all studies for columns and the cornice above, rather than studies for whole buildings, and are all based on a column diameter, or upon some part of the Order, rather than upon some external measure. It would, therefore, seem of importance in Classical architecture to have some sort of module, some unit of measurement, some system for preserving proportions and for relating part to part. Taking for instance the diameter of the Greek Doric column as a module: the capital might be one diameter high, the frieze three-quarters of a diameter high, the cornice half a diameter high, and so on. It would also seem to have been more important to use the module, whatever it might be, correctly, than that the module itself should be of any particular dimension. For Le Corbusier, and indeed for the architects of the Renaissance, this Vitruvian thesis was too limited. They were determined to derive their proportions—the measuring unit or module from which the proportions were built up—from something more specific, even more mystical. There were Renaissance architects, for instance, who based their plans upon some mystical figure such as three— symbol of the Trinity—or upon the dimensions of the body of a Man. For the Renaissance architect there was the excuse that his world was already crammed with mystic symbols and with magic, and that for him, in the most literal sense, the Trinity was an everyday reality; there was also the excuse—for him a most valid reason—that the body of a Man was the image of God. Le Corbusier should have known better.

With these architects of the Renaissance or Baroque—architects of the Age of Humanism—we discover a whole series of attempts to arrive at some system of proportion applicable not only to the Vitruvian Orders, but also applicable to the much more complicated buildings of their own time. Francesco di Giorgi, for instance, in the first half of the sixteenth century put forward a most elaborate system for relating one part of the church plan to another part (aisle to nave, nave to chancel and so on) all on a theory of 3–9–27. Meaningless and purely mystical as the figure three might be, such systems had enormous merit in that they kept what might have been chaos within the bounds of at least some sort of order. A system based upon, say, 4–16–64 might have been just as effective, but any system was better than none.

Such systems, of course, had their absurdities, including mystical figures, whether derived from the Book of Revelations or elsewhere. The most important, by no means confined to the Renaissance or to the credulous but running all through history, was that the secret of proportion was somehow to be found in the measurements of a nude man. One Renaissance system after another was based upon the proportions of a male human spread-eagled within a circle—a circle which was also shown as contained within a square. In this respect Di Giorgio, Leonardo, Alberti and others were all playing with a Vitruvian theme, developing it in greater detail. Leonardo's system—absurd though it may be basically—is expressed in all its beauty and all its clarity and foolishness in the 'ideal' church of Santa Maria della Consolazione at Todi. One has to admit the system would have been equally valid if the church had been, say, a quarter or even one hundredth its size. The system would also have been valid if it had been based upon a five-foot or a seven-foot man. The church at Todi is, in fact, 'ideal' only in its absolute conformity to system. Its absolute symmetry, for instance, is in defiance of the varying functions of the parts which, because of the system, have nevertheless to balance each other with exactitude. The central dome is over a central space, but the climax of plan is not this space but the altar within an apse . . . and so on. It is often only too easy to demolish, by this kind of argument, many of the attempts made through history to arrive at some 'eternal' system of proportion. It is doubtful whether such a system can exist; its integrity has vanished as soon as the building is viewed in, say, sharp perspective or a strange light. What matters—and perhaps a genius like Leonardo or Le Corbusier realized this—was that there must be *some* system if only to provide order rather than chaos, and that that system, to be workable, must be codified so as to become a useful tool.

A more curious fact is that Le Corbusier, the supreme architect of the modern world, clung so obstinately to the supreme belief of the Baroque world, that in the dimensions of a man lay the starting point of any sound proportional system. But if a man, why not a woman, why not a dwarf or a giant, why not an oak tree or a butterfly, both of which are almost always beautiful although a man is only occasionally so? It was all very well for the mediaeval or Renaissance worlds, under the intellectual guidance of the Church, to hold such theories about Divine Man, Adam, God's image and so on; Le Corbusier was fully aware that Man was only a biological species on a particular planet at a particular moment in evolution, and that aesthetically he was of no more significance than any other aspect of a universe filled with objects both beautiful and hideous. For some incomprehensible reason this allegedly unique character of the human dimension still haunted him, and did so to the end. What did matter, of course, was that the basic dimension, the starting point of any modulor or 'harmonic scale' of dimensions, should be easily comprehended—neither macroscopic nor microscopic—and that it should seem to credulous men to have some origin in the Divine scheme of the Universe. By the oddest chance Le Corbusier did in the end hit upon a dimension which satisfied him and which satisfied all these criteria. On the basis of that dimension he based the final version of the Modulor.

For this key dimension in the Modulor scale the height of a man—if that appealed to one—would seem to be as good as anything, although not necessarily better. Men vary; Man, as Le Corbusier had pointed out, is never a precise number of metres high, so that on this point God who presumably made Man, and the French savants who certainly made the metre, were at odds with each other. This worried Le Corbusier quite a lot until one day it was remarked by one of his assistants that in English detective novels the 'good-looking man'—the hero or the policeman—is always six feet tall! That assistant in the Rue de Sèvres might have thrown in the guardsman for good measure! Anyway, that was how, comically enough, Bulldog

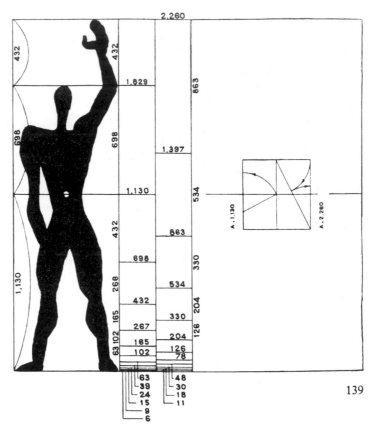

Figure 2 Le Corbusier's Modulor figure.

Drummond came to be the starting point of the Modulor—that system of dimensions in harmonious progression which bids fair to modify the architecture of the world for generations to come.

It was funny but it didn't matter. It satisfied Corbu's inexplicable obsession with Baroque systems—systems based upon an entirely different and mystical way of thought. And of course six feet was a nice round number: better if it had been ten or the sacred three, but still it would do. Also, some other totally different dimension, if it had happened to give a nice looking set of proportions on the Modulor scale, would have done just as well. The pace of the Roman legionary and the length of Henry III's arm are, for instance, both incorporated into Anglo-Saxon linear dimensions and are just as likely to be mystically valid as the kind of dimension to which Le Corbusier now became committed ... the image of God as reflected, for instance, in the hero of romance. In any case that theoretical six feet of the English hero—and of course in practice it was always just as likely to be six feet one inch or five feet eleven—before it could be used on the drawing boards of the Rue de Sèvres, had to be translated into 182·88 cm. Le Corbusier took this 182·88 cm. quite seriously and has explained to us at length how the series of harmonious dimensions at which he had already arrived during the Occupation, could now be finally and forever adjusted, 182·88 cm. being the starting point. To his delight these figures of the new post-war Modulor, although quite arbitrary in terms of metres, did in fact work out at round figures of feet and inches. That was his claim, and it is a claim that must be conceded if it is also conceded that a figure of, for instance, $27\frac{1}{2}$ inches, is a round number. Le Corbusier now had no doubts whatever: this was the finalization in precise form of all the mathematical work that had been done during the war, crystallized into a workable linear notation with help of the English guardsman:

> 'We tried to apply this standard [i.e. the six-foot man]: six feet$=6\times30\cdot48=182\cdot88$ cm. To our delight, the graduations of a new "Modulor", based on a man six feet tall, translated themselves before our eyes into round figures in feet and inches!
>
> 'It has been proved, particularly during the Renaissance, that the human body follows the golden rule. When the Anglo-Saxons adopted their linear measures, a correlation was established between the value for a foot and that for an inch; this correlation applies, by implication, to the corresponding values in the body. From that moment onwards, we were dedicated to translating our new "Modulor", based on a human height of six feet (182·88 cm.), into round figures. We were thrilled. Soltan drew a new graduated strip, this time in its final form, which replaced the old one in the little aluminium box at the bottom of my pocket.'[31]

Henceforth all pictorial explanations of the Modulor—and a huge one is cast in the concrete at Marseilles, rather like the incised figures on the pylons of Egyptian temples—show the Modulor scale related to the parts of a most curious silhouette of a nude and muscular creature with an upraised arm, raised just enough to give the correct dimension at that point in the series. . . . The Modulor Man, hero of a thousand English detective stories!

Although Le Corbusier was naïve enough to succumb to the age-long delusion that some mystical or divine proportion could be derived from the human body—a proportion which in any case can exist only when the body, a three-dimensional object, is drawn out flat and in a particular posture—he was at the same time clever enough to know that that in itself was inadequate, that if it was valid at all it was only as the starting point of a system, his own system of dimensions on a 'harmonic scale'. His early worship of the Parthenon should in any case have told him that there is no such thing as a divine measurement, only some over-riding or governing measurement such as the Greek module or diameter of the column, serving to bring the whole building within a discipline, avoiding visual tumult. Le Corbusier must also, surely, have realized that his own Modulor—whether 182·88 cm. was derived from God or not—would only have been invented by a sophisticated intellectual such as himself, someone with an incredibly sensitive eye for proportion, and could therefore be operated only by a great artist. In other words, the Modulor might be a tool for a very skilled worker; it was never a magic spell.

In fact this business of the dimension derived from the human body turned out to be the least important element in the whole of Le Corbusier's Modulor. It may even have been something of a red herring, a picturesque idea, almost a trade mark. Le Corbusier, one must remember, was always a good publicist. The *réclame* of the Modulor Man has been terrific. The Modulor Man, however, was also something of a Procrustean bed, an arbitrary thing to which the fine Modulor Scale of harmonious progression would seem to have been made to fit; or would it be more accurate to say that that Man's anatomy was ingeniously juggled to fit the Scale? To the theory of this divine Man we shall return in a moment, but first we must look at all the other elements in the Modulor.

The Modulor, as eventually used by Le Corbusier, the working tool enshrined on the tape in his pocket, was derived from five principal elements. (1) The important place of the right-angle in any sort of architecture; that unique angle, unique because it is the angle subtended by the force of gravity whereby everything falls at a right-angle to the surface of a flat earth. The obviously unique character of the right-angle, differentiating it from all other angles, is the most mysterious thing about it. It played a major part in the work of Hanning and Mlle Maillart when they evolved their series of rectangles based upon the first Modulor scale. (2) The fact that man had never treated visual beauty as he had treated musical beauty—something capable of precise division, harmonious progression and, above all, of precise notation (the bar, the octave, the scale and so on)—a great building on a Modulor basis being the equivalent of an orchestral score. The Greeks may have come within an ace of this but could never have codified it, not as music was codified in the time of Bach. (3) The old and well-known fact that a certain proportion such as, for example, 8:3, or the Golden Cut, or a rectangle so designed that its long side is equal to the diagonal of a square based upon its short side, are mysteriously pleasing to the eye, whether in small things such as window panes or big things such as whole façades, or even town squares. (4) That some such proportion as the Golden Cut should be the starting point for a whole series of dimensions arranged in a simulacrum of musical notation. Each dimension, as set out on Le Corbusier's tape or alongside the Modulor Man is bigger than the one next below it in the 'harmonic scale', but always bigger by a proportionate amount. The vital point, of course, is that any one of these dimensions can be made to form one side of a rectangle, with any other one as the shorter side, and the rectangle will be of a perfect proportion. (5) That against this Modulor scale—or 'harmonic scale'—it should be possible to fit that curious Modulor Man. The various parts— foot to navel, navel to shoulder, shoulder to head, head to top of uplifted arm—are all successive dimensions of the scale. Le Corbusier would of course disagree with this statement; he would claim not that the Man was fitted to the dimensions but that the dimensions were derived directly from the Man.

A word must now be said about each of these elements of the Modulor, and of how each came into existence: first, in a general way during the course of Le Corbusier's life—all the time he was moving towards the Modulor; and second, how each, in a more specific form, was arrived at in the 'hide-out' during the years of the Occupation, and then after the Liberation, back in the Rue de Sèvres, in a more final form.

In *Le Modulor* Le Corbusier has told us, in almost Ruskinian fashion, how his first boyhood studies were made in the mountains of the High Jura, under that excellent mistress, Nature. He illustrates his point with an even more Ruskinian, more boyish, sketch of a little fir tree, the spacing of the boughs up the trunk being already a kind of Modulor progression. Then, he says, he went out into the world where, as architect and painter, he practised an art in which *all is measured*. It might be a world where all was measured, and moreover measured with a precision and hard practicality unknown to Nature; all the same it seems strange that Le Corbusier, having reproduced his little sketch of the fir tree, failed to realize that a well-formed tree trunk, putting out a bough each year but with the spaces between those boughs progressively increasing as you go down the trunk—a year's growth being added annually to each—might well form a better starting point for the Modulor Scale than the tortured anatomy of the Man, tortured to fit a theory.

At the age of twenty-three, when he was sorting out picture postcards on the table in his little attic in the Rue Jacob, the corner of one card happened to lie across another, a picture of Michelangelo's Capitol in Rome. Le Corbusier, like Saul of Tarsus, was struck by a blinding flash: the whole composition of the façade and all its parts, wherever you placed a diagonal across it, was governed by the right-angle. 'The *lieu de l'angle droit* was a revelation, a certitude.' He then tested it on a painting by Cézanne; it worked. In Auguste Choisy's *History of Architecture*—a classic in those days—some pages devoted to the *tracé regulateur* of various compositions again confirmed him in his Pauline conversion. Then and there he wrote a poem to the Right Angle!

And that same year, aged twenty-three, he had been designing the elevation of a house on his drawing-board.

> 'A perturbing question arose in his mind. "What is the rule that orders, that connects all things? I am faced with a problem that is geometrical in nature; I am in the very midst of a phenomenon that is visual; I am present at the birth of something with a life of its own. By his claws shall the lion be known. Where is the claw, where the lion?" . . . Great disquiet, much searching, many questions.'[32]

It was in 1921, at the Galerie Druet, that Le Corbusier first exhibited his paintings. The best of them, painted in 1919, together with a series painted in 1920, he described as 'almost good . . . an improved form, with a categorical design to hold it together, enclose it, give it a structure. . . . Two mathematical expedients were used in these paintings: the place of the right angle and the golden mean'.[33]

All the buildings that Le Corbusier designed in the twenties bore witness to his then rather rudimentary conception of an architecture based upon some sort of proportional system. This applied to such comparative juvenilia as the *Pavillon de L'Esprit Nouveau* (1925), the Villa Stein at Garches (1927), the Villa Savoie at Poissy (1929–31) and, of course, to the *Pavillon Suisse* in Paris (1930–2).

In these cases, however, Le Corbusier admitted that his use of the right angle and the diagonal of the Golden Cut for arriving at a harmonious composition was purely two dimensional. It was a matter only of arranging the proportions of the façade, the shapes and sizes of windows and so on—something that had always, to a greater or lesser degree, been done by architects throughout history. The English Georgian window pane, for example, was often based upon the 8 to 3, or the Golden Cut. To use a proportional system in this way did not take architecture any further, but it was something. All this was true, one suspects, right up to the time of Marseilles, and it was only then—with the preliminary Occupation period work on the Modulor in front of him—that Le Corbusier could use his system to fix all the dimensions of a building: its total form and shape, its volumes as well as its planes, its spaces as well as its solids. At Ronchamp, at La Tourette and at Chandigarh the whole building, in mass and detail, was conceived *wholly* in terms of the Modulor. That is why Ronchamp is a little building which is nevertheless impressive; that is why the tall and elegant windows of La Tourette are so vibrant; that is why the vast spaces of Chandigarh are not deserts but part of a city.

In the twenties, however, the system, in the very embryonic form it had then reached, was also used by Le Corbusier in his many town-planning projects. In such projects as the *Plan Voisin* or the *Ville Contemporaine*—never of course intended to be built —it was used for fixing the whole mesh of roads, spaces, houses, etc. This was probably an error. It is an unconvincing use of any system, since such proportions on a town plan are never discernible to the human eye, only from the air. He realized this. By the time he was designing St Dié and Chandigarh, which *were* intended to be built, Le Corbusier was thinking of the proportions and shape of the town as something beheld by a man in motion, a man walking through the town. It was in this context, that of the 'man's eye view', that St Dié and the whole city of Chandigarh were conceived, and in that context that the Modulor was correctly and profitably used, to marvellous effect.

In addition to the aesthetic advantage of some kind of Modulor System, there had always bulked large in Le Corbusier's mind, as was bound to be the case with anyone building in modern materials, the fact that this was a 'machine age'. As early as 1921 he was writing: 'Mass production, machine efficiency, cost price, speed. . . . All these concepts call for the discipline of some system of measuring.' Since standardization there would have to be—the machine demanded it—better the standardization of the artist than of the mechanic. And, above all, since it was clearly necessary to standardize, it was also necessary to standardize not a single proportion but a whole series of proportions. . . . Or rather a means of arriving at an infinite number of well-proportioned parts. That was the ultimate goal of any system or, if you preferred to put it another way, that was Divine Proportion.

That goal, in the fullest sense, was attained only with the full codification of the Modulor. Le Corbusier had always known that before that goal was reached there would be a lot of mathematical work to be done, both on the harmonious series of dimensions and on the rectangles to be made from them. It must be possible to create shapes and volumes of all kinds within the discipline of the system, as a symphony is created within the discipline of the harmonic scale.

Le Corbusier and Hanning had been working for years on these mathematical problems, working towards their dream.

> 'My dream is to set up, on the building sites . . . all over our country one day, a "grid of proportions", drawn on the wall or made of strip iron, which will serve as a rule for the whole project, a norm offering an endless series of different combinations and proportions; the mason, the carpenter, the joiner will consult it whenever they have to choose the measures for their work; and all the things they make . . . will be united in harmony. That is my dream.'[34]

The dream never quite came true, but nevertheless that 'Proportioning Grid' was born—the ASCORAL Grid. Virtually it consisted of a series of rectangles—mainly the work of Hanning

—based primarily upon the Golden Cut, but also related to the Modulor Scale. Hanning's rectangles, with an arrangement of interlocking diagonals assuring that each should grow out of the adjoining one, were well proportioned in themselves and also, being related to the Modulor Scale, confirmed the aesthetic validity of that Scale, however absurd the origin of the Modulor Man and his anatomy might have been. If that ASCORAL Grid was never in fact used 'on building sites all over the country' as Le Corbusier had hoped, 'it did at least supply an abundance of harmonious and useful measures for the planning of rooms, doors, cupboards, windows and so on . . . to lend itself to infinite combinations of mass production, to take in the elements of prefabricated buildings and to join them without difficulty.'

It was not a simple or an easy matter, and this is not the place to expand upon the mathematics of either the Modulor Scale or the ASCORAL Grid. As Le Corbusier said: 'To tell the truth, we were not yet in full agreement,' and it was not until 1945 that the Proportioning Grid was finally agreed upon, and that it was brought into harmony with the subdivisions of the Modulor Man. A complete and, it must be admitted, very marvellous proportional system now existed, if the world, not just architects, but engineers, builders, designers of all kinds, cared to use it.

It had taken time. Le Corbusier and Hanning had not really applied their minds to the subject until the war, and in the end it was over thirty years from the day in 1910 when the young Le Corbusier could ask himself, 'where is the claw, where the lion?' to the day when the Modulor tape could at last lie by his drawing-board with the protractor and the compasses.

The acceptance of the Modulor by the world was another matter—swinging from enthusiasm to incomprehension. The patent engineer who examined Le Corbusier's numbers, figures and diagrams, said: 'In my life as a patent engineer this hour spent with you shall be a landmark.'

In 1947, in the midst of the United Nations Building controversy, Le Corbusier addressed the American Association of Architects upon the whole subject of Proportion and the Modulor. He did so in the crowded amphitheatre of the Metropolitan Museum in New York. On the voyage over, in the Liberty Ship *Vernon S. Hood*—a nineteen-day crossing—the passengers were in dormitories. Le Corbusier and the French Minister of Reconstruction, Claudius-Petit, borrowed a cabin from one of the crew for a few hours each day. It was there that Le Corbusier developed the whole theory further, making one form grow out of another—one-dimensional and three-dimensional volumes as well as shapes. One day they noticed that the bridge and other parts of the ship were most agreeably proportioned. Out came the magic tape. Yes, the ship had apparently been designed upon the Modulor System! This took one right back to the days of *Vers une Architecture* and *L'Esprit Nouveau*, to the discovery of the machine age, to Van de Velde's 'the Engineers are our Hellenes', to liners, cars and turbines as the greatest exemplars of design. One had come full circle: the Modulor had, in effect, proved the thesis of *Vers une Architecture*.

The effect of *L'Unité d'Habitation de Marseilles* upon the collective mind of the architectural world was shattering. Le Corbusier was explaining the Modulor everywhere. In London he pinned up large sheets of paper, and with the help of a big pencil, explained it to the students. When he had finished, they tore down the sheets and auctioned them. After New York he gave a similar address to Colombian architects at Bogotà, while the VIth Congress of CIAM at Bridgwater in England devoted itself almost entirely to the subject.

Finally, whether officially intended or not, the 1951 Triennale at Milan was dominated by the subject. . . . It was in the air. The Italians, after all, for at least 2,000 years have understood and enjoyed form and proportion better than anyone in the world. It has been their 'thing'. At the Triennale of 1951 the famous Studio BPPR, under the guidance of Ernesto Rogers, arranged an extraordinary display. The basis of this display was Carla Marsoli's remarkable collection of books showing the theme of Proportion from the setting out of the Pyramids through the Hellenic, Vitruvian and Palladian epochs . . . to Le Corbusier. The Modulor had certainly been the spark to fire this particular mine. It was also the focal point for a very crowded international congress. This Congress was officially organized by the City of Milan. It was called DIVINE PROPORTION. An international congress, organized by a modern industrial city, on Divine Proportion! Le Corbusier had perhaps obtained almost more than he had bargained for.

If there was a God then God, surely, was the supreme mathematician. 'Mathematics, daughter of the universe,' he said; and later, in his letter to the Bishop at the Ronchamp consecration:

'. . . all-embracing mathematics which is the creator of that space which cannot be described in words.'

In the Third Chapter of *Le Modulor*[35] he wrote this:

'*Passée la porte des miracles* . . . Mathematics is the majestic structure conceived by man to grant him comprehension of the universe. It holds both the absolute and the infinite, the understandable and the forever elusive. It has walls before which one may pace up and down without result; sometimes there is a door: one opens it—enters—one is in another realm, the realm of the gods, the room which holds the key to the great systems. These doors are the doors of the miracles. Having gone through one, man is no longer the operative force, but rather it is his contact with the universe. In front of him unfolds and spreads out the fabulous fabric without end. He is in the country of numbers. He may be a modest man and yet have entered just the same. Let him remain, entranced by so much dazzling, all-pervading light.'

Six

building for
Christic

'I was glad when they said
unto me, Let us go into the
house of the Lord.'
Psalm 122

The story is well known: how John Henry Newman, a century
ago, having been traduced, misunderstood and misrepresented
throughout his long life, was at last made a Cardinal of the
Roman Church; how he exclaimed in ecstasy: 'Now the cloud
is lifted from me forever.' Although the circumstances in 1950
were widely different, the moment not so precisely defined,
nevertheless Le Corbusier could have said the same: 'The cloud
is lifted from me forever.'

In 1950 there was a great miracle. Le Corbusier was invited to
become a member of the Institut de France (Académie des
Beaux-Arts). He declined: 'Thank you, never.' His name, he
said, would be used to hide the utterly superficial movement of
the École des Beaux-Arts towards 'modernism'. The years have
proved him right. 'One gets nominated,' he said, 'to academies
all over the world without being asked, but Paris is something
altogether more serious. Alas for Paris, the wasteland, the ruthless battlefield! One day the crust of your harsh earth will yield,
and roots will spring ... the roots of Paris, great mute city,
secret and supreme.'[36] But of course that harsh earth, as he well
knew, would never yield to academies. It was about that time,
too, that Lewis Mumford, one of the wiser men of this century,
addressed a London architectural school as 'students of the post-
Corbusier Age!' Would he, say five years later, still have said it?
Looking at Le Corbusier's work in the last decade of his life one
can but wonder.

128

Looking back with hindsight, the extraordinary achievement of *L'Unité d'Habitation de Marseilles* would seem to be a watershed. Never in the years that remained to him would there be any more such agonizing and stupid episodes as the abortive Palace of the Soviets or the League of Nations Building, and they are merely two examples. All that was now behind him. At sixty-five he was master of his destiny! Never again would he have to build for men whom he mistrusted or who mistrusted him. The time left to him was short, but it was to be filled with achievement. There was even, at long last, to be a great city. We said that when Le Corbusier's apprenticeship—those years with Hoffmann, Perret and Behrens—was over, that he was ready to build. It would have been truer to say that, knowing what he wanted, he was ready to fight, ready to act upon that family maxim from Rabelais: 'Whatever you do, see that you do it.' That fight had been going on for over forty years. Marseilles was the turning of the tide.

Now at least he could feel that he was either rejected or accepted. He need not go where he was not wanted. England was one of the few countries of the civilized world where he had never been invited to build. That sort of thing no longer mattered; he need build only for those who were ready to accept him for what he was, a very odd but quite incorruptible artist.

It was Christmas time in Paris, 1950, when the present writer was hauled out of bed at dawn to answer the telephone. It was a summons to the studio in the Rue de Sèvres. That long, white, cool and vaulted studio, above the old cloister, was very quiet. There was a secretary and a telephone, but none of the other paraphernalia seemingly so necessary to modern efficiency. On one table there was still the bowl of confetti that had been stirred around until the combination of colours gave just what was wanted for the painted jambs of the Marseilles balconies. On one large, clean drawing-board were fewer than a dozen lines fixing irrevocably the modulor proportions of the next *Unité—L'Unité d'Habitation de Nantes-Rezé*.

At one end of the studio was the little office used for interviews. His own thinking, research and drawing were all done elsewhere—at the other end of 'a well cut off telephone'—in the sacrosanct privacy of his own little studio at Auteuil. This office off the Rue de Sèvres studio was a mere cubby-hole. In his austere manner he was excited. The Archbishop of Besançon and even, so he said, the Pope, had approved the first model for a pilgrim chapel to be built upon a high hill in the Vosges, just off the road from Belfort to Vasoules. This was the birth of Ronchamp—the Chapel of Notre-Dame-du-Haut de Ronchamp.

Also, on the previous day a delegation of the Punjabi Government had arrived in Paris. They had come there to see Le Corbusier, to ask him to form an international team which, under his command, would build a new capital of the Punjab, at the very foot of the Himalayas. This was the birth of Chandigarh.

Le Corbusier wanted information about young English architects who might, just possibly, become members of the 'international team'. He was given that information there and then, a fair and impartial but rigorous assessment of half a dozen more or less brilliant architects—their technical ability, their achievements, their personalities, their aesthetic sensibility. He had met most of them from time to time at CIAM gatherings all over the world. On that 'short list' there was, of course, the name of the famous Maxwell Fry-Jane Drew partnership. Almost inevitably there came the Frenchman's gesture of doubt about a 'woman in business'. The fact is that Le Corbusier's life had been dogged—almost wrecked—by 'teams' and 'committees'. He was having none if it, but with the bitter experience and wisdom of the years was not saying so. Therefore, funnily enough and in the end, the Chandigarh 'team' consisted of himself, his cousin Pierre Jeanneret —an old partnership within which the two men understood each other—and . . . Maxwell Fry and Jane Drew. To Max and Jane, as we shall see, he gave the housing work at Chandigarh, of which, needless to say, they made a brilliant job. Note, however, that the Punjabi idea of a 'team' had all ended up with Le Corbusier in supreme command of the whole city—the Master Builder of Chandigarh.

So, looking back, one can see that Christmas in Paris as being a rather critical time in Le Corbusier's career. Ronchamp and Chandigarh were both being born, and out of Ronchamp, three years later would come the great Dominican Monastery of La Tourette. These three great works would fill the last seventeen years of his life. The cloud had indeed been lifted. In the Archbishop of Besançon, in that great Dominican, Père Couturier, and in Pandit Nehru, he had found three great patrons. For the Marxist, the Cubist, the Atheist, the Anarchist, the Nihilist—

33   House for Dr Currutchet, La
Plata, Argentine. 1949

34, 35   Ministry of Education
Building, Rio de Janeiro.
1936–45. The Portico

Palace of Assembly, Chandigarh.
36 The Portico   37   From the west

38 Palace of Justice, Chandigarh:
main entrance

39 The Palace of Justice

40 The Secretariat, Chandigarh

41 The Secretariat: detail of
brise-soleil grille

42 Villa Shodan, Ahmedabad. 1955

43 National Museum of Western Art, Tokyo. The Museum houses the famous Matsukata Collection; internally it is planned as a 'square snail'

and perhaps at one time or another he really had been all of them—this would seem to the conventional mind to be odd indeed; to the more perceptive it may seem extremely appropriate, a curious consummation of all that Le Corbusier had stood for in his incorruptible opposition to Western materialism.

The cloud may have lifted. . . . And yet even Ronchamp was a child of disappointment. In 1948 the world's response to Le Corbusier's plans for the Retreat of La Sainte-Baume—an almost forgotten project now—had hurt him deeply. M. Edouard Trouin, a geometrician, owned some land at La Sainte-Baume, in the hills between Marseilles and Toulon. There was a legend that among those hills Mary Magdalene had passed her last years. The inevitable relic, her skull, was believed by the faithful to be preserved in the grotto of the basilica at the foot of Mont Saint-Pilon. It was there that M. Trouin wished to found a place of forgiveness and peace. Whether it was the influence of Père Couturier, the work going on at Marseilles or the architect's mystical conception of mathematics—God is a mathematician—that appealed to the geometrician, we do not know. Anyway he invited Le Corbusier to crystallize his idea in some architectural form. The site was an extraordinary one, with the peak of Mont Saint-Pilon rising precipitously above a wooded plateau. The grotto was to be transformed into an underground church, while at the edge of the plateau Le Corbusier planned buildings for hermits' cells and also an hotel for pilgrims. The plan was good, beautifully subordinated to the dramatic landscape, and everything seemed to be set fair. Then, for reasons incomprehensible to Catholic and Atheist alike, the very idea of a 'modern' hermitage began to be denigrated as 'scandalous'. This time at least Le Corbusier had every reason to feel aggrieved; it was his patron who was being attacked, and without reason.

It was two years later that Le Corbusier was invited to design a new chapel at Ronchamp—a pilgrim chapel of Notre-Dame-du-haut—to replace the old one which had been destroyed by allied artillery. In the bitter aftermath of La Sainte-Baume Le Corbusier had no very kindly feelings towards the Church. He declined. Fortunately, by happy chance, Canon Lucien Ledeur, who had come from the seminary of Besançon, in the Ronchamp diocese, was now secretary of the Commission for Ecclesiastical Art, a Corbu enthusiast and a native of Ronchamp. It was Canon Ledeur who pursuaded Le Corbusier to change his mind. Le Corbusier was able later to describe him as 'the real spur' to Ronchamp. The first model was prepared—in all fundamentals it remained unchanged—and in May 1950 a delegation arrived at the Rue de Sèvres. Canon Ledeur brought with him M. Jardot of the Archives Photographiques de France; M. Mathey, now director of the Museum of Decorative Arts in Paris; and the Archbishop of Besançon. Also present, possibly at Le Corbusier's invitation, were the Minister of Reconstruction, M. Eugène Claudius-Petit, who had originally commissioned Le Corbusier at Marseilles, and also Le Corbusier's old Friend Père Couturier. It was Couturier who probably acted at this conference as the architect's advocate. If Le Corbusier was able to call Canon Ledeur the 'spur', he called Père Couturier the 'real awakener'.

From time to time this Père Couturier was destined to play a significant role in the affairs of Le Corbusier. He was a Parisian Dominican. As long ago as 1925, in collaboration with the Capuchins of Blois, he had initiated the Union des Artistes Modernes which was meant to turn the attention of artists and craftsmen to ecclesiastical art. If Père Couturier's action did not lead to a great renaissance of art within the Church, it did at least, as many will remember, lead to a genuine revival of French tapestry. For this Union des Artistes Modernes, Père Couturier enlisted the aid of Le Corbusier—a friendship which, in the long run, did more for ecclesiastical art than any Union or other organization could have done. A quarter of a century later Père Couturier was supporting M. Trouin in his patronage of Le Corbusier in the sadly abortive scheme for La Sainte-Baume. And now, in May 1950, here he was yet again, as the 'awakener' of the Ronchamp project. Three years later he would be expounding to Le Corbusier the whole philosophy of the Dominican Order as a preliminary to the building of the great Monastery of La Tourette. For the moment, however, his burning cause was that of a pilgrim chapel at Ronchamp.

Le Corbusier was no longer fighting for work. These men were not in his studio as patrons. They were there to beg of him: 'Go to Ronchamp, Corbu, and do a great job. Out of *L'Unité d'Habitation de Marseilles* you made a temple for the family. Here your work will bear different fruit.'[37] We do not know what conditions, what freedom, were insisted upon by the architect, but whatever they were—perhaps with the support of

Couturier—they were granted. And naturally, therefore, in due course everyone was rewarded, not least the whole world by the sight of one of Le Corbusier's finest buildings.

What we do have is the letter[38] which Le Corbusier addressed to the Archbishop five years later, when the Chapel was consecrated:

> Excellency:
>
> In building this Chapel, I wished to create a place of silence, of prayer, of peace, of spiritual joy. A sense of what was sacred inspired our efforts. Some things are sacred, others are not—whether they be outwardly religious or otherwise. Our workmen, and Bona the foreman, Maisonnier from my office, the engineers and calculators, other workmen and firms, and also Savina the sculptor, are among those who have brought this project into being. It was a project difficult, meticulous, primitive, made strong by the resources brought into play but sensitive and informed by all embracing mathematics which is the creator of that space which cannot be described in words.
>
> A few scattered symbols, a few written words telling the praises of the virgin.
>
> The cross—the true cross of suffering—is raised up in this space; the drama of Christianity has taken possession of the place from this time onwards.
>
> Excellency: I give you this chapel of dear, faithful concrete, shaped perhaps with temerity but certainly with courage in the hope that it will seek out in you (as in those who will climb the hill) an echo of what we have drawn into it.
>
> *Le Corbusier:* 25.6.55.

Note how, in this letter to the Archbishop, Le Corbusier says not only that the project was 'difficult, meticulous'—which is obvious—but also that it was 'primitive'. This does not mean that Ronchamp was a building in some vernacular or that it was in any sense 'folk art'. On the contrary, it used more than one technique hitherto unknown to architecture. Ronchamp is timeless.

'Timeless' is not a word to be used without thought. There is much good architecture, some of the very best, that is good without being timeless. The houses of Frank Lloyd Wright, for instance, may be seen as a very precise bridge between the earlier Ruskinian-Morris romanticism and the later pioneering buildings of the Modern Movement. The finest work of Mies van der Rohe will almost certainly endure but may be instantly dated; almost its whole justification is that it was very necessary to show that steel—utilitarian steel—could be handled with all the pure artistry of Athenian marble. In this sense, Le Corbusier's later works, although modern in their techniques, are truly outside time. Timeless.

Ronchamp, then, is timeless. It is almost primaeval. It is primaeval and strong, but not in the 'cyclopean' sense of the Marseilles *piloti*; primaeval and strong simply in the sense that it is very bold and, although in reality incredibly sophisticated, also very simple. It stands up to the supreme test: nothing can be added, nothing taken away. It is the work of a great master but it is also, fundamentally, a village chapel, a possession of the peasantry. It is also, if one will, a return to the old architecture of the wall, but definitely—most definitely—*not* to the architecture of façade. On the contrary, Ronchamp is perhaps the most three-dimensional object ever conceived and built. It is not only that one can walk round and round it in order to enjoy it, as if it were some marvellous piece of abstract sculpture; it is also architecture, and so it has an additional dimension. One walks round it, but one also walks through it. One experiences both form and space—literally the shape of space. Ronchamp thereby becomes an architecture that scores over all sculpture. It is timeless because it is primitive, but not because it owes nothing to time. It owes almost everything to time.

It has, needless to say, no stylistic bits and pieces whatever, and yet, being timeless, it belongs to all times. It is, for instance, very Greek, owing more than one can know to those months when the young Le Corbusier was alone up on the Acropolis, seeing things that no one had ever seen before: how small, for instance, everything was, and how everything was 'a cry of inspiration, a dance in the sunlight. . . .' And then, too, the Ronchamp site is after all almost an Acropolis in itself. There is nothing very Roman about Ronchamp, it is true, but some observers have felt an aura of a Christianity so primitive as to make them think of the catacombs. Then too—it is obvious—Ronchamp is very Byzantine; one can think quite easily of some little church in the Balkans, in Russia or on some Aegean island. As one looks at those three white towers one remembers that forty years earlier Le Corbusier had lived for a time in Athos and filled a sketch book with these little Greek churches. There is no hint of actual Gothic. The little coloured windows are painted transparencies, not stained glass in the true sense; he was determined to avoid any such direct historical association.

And yet of course one does, inevitably, think mainly of the great stone monasteries of a thousand years ago.

Above all, one is where one really is—in Catholic France. We know nothing of Le Corbusier's 'religion'—whatever that word may mean. He was born a Swiss Waldensian, and thereafter became a man of his own time. If he thought about the nature of God, it was almost certainly to think of God as a superb mathematician. Beyond that Le Corbusier has told us nothing, except for a significant phrase when writing about Ronchamp: 'the language of architecture . . . the compass needle pointing to that infinite space which is beyond description.' And yet this chapel, in the end, is above all things a thing of France, of the very heart of mediaeval France. France is 'the eldest daughter of the Church', and this chapel is almost an embodiment of what Hilaire Belloc used to call 'The Faith'. None of these architectural reminders of either God or of other epochs must, however, be taken too literally; they are sparks in the mind which die as they come. One cannot pin them down. It is merely that Ronchamp seems momentarily possessed of the spirit of such things; one senses them and they have gone. Le Corbusier had absorbed all the architectures of history—*as an artist, not as a historian*; but he had probably also absorbed all the religions—*as an artist, not as a believer*; and then, at the end, he distilled them into this chapel.

In the last analysis, Ronchamp, being timeless, must also of necessity be modern. Even in a Catholic chapel *la vie commence demain*. Ronchamp is in fact mysteriously and perfectly attuned to the modern crowd, to the modern pilgrims. They swarm; the chapel remains serene, silent, aloof, and yet at the same time it accepts and embraces them. Moreover, being modern, it has the enormous advantage that to the pilgrims it can never be a relic from history, never just one more cathedral from the guide-book. In this place, if their faith springs from sentiment, association, history, it cannot survive; if it is real, then the Chapel embraces them and they accept that embrace as if, in their primitive imaginings, it were indeed the embrace of their Virgin.

There is another sense in which Ronchamp is 'primitive' as well as modern. It was the creation of craftsmen, not of a contractor—a team of craftsmen created by Le Corbusier himself, and then used by him as if that team was a most remarkable tool. He loved them—an unexpected trait in Le Corbusier—and understood them, and they loved him: a foreman, Bona, a father and two sons, and four others—eight strong and skilful men of the Franche Comté, a land that had once bred the greatest craftsmen in the whole world.

Ronchamp is a village at the foot of a splendid hill, one of the last spurs of the Vosges mountains, looking out across the plain of the Saône. For many centuries pilgrims had made their way to the chapel, seeing it from far off, like the Parthenon, white against the sky. That hill has suffered much in its time from the elements, from lightning and from war. In the end it was the guns that left the old chapel a pile of rubble—so that the story of Ronchamp could begin again.

In the summer of 1950 Le Corbusier climbed the hill and spent many hours studying his site, the ruins and the four horizons; one to the east, the Ballons d'Alsace; one to the south, the vale; one to the west, the River Saône; and one to the north, the village of Ronchamp. And there on the hill, when he had made his sketches—they have since been lost—he met the committee: M. le Curé, the Mayor, the lawyers and the rest. No, they told him, there was no practicable road for taking lorries up the hill. Very well, he would build with sand, cement and the cracked and calcined rubble. It would do excellently for 'fill' and for concrete aggregate. In that hard fact, in that landscape and surrounded by those far horizons, 'an idea was born, wandered and developed . . . 4th June, 1950—Give me charcoal and paper. The idea crystallized: in these conditions at the top of that lonely place, here we must have one all-embracing craft, an integrated team, a "know-how" composed of men, up there on the hill, free and masters of their craft. Good luck to them!'[39] And so it was.

Mr Peter Blake, in his admirable study of Le Corbusier, has said that after 1950 Le Corbusier's buildings 'have a plastic inventiveness and grandeur comparable with the most powerful monuments produced by man since the beginnings of recorded history'.[40] This is a tremendous claim. There are moments when Ronchamp imposes itself, when—as has been said—it embraces you in such a manner that the claim stands. It embraces and imposes itself by the pure power of architecture. That tremendous claim, in any case, would almost certainly have been understood and conceded by, say, Imhotep, Michelangelo, Roger of Chartres or by Henry Yevele, but by no one else who has lived since.

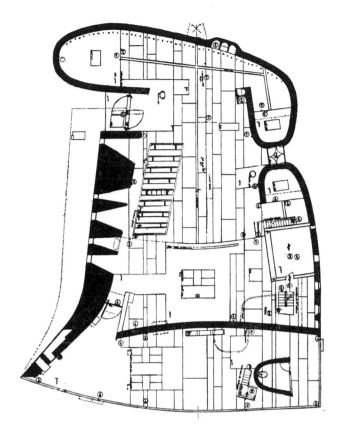

Figure 3 The Chapel at Ronchamp.

It is a very little chapel (Fig. 3; Pls. 22–6). There are a few benches in the nave, but most of the people, a bare 200 anyway, stand, leaving the fine paved floor uncluttered by such things as chairs or pews. This bare and uncluttered floor is a foil to the curving roof and the curving walls, just as the empty paving of mediaeval cathedrals must once have been a foil to the clustered piers and ribbed vaults. The nave is only 81 feet long and just over 42 feet wide. The ceiling, with its great sweep of a down-ward curve, contrary to all the vaults of history, is 32 feet above the floor at its highest point but falls to as little as 14 feet. This down-curving ceiling is of course the convex side of the 'crab-shell' which is the roof itself. Dimensions such as these, however, do not really help one to envisage the building. The curves, inside and out, combined with the fact that every dimension is related by Modulor to every other dimension—all part of a harmonious progression—has the astonishing effect of destroying all sense of size. As Le Corbusier said, some things, such as the little side chapels for instance, are quite ridiculously small, but this smallness, since one is unaware of it, is not felt as such, although it harmonizes everything. 'I defy a visitor,' wrote Le Corbusier, 'to give offhand the dimensions of different parts of the building.'[41] To design big things big and small things small is of course the oldest recipe in the world for attaining good scale in design; here, at Ronchamp, it is not only more subtle than before, but also, through the Modulor, systematized. The smallness, although disguised, humanizes everything, and at the same time prevents one from feeling crushed, overwhelmed, by the big things such as the sweeping curves or the broad eaves. Every thing is both humanized and harmonized. Parthenon, *L'Unité*, Ronchamp are all among the buildings of the world that have this quality, the architectural understatement. It is this ridiculous smallness of the smaller parts that causes the larger elements of what, after all, is a small building, to seem so impressive. It is this subtle relationship of sizes, achieved through his Modulor, but of which one is not conscious, that Le Corbusier has called 'ineffable space'. 'The appreciation of dimensions is abolished in the face of the imperceptible.'[42]

To give the reader dimensions, therefore, is to give him no idea whatever of either the exterior, which is sculptural and abstract —an arrangement of large curves and large shadows—or the interior where one is enclosed in a volume of air. This is hollow sculpture, space demarcated by a few curves. These curves, very subtly, lead the eye to that focal point where, once again with great subtlety, the interest is not divided but is, rather, balanced. It is balanced between the Sacrament upon an altar of white Bourgogne stone, and the full-size wooden cross which is not on the altar, but alongside it.

The plan of Ronchamp, although strictly in accordance with the Modulor, contains virtually not a single straight line. Even the floor slopes downwards towards the altar, thereby following the slope of the ground. The plan—although a plan in itself is only a two-dimensional diagram—is a most extraordinary object, a species of convoluted organism. Study it, walk about in it with imagination, and relate it to the walls, the roof and the towers.

Le Corbusier had picked up a crab-shell on the beach of Long Island, and this shell lay by his drawing-board while he was designing Ronchamp.

This shell, and perhaps more elaborate shells such as the Giant Murex—and one recalls the collage of marine biology on the wall of the *Pavillon Suisse*—must have been the beginning of the inspiration of Ronchamp. If the whole building is organic and convoluted, as it surely is, then the crab-shell from Long Island, convex side downwards, is almost literally the roof. Actually, when turned into a real roof the shell is found to consist of two membranes separated by a space some six feet wide and covered externally, on top, by aluminium sheathing; the roof is thus both light and thick, its thickness allowing of those enormous rounded edges to the eaves, surely the broadest eaves in history. These eaves are, so to speak, the edges of the crab-shell and are by no means the least characteristic feature of Ronchamp.

This crab-shell roof, with its big upturned edges, rests on those absurdly but magnificently thick walls. And yet it does no such thing; it is actually raised above the wall on thin reinforced concrete columns, set so far back in the thickness of the wall as to be invisible from below. The roof, therefore, belying appearances, does not touch the walls. There is a six-inch crack all round the building between walls and roof, a continuous line of light which amazes. One recalls the dome of Santa Sophia, the ring of windows at its base giving rise to the legend that it was suspended by a chain from heaven.

Frank Lloyd Wright, when building those wonderful houses of half a century ago—wonderful but very dated now—coined the phrase, 'organic architecture'. This really meant no more than what would now be universally accepted: the organic growth of the plan out of function, and the organic marriage between a building and its site; that a building grows from the landscape rather than being merely put there. Le Corbusier's Ronchamp does also of course, like any decent building, have a highly organic link with the landscape, up there on its hill, but the building itself is also an organism. Long years before, in the Paris Exhibition of 1937, the Modern Movement was said to have abandoned the formal façade and to have become three-dimensional; now, at Ronchamp, even the old 'four walls and a roof' and the rectangular compartment have vanished; they have been replaced by a single piece of, as it were, hollow abstract sculpture; they have been replaced by this—one repeats it—this 'convoluted organism'.

Apart from the shell-form of the roof, the whole structure is fascinating. The walls are of Vosges stone taken from the rubble of the old chapel. They are without buttresses; the roof exerts no pressure; it is a kind of space-frame and, as has been explained, is lifted up on its columns six inches clear of the wall top. The walls acquire stability from being not straight but curvilinear, following the curvilinear lines of the plan. In spite of the cracked and calcined nature of much of the stone, this is a strong structure. The walls are so thick—in places up to ten feet—that they can also be taken up quite simply to form the three white towers of Ronchamp, with their domed caps, and those towers in turn are used to throw down light into the little side-chapels which are hewn, as it were, out of the thickness of the walls.

These tiny chapels—and they are among those things that are even smaller than one suspects—are in the north wall, virtually in its thickness. It is, however, the south wall that is so astonishing. Buried within it, of course, are the columns, already referred to, which carry the roof. This south wall is also patterned apparently at random, with some two dozen square openings. These openings seem to be not so much windows, in the ordinary sense of the word, as a series of rectangular holes punched through the great thickness of the wall, giving deep embrasures, jambs and cills. Some of these windows are very small square holes, only inches across, while the largest are no more than two or three feet. Each window was set and sealed by Alazard, a craftsman in mirrors. The panes are of tinted glass, casting a very soft light on the interior, while through them one can see the moving clouds and the trees, even passers by. Externally these windows form a fascinating and staccato pattern on the big plain wall, which is a backcloth to the outdoor mass.

The three side-chapels, one just inside the entrance and two within the thickness of the north wall, are, as has been said, remarkably small. They are of great intrinsic interest, and the fleeting glimpses one has of them from the nave contribute greatly to the Chapel as a whole. One is an intense red, while a little farther on the wall leading to the sacristy is painted violet. These chapels are most ingeniously lighted. The light from the towers above comes from three directions; upon the altars it falls vertically and is more brilliant than in the main chapel, thus accentuating the unorthodox shapes within these little shrines. We shall see in the monastery of La Tourette the length to which Le Corbusier was prepared to go in this matter of controlling the intensity, the colour and the direction of light.

Apart from these side-chapels and the *vitrages*, colour is sparingly used. Certain parts, where both the interior and exterior altars are placed, are of a beautiful white Bourgogne stone, as are the altars themselves. The towers are of stone rubble, but the walls generally, inside and out, are surfaced with mortar sprayed on with a cement-gun. Rubble of quality could not be retrieved in sufficient quantity for the entire building. This sprayed-on mortar slurry has a rough texture and is whitewashed; it is effective and, in a way, 'primitive'. Walls, then, are all white, the ceiling and the external eaves are grey. The benches are of a grey African wood and were made by Savina who had so often co-operated with Le Corbusier upon sculptural projects. The communion rails are of cast iron and were made in the nearby foundries of the Lure. The floor is of cement paving poured between battens to form a pattern based upon the Modulor. The main axis leading down the length of the chapel to the altar is marked in the floor by a cement band. One may, perhaps, question this, since it seems to give a symmetry of sorts to a building where symmetry is otherwise studiously avoided.

One noble piece of craftsmanship is the great processional door. This is ten feet wide and ten feet high. It is pivoted on its centre. It is covered on each face with eight panels of sheet steel enamelled by Le Corbusier himself in vivid colours. The final enamelling process was then carried out at a temperature of 860° C., thus bringing a new technique from industry into architecture.

Processions may take place within the chapel; they may also pass out of the chapel through the great doors. One of the most important things about Ronchamp is that it is not only a chapel for services but also a stage, a rostrum, a proscenium—what you will—for outdoor ceremonies. A theatrical producer could do marvels with it. The white walls, the overhanging eaves like some curious proscenium arch—the whole thing is designed for drama. While two hundred people may be congregated within the chapel, mass can also be celebrated beneath the huge shadows of the eaves and against the softer shadows of the curving walls.

White walls and big eaves; the walls bend round gradually

from shadow to full sunlight, while also receiving the very deep shadow cast by the eaves, while the eaves themselves, at the edge of the 'crab-shell', bend upwards out of the darkness into the light. The line of the roof sweeps up, since the eaves do not run level, to where, at a corner of the chapel, two walls meet at an acute angle. 'Observe,' wrote Le Corbusier, 'the play of shadows, learn the game. . . . Precise shadows, clear cut or dissolving. Projected shadows, sharp. Projected shadows, precisely delineated, but with what enchanting arabesques and frets. Counterpoint and fugue. Great music. Try to look at the picture upside-down. You will soon discover the game.'[43]

'*Dedans: tête à tête avec soi-même; dehors: 10,000 pèlerins devant l'autel.*'[44] With the chapel as a background to the altar, and those far horizons all around, the outdoor ceremony is memorable. Indeed, on the completion of the Chapel at Ronchamp a strange unanimity inspired world opinion, including even the Church of Rome. Ronchamp was made a place of fixed pilgrimage on fixed dates, also a place of pilgrimage for men and women from all over the world. It was all a far cry now from the *avant garde* students of the thirties, the Palace of the Soviets and the League of Nations.

From Ronchamp, for over a hundred and fifty miles, in the wide valley that lies between the Bourgogne and the Franche Comté, the River Saône flows south to join the Rhône at Lyon. Sixteen miles west of Lyon, on a slope above the village of Eveux-sur-l'Arbresle, is the Dominican monastery and college of Sainte-Marie de la Tourette. In one direction it is possible to look towards these great rivers of France, in the other towards the sources of the Loir. The monastery itself, in a secluded land between forest and meadow, looks mainly westward to the blessed vineyard country of the Beaujolais. As Le Corbusier described it, 'the site was a steeply sloping valley, wreathed with woods and opening out onto a plain'.[45]

Ronchamp is a small building set high upon a hill, a hill that is almost a peak. Seen from far off, and from every side, Ronchamp might, very superficially, be likened to Mont St Michel; as a silhouette in the landscape and as a building on a mount, it had to draw itself up, as it were, into a cluster of towers, distant banners to the pilgrims. Ronchamp's whiteness and vigorous skyline are more than a compensation for its smallness; they are also a way of proclaiming its presence to the devout. La Tourette is quite different. A monastery need not, and should not, proclaim itself, or rather it need proclaim only its monastic nature. It may appear almost as a fort, secluded against the world, aloof and unwelcoming, defying the world, repelling rather than summoning the visitor—although with charity rather than violence. The chapel of Notre-Dame-du-Haut at Ronchamp glories in the beauty of its towers; the monastery of Sainte-Marie de la Tourette commands the landscape with a severe silhouette. One little bell-turret is all that breaks the level line. 'The roof,' wrote Le Corbusier, 'has a grand, all-commanding horizontality.'[46]

Apart from skyline and landscape, Ronchamp is rich not only in architectural forms but also in craftsmanship and colour; it is a place for the devotions of simple people who ask these things of their architecture. La Tourette is rigidly austere; it has the ruthless poverty that has always given infinite and real richness to the buildings of Franciscans and of Dominicans. This is a Dominican monastery, repudiating wealth not only for the individual friar but for the whole community. La Tourette was paid for entirely from the sale of old buildings and from charitable gifts; no real building fund ever existed.

And yet and this is the whole key to La Tourette—in spite of plain forms, rough and unfinished surfaces, the sparing use of colour, the absence of all ornament and all images except the body of Christ on the altar cross—Le Corbusier endowed La Tourette with a richness which seems to be not of this world. It is mysterious and intangible. For one thing, in a building where everyone dresses alike, the place of carvings and images is taken by living men, men who believe themselves to be made in the likeness of God, moving silently along austere corridors in their black and white habits. The architectural richness is outwardly no more than a few touches of brilliant and occasionally dramatic colour and equally dramatic lighting—all most strictly confined to the monastery church, and indeed almost wholly to the immediate neighbourhood of the altars. At those points, while restrained, it becomes almost exotic. That, and the fact that Le Corbusier's Modulor proportions—as used for instance in the spacing of, say, window bars—is something vibrant, something that almost seems to sing to us.

It was in 1953, when Ronchamp was already beginning to

reveal itself as a wonderful thing, that Père Couturier came once more to the Rue de Sèvres. This time it was to ask Le Corbusier on behalf of the Dominicans of the Province of Lyon to build a monastery and a college at La Tourette.

In his earlier years, as a travelling student, Le Corbusier had studied carefully the Carthusian monastery at Ema, so ample, so beautiful and yet so functionally and austerely conceived. As a spectator, living in the world, he had retained his interest in monasticism, to the point of fascination—fascination with the relationship of the individual to the community. Whether in a monastery or in marriage it is the relationship of human to human that is the heart of the matter, upon which all else depends. And now, years later, but with the Carthusians of Ema still in his mind, Le Corbusier was sent to the Abbey of Le Thoronet, which Père Couturier described to him as having the very essence of monastic life. At Le Thoronet Le Corbusier would be able to study a mediaeval monastery still dedicated to silence, poverty, meditation and devotion, and also virtually unchanged both in its buildings and in its life. Père Couturier hoped that La Tourette, like Le Thoronet in its day, would be 'in its poverty one of the purest and most significant works of our time'.[47]

Le Corbusier studied the site, sketching the far horizons as he had done at Ronchamp. He then took three years to prepare his plans and models. The result was indeed one of the most significant works of our time; and of course very much of our time. The Dominican Constitutions, formulated in the thirteenth century, had dealt admirably with the whole problem of building a monastery, the whole problem of architecture. They took the monastic types of building as they knew them; they did not revolutionize them, but they simplified them and stripped them of every superfluity, imposing a greater austerity. For instance, the towers—one of the glories of the Middle Ages—were reduced by these Constitutions to the status of a small bell-turret. A friar who had studied these matters was to expound the 'programme', as we would now call it, of a new building, but the architect was to be a layman. The friars of La Tourette asked for a church, an oratory, a refectory, an atrium, a chapter room, lecture rooms, a library and a hundred cells. All that, however, was to do no more than state the bare requirements of the community. The schedule of accommodation had of course to be planned, as had any building. It had not only to be arranged functionally, economically and beautifully; it had also to exploit fully the possibilities of a steep, difficult but very magnificent site. All that is the minimum task of architecture. More important: into that bare schedule Le Corbusier now had to breathe the whole life and spirit of Dominicanism. The friars had told him their needs. They left the shape and planning of their monastery to Le Corbusier, giving him freedom to depart, if necessary, from the strict tradition. As one friar said: 'Le Corbusier knows what we are and what we want.'[48] He took advantage of the freedom he was given—although to some extent the steep site may have forced it upon him—to depart in *many* ways from the strict tradition. In doing so he may have come nearer than he knew to a very real interpretation of the monastic rule. No other building, it is said, had ever caused Le Corbusier so little vexation.

Herr Anton Henze, in his book on La Tourette, has admirably summarized the link between the Dominican rule and tradition on the one hand, and the building of a modern monastery on the other hand. The Dominicans, like the Franciscans, are a mendicant body, repudiating wealth; but whereas the Franciscans have been a liberal force in the Church, almost a democratic one, holding the example to be more important than the word, the Dominicans have been more concerned with the fiery defence of orthodoxy, dogma and canon law. Some even served the Inquisition. In the modern world the task of the Dominican must be harder than that of the Franciscan; the exclusion of the world, the inviolability of the religious life, quiet study—everything that Dominicanism stands for is reflected in every line of Le Corbusier's plan for La Tourette.

In spite of aloofness from the world, the Dominicans not only live in obedience, chastity and poverty, but are also preaching friars. In the thirteenth century they had emerged from a community of priests so devout that in 1215 St Dominic had been able to transform them into an Order dedicated to spreading the Faith by word of mouth. In order to preach, however, the Dominicans had to go among men, to build their monasteries in cities. Unlike, say, the Benedictines who, as scholars, farmers and artists—sophisticated and civilized—conducted an almost Vergilian dialogue with the landscape, placing their churches poetically in, say, the Vale of Severn or of Seine, the Dominicans were more ruthless, more primitive, more dedicated, more holy, living behind great locked doors and a grille, in the narrow streets of old towns.

When, therefore, the Dominicans of the Province of Lyon built La Tourette in the remote country above Eveux-sur-l'Arbresle, they deliberately broke with one tradition, but they also at the same time strengthened another. They broke with the tradition that they should build in cities. This was sensible, since it was no longer necessary. City and country are no longer separate worlds; travel is no longer perilous either to body or to soul. Where a man must preach, there he can go.

To build in cities had ceased to be important. On the other hand the great tradition of preaching must remain at all costs. If the Benedictine monasteries had once been beacons of enlightenment in a rough world, and if the Franciscans had once tried to convert men by the example and even the charm of their own lives, then the aim and determination of the Dominicans had always been to convert the heretic and the sinner by reason, by persuasion, by sheer logic. This implied in the preacher a scholarship more intense, if less wide and less poetic, than Benedictine learning had ever been. It implied a most rigorous training through years of study.

St Dominic was a Castilian, and it has been said that the Dominican ideal was rather like the Castilian landscape, poor and arid but also bold and clear. Behind the words of the preacher, however eloquent, there must always be precise thinking and a very exact knowledge of Holy Scripture. La Tourette, therefore, is not only a monastery, it is also a college. Almost half the monks are student-brothers or student-priests, committed to seven years study of the Scriptures, of philosophy and of theology, to which are added the learning and scholarship of the Arab and the Greek —the entire system, in fact, which the Middle Ages knew as Scholasticism.

This, therefore, was to be no ordinary monastery. Perhaps one might say that the emphasis was to be upon the rigorous training of the preacher rather than upon the preacher himself. Apart from the black-cowled fathers who govern the community, the population of La Tourette is youthful. The young novice, with seven years ahead of him in the library, the lecture room and the solitude of his own cell, has no reason to be in the world or even in a town. He has, as yet, no mission in that world, no reason to be among men. The quiet, the peace, the light and the air are the things that are best for him. La Tourette, therefore, brings Dominican life into the twentieth century but, at the same time, gives the scholar the quietude which is that century's greatest need.

Unlike the Franciscans, the Dominicans, except as preachers, may have had little contact with their fellow-beings. They are aloof. They are a close Order, or as strictly closed as is consistent with preaching to the world. Only within their own walls do they have a peculiar democracy of their own. Their founder exhorted them to 'live in harmony together and to be one heart and soul in God'.[49] This is shown every evening when the friars meet in their chapter room to discuss their communal life and to make decisions as to the ordering of their affairs. This meeting is of the whole chapter; but since student-brothers and student-priests are not members of the chapter, Le Corbusier was able to make the chapter room a fairly small place. It is only in the church and in the refectory that the entire community is ever gathered together. The chapter room, however, is given a central position on the plan because of its importance. Moreover it is approached through the atrium. This atrium is the real core; it is an almost ceremonial ante-room, open to the cloister, and the one approach both to the chapter room and to the refrectory. It is the point where the friars can gather before going in procession to the church or to meals. The atrium, refectory and chapter room, therefore, are *en suite* and are considered, apart always from the church, as being the heart of the monastery. Le Corbusier has given them the most central position, and also that magnificent view over the vineyards and the rolling hills.

The whole problem which the friars laid before Le Corbusier, in conjunction with the fine but sloping site, explains the general form of the building. We have just seen how the Dominican system of self-government was reflected in one part of the plan. And now, in greater detail, it will be seen how each room— from the great church to the cell of the novice—is a precise reflection of the whole life and spirit of the Dominican Order.

The steep slope in any case, whether Le Corbusier had wanted it or not, would have ruled out the orthodox or traditional monastic plan. Certainly the traditional cloister, as a closed garden alongside the main buildings, was just not possible. Nevertheless Le Corbusier did plan the whole monastery around a large rectangular court, the whole building being contained within a square of approximately 200 feet. The buildings on the east, south and west sides are conventual, for living and for study, while the whole of the north side is given to the church, together with the sacristy, the blessed sacrament chapel and the amazing lower church or crypt.

Owing to the slope of the ground it is a little difficult to describe La Tourette (Pls. 27–32). The eastern wing, forming the whole of the eastern side of the court, is at the highest part of the site and is only three storeys high. The western wing, however, forming the whole western side of the court, is five storeys high; so quickly does the ground fall away. One enters, therefore, on the 'ground-floor' of the eastern wing, but in actual fact one then goes *down* the spiral stair from this entrance level to the two lower floors, of the western wing. The five levels, working downwards, are here described as: 1. The Entrance Floor; 2. The Refectory Floor; 3. The Domestic Floor, and then, returning to the upper floors: 4 and 5. The two Cell Floors.

The north wing, the church, occupies the whole of the north side of the court. It is accessible only at one level, the refectory and atrium level, and runs the full height of all the other floors. It may, therefore be considered quite separately.

1 THE ENTRANCE FLOOR

The Approach: The visitor approaches La Tourette by climbing the hill. He is faced during his ascent with the long, blank north wall of the church. That great area of rough concrete, nearly two hundred feet long, speaks volumes. It is impressive. It is not welcoming. When the visitor reaches his goal he will find himself, first, at the foot of the tall eastern gable of the church, topped with its little bell-turret, the only break in the horizontality of La Tourette. Also at this point is a small door. This is the only external door in the monastery apart from the main entrance; it is the layman's access to that part of the church where he may share in the mass, receive Holy Communion and make his confession. Then, beyond this eastern gable of the church, there extends the long eastern wing. On the ground floor there is nothing but an unbroken corridor wall with a narrow band of horizontal slit windows. Above this for two floors (the fourth and fifth) there is the characteristic fenestration of the cells; these are really small loggias or balconies, the windows of *L'Unité d'Habitation de Marseilles* in miniature. Here too, immediately

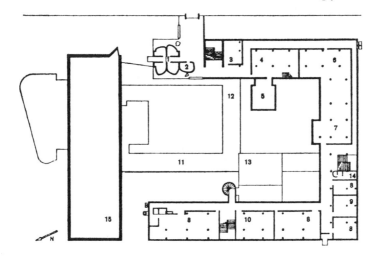

Figure 4 La Tourette: plan of the entrance floor.

1 Parlatorium; 2 Porters; 3 Room for the lay brothers; 4 Common-room for the student brothers; 5 Oratory; 6 Reading-room; 7 Library; 8 Lecture rooms; 9 Common-room for the student brothers; 10 Common-room for the fathers; 11, 12 Cloister; 13 Atrium; 14 W.C.; 15 Church.

beyond the church gable, is the main entrance to the monastery. If the days of the barred door and the iron grille have gone, Le Corbusier's frame, lintel and plate-glass door, set in a plate-glass wall, somehow make it quite clear that one goes no farther. Perhaps the secret lies in the glimpse of life beyond the glass, the life one may not share. Just beyond the glass, however, lies La Tourette's positively last link with the world, the Parlatorium.

The Parlatorium: At this point of the eastern wing, in Le Corbusier's usual manner, we find that the upper floors are carried on *piloti*. Normally one would, therefore, look right through the building from the road outside into the inner court. That view, again, is only a tantalizing glimpse. It is partially blocked by five curious little pill-box structures inserted into the main building almost like pieces of sculpture. These 'kiosks', as abstract form and by reason of their small scale, are a delicious foil to the bulk of the main building, also an example of richness subtly achieved without ornament of any kind. One of these kiosks, guarding the entrance, is for the monastery porter. The other four are each equipped with a seat, and it is there in privacy, rather than in the old-style monastery 'parlour', that a friar may be allowed to conduct a family or business conversation with the occasional visitor. Hence the word 'parlatorium'. The benches give scant comfort and are not intended to prolong such an indulgence. The design of the kiosks—almost free-standing—as well as their position at the entrance, make it clear that they are not truly part of the monastery. As Anton Henze has said, 'in the parlatorium the world has pitched its impermanent tents before the monastery gates'.[50]

Common Rooms and Library: The remainder of the Entrance Floor, apart from one small but notable exception, is made up largely of various kinds of day-room: a room for the lay-brothers, the common room for the student-brothers, the library and the reading-room, lecture rooms and the common-room for the fathers. This last looks out over the country, but the rest of these day-rooms, including the library suite, look inwards to the quiet seclusion of the court. On that side they have almost a whole wall of glass. This is fenestrated with a fascinating chequer-board pattern designed on a Modulor basis. Again, richness born of austerity. The library is a fine room, the heart of that gruelling seven years of Scholasticism; it is light and simple with one part going up double height. This means that the book stacks are tall but that the more intimate places for study are quite low.

The Oratory: This is the single and remarkable exception to the simple and utilitarian nature of this floor. The one unique and transcendental feature of this floor is the oratory, deliberately placed among these workaday rooms. It opens directly from the student-brothers' common-room. It projects into the court as an almost isolated chapel and is therefore to be seen from all the upper windows as well as by friars passing through the court itself. It is instantly identifiable. It is almost free-standing. It is cubical, and it is small, although crowned with a pyramidical roof. 'In the oratory or house of prayer no one shall do anything other than the purpose for which it is there.'[51] That purpose is private prayer. It is designed to concentrate the mind of youth at his devotions, perhaps the mind of a student still uncertain of his vocation. It is a dark little cube, but one bright shaft of light strikes down from the roof . . . 'The solitary worshipper who cries to the Lord from out of the depths.' Once again, simply by the arrangement of simple forms in bare concrete, and by the distribution of light, Le Corbusier has given us an effect no less dramatic and appropriate in its own way than all the fretted ornament to which, say, Tudor or Baroque art could have aspired.

2 THE REFECTORY FLOOR

The Piloti: From the Entrance Floor we now descend the spiral stair to the Refectory Floor. A great part of this floor, once again because of the slope, is as it were a vacuum—space beneath the common rooms and library on the floor above. This

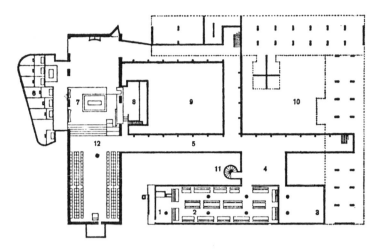

Figure 5 La Tourette: plan of the refectory floor.

1 Pantry; 2 Refectory; 3 Chapter-room; 4 Atrium; 5 Cloister; 6 Lower Church; 7 High altar; 8 Sacristy; 9, 10 Courtyard; 11 Spiral staircase; 12 Church.

space is the ground between the *piloti* which support so much of that Entrance Floor. The use of the *piloti* at, say, the *Pavillon Suisse* or at Marseilles was highly functional, serving many purposes; at La Tourette it is architectural or aesthetic, seeming to lift a solid and bulky rectangular mass—or what might have seemed such—into the air. On that site, and with that ruthlessly horizontal building to cope with, La Tourette without its *piloti*, as one sees it in the landscape, would be unthinkable.

The Cloister: The most important part of this Refectory Floor is the cloister. As has been said, an orthodox cloister garth was hardly possible. The so-called cloister—the court—is actually divided into four small gardens, by glazed cloister-walks in the form of a cross. The cloister or court, therefore, instead of being the place of meditation, is here the very centre of all communications. A study of the four arms of the cross makes it clear that this floor is indeed the *piano nobile* of La Tourette. These cloister-walks link together, mostly by the shortest route, all the salient parts of the plan. They make it organic. From the very centre of the monastery, one arm of the cross leads to the entrance; a second arm gives access, by way of a small stair, to the library and common-rooms; a third arm is itself the atrium from which the main spiral stair, the chapter-room and the refectory are all immediately accessible. The reasons for this have been explained. The fourth arm is the processional way into the church. Having already discussed the atrium as the ante-room or assembly place for the refectory and the chapter-room, we now find that it is also the point of assembly for the procession, the preliminary act before the supreme moment of the Dominican day.

The Refectory: The refectory is a simple but rather splendid room. It is, in a way, the festive room of the monastery. It has a panoramic view of the countryside in one direction, and in the other has a glass wall of chequer-board pattern onto the court. It is a long room, and down its whole length are the tall windows of 'undulating glass', virtually a system of large vertical glass louvres. It is in the subdivision of these windows into variable widths that the Modulor seems to sing to us. The room is three-aisled, with plain cylindrical columns. The friars, three at a table, sit silently at their good food and their Beaujolais. The tables are in the aisles, facing inwards towards what in a church would be the nave. The 'nave' is empty, but somehow this modern aisled refectory has something of the aspect of an Early Christian basilica. The meal is silent ... 'When you go to table, until you stand up again, listen to the regular reading without a sound and without dispute; for you shall take in nourishment not only through your mouth, but your ears shall be hungry for the word of God.'[52] The reader stands at a pulpitum which is placed at one end of the long room, thus increasing the Early Christian feel of the place.

3   THE DOMESTIC FLOOR

The spiral stair goes down once again, this time to the lowest level. In fact this Domestic Floor fills only a very small part of the total area of ground occupied by the monastery. Part of that area is non-existent at this level since it is, so to speak, absorbed by the slope of the ground. Another part is taken up by the *piloti* and the space between them, leaving only the area immediately below the refectory for practical use. It is here, looking out over the country, that we find the kitchens, laundry, stores and so on. They are all light, clean and well-equipped.

4 and 5   THE CELL FLOORS

The whole of the upper part of La Tourette—that striking part that overhangs like a fortress—consists of two floors, identical with each other and devoted entirely to the friars' cells. There are just over a hundred of these. Externally these two

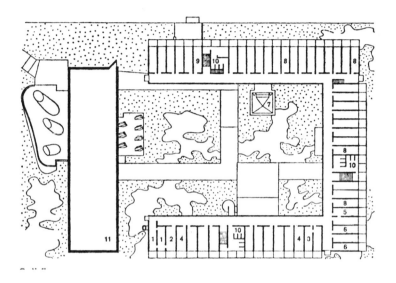

Figure 6 La Tourette: plan of the cell floor.

1 Cells for the sick; 2 Nurse's cell; 3 Cells for visitors; 4 Fathers' cells; 5 Cell for the friar in charge of the student brothers; 6 Student priests' cells; 7 Oratory; 8 Student brothers' cells; 9 Lay brothers' cells; 10 Sanitary offices; 11 Church.

floors, of a more rugged and solid design than those below them, act as a wonderful foil to the tall and elegant 'undulating glass' windows of the common rooms and refectory. It is not part of the Dominican rule that a man should live entirely in community. He may have private prayer in the oratory, he may celebrate mass privately at one of the altars of the lower church, but he must also be able to meditate and to study. The cell, unlike those of some Orders, must therefore be rather more than just a place for sleep. Drawing on his experience of the students' rooms at the *Pavillon Suisse* and the balconies at Marseilles, Le Corbusier arrived at the almost perfect monastic cell.

The La Tourette Cell is small, but it has a table in the window for study; it has bookshelves, a cupboard and a bed; also a washing recess at the back of the room. Every cell gets some sunlight for some part of the day—it is only the big blank wall of the church that looks north—as do the much larger balconies of the flats at Marseilles. Each balcony is private, being cut off by a fin wall from the one belonging to the next cell; each balcony is therefore called a loggia and also acts to some extent as a *brise-soleil*. The value of the Modulor in making a small room seem larger was quite clear in the little side-chapels at Ronchamp; it is equally clear in these cells at La Tourette. They are of a minimum size for their purpose, but they seem almost spacious and, as Anton Henze has said, 'they fit like a well-made garment'.[53]

Externally the result of these individual balconies or loggias is to give a fenestration pattern based upon a series of separate openings—a staccato pattern of black holes—all along the two upper floors, as contrasted with the tall windows or blank walls of the floors below. This stronger pattern of the cell floors—holes framed in rough concrete blocks—receives additional emphasis from the fact that they overhang the floor below, like the memory of some mediaeval fort.

THE CHURCH

The Church: The church, occupying the whole northern wing of the monastery, together with its sacristy, chapel of the Blessed Sacrament and lower church, is—with Ronchamp—Le Corbusier's most memorable work. It is good to think that in these last years this man actually did build two churches, always the supreme test of any architect.

In the age 'when the cathedrals were white' the whole energy of a virile society was directed into church building, with the results which we all know, results that are part of history. In our age the total energy of society is directed elsewhere. No modern church—prior to Ronchamp and La Tourette—has been truly significant. We have long since left behind us the era of stylistic imitation—St John the Divine in New York or the Anglican cathedral in Liverpool were almost the last of that genre—only to replace it with such churches as Perret's Le Raincy in Paris or Spence's Coventry, where smooth modern techniques are used simply to iron away the more obvious stylistic excrescences, while leaving the really basic bones as Gothic as ever—Gothic, the unmentionable inspiration, the death-wish of every well-meaning church architect.

At La Tourette Le Corbusier, like a master mason of the thirteenth century, was able to build for a fanatically and fiercely religious society, quite different from the Anglican clergy of Coventry. That that society was a community of only a hundred men—since it was self-contained—was neither here nor there. That they were poor seems to have been a positive advantage, a challenge to be overcome.

The great church is a single chamber about 200 feet long and 50 feet high. Its proportions are as if there were eight cubes, a row of four being laid on top of another row of four: four cubes long and two cubes high. This is the long-shaped hall ever beloved of mendicant orders in the Middle Ages. There are no aisles, no vault—a flat ceiling. The rough concrete walls, as rough as they come from the shuttering, rise unimpeded, uncarved and unbroken from floor to ceiling on all four sides. In the orthodox sense there are no windows, but the lighting is very subtle, both in its placing and in its colour, as well as its intensity or softness.

The church is traditionally orientated. On the short western wall is the organ, an inconspicuous panel. In this western half of the church the benches for the friars are arranged in the manner of a choir or college chapel, with an ample area of clear floor in the centre for absolute prostration at the elevation of the Host. In the wall behind the friars' benches are horizontal window slits giving them light on their books. These are low down in the church, but the light from them is carefully tempered with blue, green and yellow glass. On the short eastern wall the confessional glows red. In the ceiling is one square panel of glass, and round the top of the walls—Ronchamp fashion—is a slit of light between wall and ceiling. All uncoloured light falls from above; at no point is the eye distracted by glare. At first the church seems dim, but in fact, from the working point of view, it is well lit and very beautifully lit.

The High Altar: Five steps separate the friars' nave from the altar. The altar, of white Bourgogne stone, is on a kind of rectangular island. Physically and visually it separates the monks in the western part of the church from the laity who are beyond the altar in the eastern part. In this remote village the lay congregation is small, a mere handful; but even so, as has been explained, they have their own access door to the church. Only the server is in contact with the two halves of the congregation.

A few feet from this altar, the high altar of the monastery, is the big cross. It is full size. It is made from two bars of iron. To the south of the altar is the sacristy where, in silence, the communion meal is prepared and the priest robed. It is lit by seven of Le Corbusier's 'light guns'. These are, as it were, wide tubes or barrels passing through the roof and directed to the sky at various angles, like some novel form of telescope, so as to receive the beams of sun at various times of day as it passes across the sky. These barrels send down dramatic shafts of light into the sacristy.

Chapel of the Blessed Sacrament: To the north of the high altar, on the opposite side of the Church from the sacristy, is the Blessed Sacrament chapel. In accordance with a rule of monastic and episcopal churches the Sacrament is not reserved in a tabernacle on the high altar, but on this altar of the special Blessed Sacrament chapel. The chapel is tinged with a warm-coloured light that filters downwards through yet another of Le Corbusier's 'telescopes'. The layman has access only to his own part of the church—east of the high altar—but the glow from the Blessed Sacrament chapel can be seen by the whole congregation. . . . 'Thus is the mystery of the deep linked to the Church which is open to the world.'[54] The tall iron cross by the high altar, already mentioned, serves as a kind of pyschological barrier, imposing a pause upon the priest as he moves from the church to the Blessed Sacrament chapel. On the altar of the latter the small crucifix bears the body of Christ; this is the only piece of modelling or carving in the whole of the monastery. Its effect in consequence is shattering; one had almost forgotten that carving could exist.

The Lower Church: Anton Henze has said that the church of La Tourette is a ship, while the lower church is a submarine; it has sunk out of this world. It is the innermost domain of the monastery. Every morning the Dominican priests say mass silently to themselves, each at his own altar. For this purpose side-chapels, in the traditional sense, would have been excessive, while portable altars would have been undignified. Le Corbusier gave the friars seven altars, each a block of white stone. He placed them in the lower church, immediately behind the Blessed Sacrament chapel. The floor of this lower church rises in a series of platforms, an altar and a block at each level—the whole thing a most remarkable piece of abstract and purely geometrical sculpture. The walls are red and yellow. The ceiling is blue. The 'telescopes' or 'light guns'—each at its own angle so that collectively they follow the sun's path—shine down as if they themselves were suns; the walls of their barrels are coloured so as to give a faint tinge, red or black, to the light that comes through them.

The Christian sees the altar as the high place where the earth arches up towards heaven, and Christ descends in the Sacrament. This image is embodied in the lower church at La Tourette. Again to quote Henze: 'They are the high places of the drama of Golgotha.'[55] Here, if anywhere upon earth, the friar believes himself to be alone with God.

Externally the great church of the monastery presents one blank wall to the court and three to the outside world; each is a plain and uncompromising cliff of rough concrete, as rough as it comes from the shuttering. Le Corbusier, for some unfathomable reason, is popularly supposed to have filled our cities with plain rectangular boxes. He built only one plain rectangular box—the church of Sainte-Marie at La Tourette.

Seven

the great city

'Another Athens shall arise,
    And to remoter time
Bequeath like sunset, to the
    skies,
    The splendour of its prime.'
Shelley

In this last busy decade of his life Le Corbusier was very fully occupied. With his wife's death success and sadness had come together and he was probably glad to be busy. In addition to the major achievements of Ronchamp, La Tourette and Chandigarh —enough, one would think, to keep anyone going—he was responsible for many other projects. Some of these materialized; some, like the great stadium for Baghdad, were abortive. A few must certainly be noted.

For the 1956–8 Inter-Bau Exposition in Berlin he was invited to design and to build as a permanent structure an *Unité d'Habitation*—the *Unité d'Habitation* of Charlottenburg—incorporating the same principles, social, structural and aesthetic, as the Marseilles Building. The site was a very fine one, on a hill-top. The building was duly erected. After that its fate might best be passed over in silence. Possibly there was too little supervision from Paris, but the conduct of the Berlin authorities was unpardonable. Le Corbusier said that 'the manner of execution was . . . incompatible with his desires'. This would seem to be a mild way of saying that his elevational drawings, especially for the fenestration, were almost completely ignored by the contractors. The building might not be worth mentioning except as a warning: Le Corbusier must not be judged by the *Unité d'Habitation* of Charlottenburg.

In 1958–9 Le Corbusier built the Tokyo Museum. We have already seen how in 1939 at Philippeville, in North Africa, he

158

designed the first 'square snail' or Greek fret museum, 'the museum of unlimited extension', where the visitor passes onwards almost imperceptibly from one section of the continuous gallery to another, rather than moving wearily through great salons *en suite*, the usual inappropriate arrangement derived from the state apartments of a Baroque palace. This 'square snail' plan was probably the origin of Frank Lloyd Wright's 'circular descending snail' at the Guggenheim Museum in New York. Philippeville came to nothing, but Le Corbusier lived to see his conception realized in a finer form, both at Ahmedabad in India and at Tokyo. The Tokyo Museum is an extremely elegant and distinguished building (Pl. 43). It was carefully placed on a beautifully wooded site, and was designed for the famous Matsukata collection of Impressionists. Ironically this wonderful collection had been claimed as a war prize by the French but was returned to Japan by negotiation, to be eventually rehoused by the most famous of French architects. Le Corbusier was more fortunate in Tokyo than he had been in Berlin; the execution of the museum was supervised on his behalf by two Japanese architects who had long worked for him in the studio at the Rue de Sèvres.

The Philips Pavilion at the 1958 Brussels Exhibition was composed of a number of cleverly united hyperbolic-paraboloid shells cast in sand moulds on the ground. The result was rather like a tightly knit group of steeply sloping and gigantic tents. These forms, at that date more novel, have since been used, with variations, in all manner of circumstances, appropriate and inappropriate, as, for instance, in the Commonwealth Institute in London. This Philips Pavilion was called 'an electronic poem' —which was rather absurd—and also, by Le Corbusier, 'a synthesis unlimited in its possibilities for colour, imagery, music, words and rhythm'. He was always optimistic about the implications of his designs for generations unborn; perhaps he was right.

The City of Chandigarh was the culmination of Le Corbusier's life. This city is like the man. It is not gentle; it is hard and assertive. It is not practical; it is riddled with mistakes made not in error but in arrogance. It is disliked by small minds, but not by big ones. It is unforgettable. The man who adored the Mediterranean has here found fulfilment, in the scorching heat of India.

Chandigarh is a seed that will certainly, in some other century than this, become one of the flowers in the garland that is a new India. It stands at the beginning of an era, not at the end. Chandigarh is not, for instance, the end of that long era of city building that began with Rome. It might have been. Some kind of Roman Chandigarh might, conceivably, have been given to the world. Eighteen hundred years ago the Emperor Trajan, at the farthest confines of his empire, passed down the Euphrates in a flotilla with purple sails, and so out into the waters of the Persian Gulf where for one night, in those hot miasmic airs, there floated the dream of a Roman India. It was not to be, but oddly enough the last city of that genre did in fact come to India. It came to India when Edwin Lutyens built New Delhi, tired Baroque swansong of the British Raj. That was as certainly the end of one epoch as Chandigarh is the beginning of another.

If it takes a century to build Chandigarh—and it well may—then equally it may take ten centuries for India to make a culture of which Chandigarh can be the heart, as Rome, Byzantium or Paris was each, so intangibly, the core of a great empire.

Chandigarh's parks are still mainly dry and arid grass; its streets are still filled with dust, its boulevards still shadeless and endless. The monsoon rains, in their season, beat into porticoes designed to keep out the sun, while the sun itself, the great enemy, has never been wholly conquered. Chandigarh still sometimes seems as brash and raw as any pioneer landscape in any new land; but whereas in the Americas, Australias and South Africas of this world no man ever managed to lay down the lines of a truly great city,* in Chandigarh, with its thousand faults, Le Corbusier has designed an indubitable capital. And on the Capitol of that capital he has placed with unerring precision a dozen great buildings, still pools between them, and all in perfect modulor and mathematical relationship to each other, to the mango groves, to the river-beds, to the wind-swept plain, and to the eternal backdrop of the Himalayas.

Chandigarh was neither conceived nor born in comfort. This city was the daughter of strife. Every great nation is founded upon a great revolution. Every great revolution has an aftermath of blood. The founding of modern India, the expulsion of the British from their short-lived 'empire', was no exception. This

---

* *Except possibly William Penn, when he planned Philadelphia in 1683.*

continent of races, languages, castes and religions was torn in
shreds. It was bound to be so. Only part, the eastern part, of
the ancient province of Punjab came to India. The western part
went to Pakistan together with the old capital of Lahore. The
Indian rulers of the eastern Punjab found themselves, therefore,
without a home, without a city. It was from Simla, haunted by
British ghosts, that they planned to build a new capital. In the
context of mid-twentieth-century India, a land so disturbed and
so uncertain of itself, this decision was a courageous one.

It was not without precedent. The world after all is littered,
if very thinly, with such cities, cities founded by decree. They
have been called 'fiat cities'. And these fiat cities were most of
them founded in glory and built in travail. Among them were
Peking, Byzantium, Petersburg, Washington, Canberra, New
Delhi, Brasilia, Chandigarh. Of this mixed bag, the last two—
Brasilia and Chandigarh—let us always remember, may well
prove to be the finest of them all.

The founding of Chandigarh was an act of courage, but it was
not irrational. Indeed it was necessary. After partition the
population of eastern Punjab had been doubled by the influx of
refugees from the Muslim west. Even the government was home-
less. There was no town where it could do its work. Simla, when
the snows came, was almost inaccessible, while Ambala, an old
military cantonment on the north-west frontier, would always
be vulnerable in war. There was no town, still less was there a
capital. As these men in Simla looked down upon the great
plain below, they could see only chaos—human and physical.
It was, moreover, chaos in a vacuum; the first necessity was a
symbol, an anchor . . . a capital city.

The problem, human and physical, was intractable. It still is.
With Pandit Nehru as the dominating figure, neither vision nor
determination was lacking. Chandigarh, like any fiat city, had
to be designed as an administrative, legal and ceremonial capital,
as well as a place where people lived. It had also to be a great
symbolic gesture. Norma Evenson, in her fine but critical study
of the city, to which I am indebted for much of the information
in this chapter, wrote: 'The Punjabi needed a lift for their
morale. The new city, coming into existence in a time of dis-
order and uncertainty, could stand as the tangible embodiment
of the will to maintain a stable society . . . the creation of a new
city is a gift to the future.'[56]

The site of Chandigarh shocks and fascinates. It was a terrific challenge to Le Corbusier, a challenge which he seized upon avidly to the exclusion of all else. The choice of site, long before Le Corbusier came on the scene to show what could be done with it, may possibly have been inspired; it seems more likely that it was perverse. It lacks almost everything that a designer of cities would ask for. One had only to think of, say, Byzantium and Petersburg, one on the Bosphorus and one on the Gulf of Finland, each at a curious contiguity of land masses, each set beside a great anchorage; one had only to think of Washington and the curves of the Potomac, to realize how unique but how harsh among such cities is the site of Chandigarh.

The site is neither defensive nor mercantile nor salubrious. It was chosen from an air survey. It is one hundred and fifty miles from New Delhi, those hundred and fifty miles across which the departed spirits of Lutyens and Le Corbusier must forever gaze at each other in utter incomprehension. The site itself, about four miles across, is a flat plain, 1,500 feet above sea level, dusty and hot and windy, its aridity tempered only by the mango groves seeking their moisture in those canyons which, like fissures in a lunar landscape, meander across the site. These belts of trees form bands of sombre green across the bare, brown earth. This wide plain, upon which they are building Chandigarh, is bounded by two rivers, one to the east and one to the west, dry and stony beds between one monsoon season and the next, only to become roaring torrents with the rains and the melting of the Himalayan snows. The architect of Ronchamp came directly from the smiling valley of Saône to this desert of the moon.

The site has two features which, at least as they were exploited by Le Corbusier, redeem all. One is the clear and luminous air of winter. This air bathes all Chandigarh and gives to it those pale and olive greens, beneath an intensely blue sky, in which Jane Drew discovered the qualities of a Giotto. The other feature, to the north-east, is the endless cyclorama of the Himalayas. Against this cyclorama Le Corbusier envisaged the whole city, but, above all, on their platform to the north of the town, he placed beside their reflecting pools the big buildings of the Capitol, stark sunlit masses seen in that luminous air and with nothing behind them but the mountains eighty miles away.

The first launching of Chandigarh was not simple. That was not to be expected. Nehru had said that the new city was to be 'symbolic of the freedom of India, unfettered by the traditions of the past'.[57] That was well. The ancient culture of India, after all, had very little to offer that was truly relevant to the building of a modern city. For two hundred years, in every trade, profession and art, the Briton had trained the Indian to execute his will, never to initiate, never to create. Initiative and imagination, so necessary to a great creative act, were hardly to be found above the craftsman level. The planner, the architect, even the school of architecture, in so far as they existed, were rudimentary.

Paradoxically this left India with great freedom of choice. She was not tied, like some European countries, to any suffocating tradition or academicism of her own. She was able to recognize frankly that she must look outside India for someone who could plan an Indian city. In this search for a master-planner the two men most concerned, men of character and determination, were P. L. Varma, chief engineer of the Punjab, and P. N. Thapar, head of the Chandigarh project from the start. Naturally enough Varma and Thapar turned first to the United States of America. Albert Mayer, of the New York firm of Mayer, Whittelsey and Glass—a man who had known India well in his time—was invited to prepare a master plan for the city of Chandigarh. Under his contract of December 1949 he drew up a detailed plan for a city of 150,000 people. Mayer, in spite of his knowledge of India, assumed that this plan would be implemented—transformed into bricks and mortar—by a staff of Indian architects. He was rapidly disillusioned. The Indian architects capable of such a thing were just not there. A number of western architects, therefore, were enlisted to reinforce the Indian staff, some working in the United States, some at Simla and some at Patiala, twenty miles south of Chandigarh.

It was inevitable that the initiative would pass, sooner or later, to the most able of these men. Among the Western architects recruited by Mayer was Mathew Nowicki, a brilliant young Pole who had been head of the School of Architecture in North Carolina. It was Nowicki's tragic death, when his plane crashed outside Cairo in August 1950, that precipitated the decision to appoint a master-planner who, unlike Mayer, would assume overall supervision for the implementation of his own plan and for the architecture of the city. This was the origin of Le Corbusier's team. Nevertheless the faint ghost of the Mayer

Plan and of Nowicki's idealistic logic can still be traced in Le Corbusier's city; Mayer's ghost was never wholly exorcised.

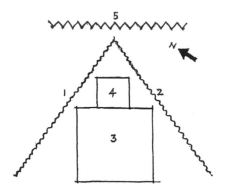

Figure 7 The elements of Chandigarh.

Very roughly and in very simple diagrammatic form Chandigarh consists of five elements: (1) and (2) are the two rivers, the Sukhna Choe and the Patiali Rao, which fork to the north-east of the city, the city lying between them; (3) is the city itself, bounded by the rivers and crossed by the mango groves, otherwise a featureless plain; (4) is the slightly elevated ground upon which, in the Mayer Plan, the Nowicki Plan and the Le Corbusier Plan, was sited the Capitol—all the monumental buildings of government; (5) is the distant range of mountains, backcloth to the Capitol. We can never know very much about the details of the architecture—whether small houses or such things as the Palace of Justice or the Assembly—which might have come from the pencil of Mayer or Nowicki. It was in the planning of (3), that big and bare central square that was the town itself, that the three men differed; fundamental differences of approach to the ancient art of city building.

Mayer, with his experience of India, recognized immediately that a 'city', in the sense which that word possesses for an American or a European, had to be ruled out. Forward-looking educated or travelled Indians might be dazzled by the Western world, but the people of Chandigarh, apart from a small governmental circle in the lush villas near the Capitol, were, at most, one or two generations removed from rural or village life. Half the cooking stoves in Chandigarh may be electric, but are placed on the floor; the w.c's may flush, but half of them are oriental rather than occidental—one squats; half the people place their light frame beds on the grass, the other half place them on the roof; half the women are in purdah. The simplest houses of all are still the village hut plus hygiene. It is a very clean city; it is also, just under the skin, a very primitive one.

Mayer was well aware of all this and yet, rather splendidly, he proclaimed that 'we are seeking symbols to restore or create pride and confidence. . . . We are seeking to build a city not in our idiom, not the city of bold-winged engineering and canti-levers, but a city in the Indian idiom, fused with our own simplicity and functional honesty.'[58] Did Mayer really mean this, or was he merely echoing the ideas which had inspired Nehru and the men in Simla, the men who had first thought of Chandi-garh? Mayer was well aware of the primitive standards for which, in the main, he would have to build. He was always anxious to avoid that Baroque monumentality which was the basis of Washington or New Delhi. Did Mayer mean what he said or was he actually somewhat afraid of greatness? Le Corbusier, being himself a great artist, was able, when he came on the scene, to conceive a great city which was nevertheless very far from the Baroque tradition. Did Mayer, on the other hand, equate great-ness with Baroque, and yet know only too well that a Baroque Chandigarh was out of the question? Jawaharlal Nehru, after all, could hardly be the founder of another New Delhi.

The Mayer Plan, therefore, fell between two stools. It has charm, a pretty domestic charm, but it lacked the essence of a great capital. It was strangely at variance with his proclamation. It really sprang from his confessed admiration for the 'garden city'—for Radburn and Baldwin Hills in America, for Welwyn in England or for Hilversum in Holland. However, it is one thing to avoid the too obvious boulevards of Haussmann; it is quite another thing to take the arbitrarily curved roads of the 'garden city'—directly inspired by the winding lanes of the tiny English village—and reproduce them over some sixteen square miles. Hilversum and Welwyn are boring enough; Mayer's Chandigarh, had it been built, would surely have been more boring still.

Mathew Nowicki, after one of the Indian conferences, wrote to Mayer in no uncertain terms. In the course of the letter, quoted at length by Norma Evenson,[59] he said: 'In planning a city for ages of its future growth it seems that we must continuously beware of trends in present taste which might not be appreciated in the future . . . the only unquestionable element in our thinking is cold logic.' Nowicki emphasized that simplicity which is allied to greatness: 'I have no better example to quote,' he said, 'than the axis Place de la Concorde, Étoile and the Bois de Boulogne.' Nowicki at least was not afraid of either the past or of bigness. This does not mean, of course, that he wanted a classic or Baroque city, only that in the disposition of masses and spaces, such as are to be seen in, say, Rome, Paris or Vienna, he knew that there will always lie the seeds of a great city. But then Le Corbusier knew this too: 'Paris, the city that I have loved!' What Nowicki's letter to Mayer does mean is that Chandigarh, in his opinion, could not be built solely on a domestic pattern, with the Capitol merely as a kind of annexe. The domestic pattern, the little houses with their little roads, their parks and pools, could exist only within a strong framework of monumentality, where it could, if well handled, act as a foil to that geometric rigidity which is a great city's skeleton. Nowicki realized this but could not hit upon the solution in modern terms; perhaps he would have done so, had he lived. Mayer, one suspects, did not quite realize it, equating formality with pomp.

The fact is, in very broad terms, that both Mayer and Nowicki were able men, and both were seeking a new form for the flat city, a form which should avoid (a) the prettiness of the 'garden city' style and (b) the outworn pomp of Parisian formality. Neither turned the trick. It was left to Le Corbusier.

Nevertheless, had Nowicki lived, the whole city of Chandigarh might have been planned and even built by him. That would have been an interesting chapter in the history of town-planning and of architecture, although not part of the life of Le Corbusier. Nowicki's own draft plan had, it is true, some of the informal charm of the Mayer scheme, but also a much greater logic. For the main area he planned a city like a leaf; the veins of the leaf were the principal roads, curving slightly in the Mayer manner, but the central vein, designated as the business area, received very strong emphasis. The Capitol was still sited on the elevated ground to the north-east; but this business area, the central vein, led directly to it, thus establishing a good link between town and Capitol. The Nowicki scheme was not only more logical than the Mayer scheme, but the central business area helped to break the monotony of the small-scale residential pattern. The scheme might be criticized, however, on the grounds that the strong central vein divides the town into two equal halves—something Le Corbusier avoided.

When he was working for Mayer at Simla, the difficulties encountered by Nowicki were endless: no blueprints, no camera plates, a staff whose knowledge was as slight as their attendance was casual. Everything was held up by farmers on the site, who said they would rather be shot than displaced—and meant it. Both Nowicki and Varma were in despair, the latter frequently threatening resignation.

It was eventually decided between Mayer and Nowicki on the one side, and the Punjabi Government on the other, that at this early stage all they could attempt was the building of one of the two dozen 'superblocks' or sectors into which the main town was divided. The 'sector' was virtually a neighbourhood unit, a block surrounded on its four sides by main traffic streets but planned within its boundaries as a more or less self-contained area with its own minor roads, services and amenities, as well as being free from fast or through traffic. The design of the first sector, embarked upon by Nowicki, involved houses of various grades for 1,175 families, several communal features of the ordinary Indian village, six nursery schools, two primary schools and one middle school, a traffic-free bazaar, clubs, a library, a park with an amphitheatre and a swimming pool. Nowicki planned all this with some skill: a good arrangement of closed and open spaces, crescents and courts, as well as an understanding of vernacular techniques such as brickwork and rough concrete. As Mayer said, Nowicki turned to this work with enthusiasm, giving all the architectural quality he could to the most 'minimum' kind of housing, while hiding his disappointment at the postponement of the great buildings on the Capitol. In fact, the few sketches we have of Nowicki's proposals for the Capitol are rather pedestrian; if they show him, at best, to have been a good architect, by contrast they show Le Corbusier to have been a very great one.

This use of the 'superblock', sector or neighbourhood unit was inherent in the Mayer Plan, was developed by Nowicki and finally incorporated, more or less, into the Le Corbusier Plan. Le Corbusier, however, inevitably played variations upon the theme, seeing to it that parkland—grass, groves and water—should meander through each sector. Also, if one were to ask whence Mayer derived the idea of the sector one would certainly find oneself going back a quarter of a century, to the *Ville Contemporaine* in the Salon d'Automne of 1922, to the *Plan Voisin* in the *Pavillon de l'Esprit Nouveau* of 1925, to the *Ville Radieuse*, and to a dozen Corbu projects scattered through the years.

The Punjabi administration recognized the worth of Mathew Nowicki. Mayer's contract has been only for a master-plan, and this he had provided. Nowicki was now asked, in 1950, to sever his connection with Mayer and to remain in India to finish the work he had begun. He accepted, and was returning to the United States to wind up his own affairs when his plane crashed.

Once again the whole problem of the planning and building of Chandigarh was thrown into the melting pot. Looking back, twenty years after, it is easy to see the Mayer-Nowicki affair as no more than an interlude. At the time, in Simla and in New Delhi, it must have been seen as a disaster. In Nowicki the Punjabi Government must have thought that they had at last found their man. That Government, however, with the full support of Nehru, now faced a new situation. They resolved it courageously and decisively.

The present writer has already described (p. 130) how he was in Paris when Varma and Thapar were first visiting Le Corbusier, and how, in discussing the merits of various English architects, the names of Maxwell Fry and his wife, Jane Drew, were mentioned. Le Corbusier had known them at CIAM meetings and elsewhere, and partnership with them was probably inevitable anyway.

The Punjabi delegates were in Paris because, through sheer shortage of dollars, they were now being forced to find an architect in soft currency countries—as it happened, a miraculous dispensation. The Punjabi delegates had drawn a blank in Rome, while in Paris they had already rejected old Perret as 'too classical'. They now offered Le Corbusier an annual salary of some four thousand pounds on condition that he should live in India for three years. Le Corbusier probably thought that the city would never be built anyway—the experience of a lifetime told him that much—while the terms offered were of course ridiculous. He did not, however, show these delegates the door. On the contrary he bought them two return tickets to Marseilles. They must inspect *L'Unité d'Habitation*. The ultimate result of all this was a condition in Le Corbusier's contract that there should be no high-rise buildings in Chandigarh. At the sight of Marseilles Thapar had been rather shocked. Indians slept on the street or on the roof, and would never use elevators; the whole idea was daft. But the two men came back to the Rue de Sèvres.

In the next scene we find Varma and Thapar in London, dining with the Frys, Varma sitting on the carpet. Maxwell Fry, like Le Corbusier, wondered whether the city would be built at all; he wondered still more about leaving his practice for three years. Jane Drew overruled him, and there and then a telephone call was made to Le Corbusier. The destiny of yet another of the world's fiat cities had been decided.

In this way the team was formed: Le Corbusier the master-planner, Maxwell Fry and Jane Drew, pioneers of modern architecture in England and in West Africa, and Pierre Jeanneret, an able architect in his own right and the cousin with whom Le Corbusier had been associated as long ago as the *Pavillon de l'Esprit Nouveau*. Salaries remained absurdly inadequate; Thapar had been proved right in his surmise that the tremendous glamour of city-building—and city-building in India—would overcome more sordid considerations. Le Corbusier, however, it was agreed, should visit India for a month at a time only twice a year. 'You can rely on us at 35 Rue de Sèvres', he said, 'to produce the solution to the problem.'[60] In February 1951 he arrived in India.

Gradually, tactfully but quite legitimately, Mayer was told that his plan must be superseded, 'specially on informal housing layout'. In other words the whole outmoded 'garden city' pattern, so absurd in a great Indian capital, was quietly buried. Equally Nowicki's sketches for the more monumental buildings on the Capitol were forgotten; they had never, anyway, been more than sketches. But for what reason had Le Corbusier been invited to India? Certainly not to revise other men's designs.

It would, of course, have been marvellous if a single mind such as that of Le Corbusier could have now created not only a city, but every part of a city, every building. There is a popular misconception that this is what happened. It is something that never has happened and—apart altogether from the time-scale of city-building—probably never could happen. At least eight architects (four Europeans and four Indians) have been responsible for various buildings within the Le Corbusier Plan. The results, inevitably, have been unequal. Maxwell Fry started by

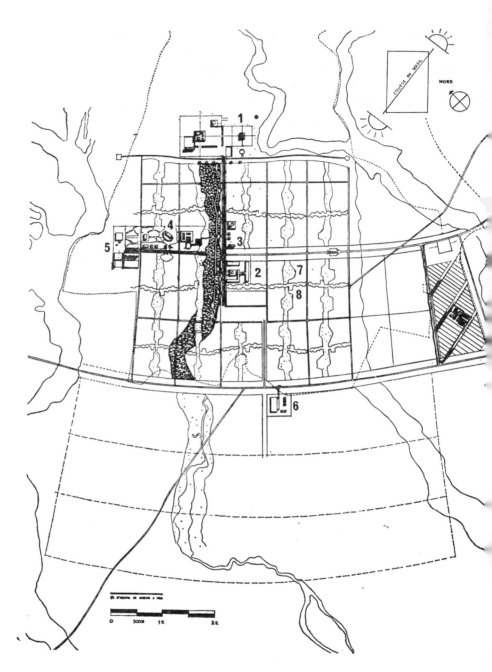

Figure 8 General plan of Chandigarh after Le Corbusier's first visit. 1 The Capitol; 2 Commercial centre; 3 Hotels, restaurants, etc.; 4 Museum, stadium; 5 University; 6 Market; 7 Open spaces with schools, clubs, sports facilities; 8 Shopping street.

deeply regretting the partial loss of the master's controlling hand. In a moment of despair, in the early days at Chandigarh, he wrote: 'Nearly I gave up the unequal task to offer myself as a mechanic, but it wouldn't work that way; there was less value in it than in making my own machine work.'⁶¹ And Le Corbusier himself, in spite of his forceful and masterful character, his intolerance in matters of design, recognized the inevitable— that some things had to be delegated. Having recognized it, he behaved magnanimously. As Jane Drew said: 'He is there for you to ask his advice: take it or not as you think proper.'⁶²

On this basis a harmonious team, united but with no loss of independence to anyone, was quickly established. In such an undertaking that was no small thing. One thinks of other fiat cities. It is too soon to speak of Brasilia, but one thinks of the squalor mixed with the glory at Byzantium as well as the centuries it took to build; of the *diktat* at Petersburg; of the jealousies which ruined Washington, and the childish squabbling of Lutyens and Baker at New Delhi. At Chandigarh there was always mutual understanding; there was happiness and consequently there was achievement. Max and Jane, for all their pre-eminent sophistication, were capable of humility, while Corbu, behind the arrogant façade, could be the most affectionate of men—at least to those on the right side.

From the start, moreover, he established an astonishing liaison with the Indians, from Nehru at the top to the squatting peasant whose way of life he so carefully studied. He declared that in his whole long experience the best patrons he had ever had were the friars at La Tourette and these Punjabis; they were rewarded with fine architecture, but what a comment upon modern Western society!

The mere presence of Le Corbusier, the knowledge that he was living in the Rest House at Chandigarh, was a tremendous stimulus to everyone, whether in Chandigarh, Patiala or Simla. They had wrestled with this problem for years and now, at last, they knew that it would be solved. Again, as Maxwell Fry wrote: 'While I was fiddling with pieces of string, parts strewn about my mental chamber, Le Corbusier was in perfect gear, a combine harvester at work on the Chandigarh harvest, covering the acres in a purposeful methodic path, concentrated essence of work in high melodic rhythm.'⁶³

Le Corbusier's reputation—and in India he must have been

one of the great modern myths of the West—convinced everyone that they were engaged upon a high historic enterprise. How different from before he came. Nowicki had had to complain to Mayer about the inadequacy of his Indian staff. Maxwell Fry, with everyone knowing that Le Corbusier was in the background, found quite a different situation. The four Indian planners and four Indian architects who worked for Le Corbusier at Simla. and others who joined them later, formed a very real community, They made their own furniture and performed their own plays. They could arouse in Max the feeling that 'youth and enthusiasm can in most enterprises be a substitute for experience'.[64] These young Indians, he thought, were better architects because they lived joyfully and fully, and would be better still when India gave them the responsibility they deserved.

Le Corbusier naturally remained the master-planner. That was his function. He had the power to initiate, to change and to veto. Happily it never worked out like that. Having accepted colleagues of great worth he also had the wisdom to give them their freedom; he knew that a man is either a mechanic on the drawing-board, or he can design; that there is no half-way house. If Maxwell Fry had carried out his threat, and had offered himself as a mere draughtsman in Le Corbusier's studio, the offer would certainly have been declined.

It cannot, however, have been easy for Le Corbusier. He knew perfectly well that not every building by this team—although every building had to take its place in his plan—would be as good as every other building. How could it be? Apart from ordinary human fallibility, the physical and human problems were almost unprecedented: a rigid caste system and an equally rigid class system, in a sweltering climate, and very little money.

It is not part of the story of Le Corbusier's life to examine in detail the work of the Chandigarh team. But since that work is a fundamental part of his city and was initiated by him, it must certainly be remarked upon before considering the plan as a whole, or the great climax of the Capitol. All these lesser buildings designed by the team were, after all, the infilling of the Le Corbusier Plan. Most of the housing in all grades, from civil servants' villas to peasants' shacks, was the responsibility of Jeanneret, also of Maxwell Fry and Jane Drew who, however, after three years' hard work at Chandigarh, returned to London in 1954. Pierre Jeanneret remained behind; he was in charge of the design office and was himself building houses, schools, clinics and hospitals. After 1954 several of the Indian architects began to emerge as distinguished designers in their own right, especially Aditya Prakash, Jeet Malhotra, M. N. Sharma, J. K. Chowdhury and Mrs. U. E. Chowdhury.

There are thirteen categories of house in the Chandigarh building programme, not counting the Governor's Palace. The highest category is the house of the Chief Minister—a 'one-off' job scheduled to cost a quarter of a million rupees. From there one may work down the scale: ten houses at about 60,000 rupees each, for Ministers, the Speaker and the Chief Justice; another ten houses at about 45,000 rupees each for junior ministers and senior civil servants. And so on through the salary scale. Each of the two dozen sectors of the city was planned to take about 2,000 houses of the two lowest categories, costing about 3,000 to 6,000 rupees each. These are for families with an income of less than 100 rupees a month, more often less than 50 rupees. These houses of the twelfth and thirteenth grades were indeed primitive, and Jane Drew performed a miracle in casting them in the form of decent, cool dwellings in architecturally decent streets.

The whole city was eminently human, even progressive, but it would be absurd to pretend that it was even remotely democratic; paternalistic perhaps, but not democratic. As has been said, all high-rise buildings were ruled out as the result of Varma's and Thapar's visit to Marseilles, and one must admit that one cannot envisage these Punjabi villagers taking the elevator to some eighteenth- or nineteenth-floor apartment. Their homes, nevertheless, as Jane Drew designed them, must be something almost unique in architecture: the seemly and hygienic shack.

Le Corbusier's own comment upon this rigid class structure and upon the absence of high-rise buildings is illuminating:

'Chandigarh's programme of construction was established by high officials who, having studied at Oxford, have known and appreciated English civilization. Chandigarh is, therefore, a horizontal city. This Oxfordian programme comprises thirteen categories of individual dwellings, from that of the peon to that of the government minister. Up to now the peon has led an extremely primitive existence, without a dwelling house. But now he has a dwelling planned and built with the same love and care as are lavished upon the houses of ministers, or on the dwellings of the twelve other classes. Do not have any qualms about the classes! They are simply a functional way of ordering things.'[65]

And so it is all through history: cultures acting and reacting upon each other across the planet. Britain and Oxford upon India, Rome upon Provence and Marseilles, until ultimately the sophisticated Parisian and the Punjabi peon come face to face. Whether or not an Oxfordian culture directly accounts for a horizontal Chandigarh is comparatively irrelevant—it would seem to be extremely doubtful—but Chandigarh may represent a subconscious Oxfordian thinking.

Le Corbusier goes on to explain the conditions which governed the works of Fry, Jane Drew and Jeanneret.

'Rome was not built in a day. There is not enough mechanical knowledge in India to make it possible to have air-conditioning during the hot season. The Indian climate thus imposes its own rules upon the city-planner—cool nights. The nights are cool and the people usually sleep on the grass in front of the houses or on the roof, and they carry their beds there, beds weighing only some seven pounds.'[66]

This statement is the clue to the very curious design of many Chandigarh houses, just as Le Corbusier's exclamation—'do not have qualms about the classes'—is the clue to the planning of each sector of the city.

So far as housing design is concerned Jane Drew's 'minimum' one-storey houses provide (a) a living-room, usually with a bed in it, (b) one bedroom, (v) a kitchen on a verandah and (d) a small yard with a shower and a w.c. in one corner. There are only two tiny windows in the whole house and these are usually blocked up to keep out the warm air, but there is a continuous band of cross-ventilation at clerestory level—a kind of open honeycomb of brickwork. This and the doors are all there is in the unbroken street façade. In envisaging the sleeping arrangements of, say, a three-generation family with a dozen children into the bargain, it is as well to remember that business of sleeping on the roof!

Other houses, all up the scale, naturally have more elaborate fenestration; but the key to the design of all Chandigarh housing, above the lowest level, is the sun-breaker or *brise-soleil*. This is usually of precast concrete. Its design becomes almost the hall-mark of the individual architect. Indeed, with such severe economy, it was almost the only feature where individualism could be given free play. Maxwell Fry, for instance, tends towards screening his windows with a comparatively delicate grille or honeycomb. Pierre Jeanneret, on the other hand, makes a rather chunky or over-emphatic use of his concrete blocks, projecting them vigorously both to shade the windows and to make a strong pattern. Some of his smaller houses, however, where this excessive chunkiness was not possible, have great charm.

Street after street in Chandigarh is a variation upon this theme of a white sculptural pattern—the zig-zag, the Greek key, arrangement of rectangles, etc.—set against red brickwork. In the sunlight it is strong and uncompromising, perhaps better when glimpsed between the mangoes. It is most definitely, however, not an architectural gimmick; it is a very necessary device to keep out the sun. It is also a logical and Indian version of the mechanically controlled *brise-soleil* which Le Corbusier had invented and used so many years before at the Ministry of Education Building in Rio de Janeiro. A logical progression: the Venetian blind, the façade at Rio, the streets of Chandigarh.

The class structure, whatever Le Corbusier may say, is one of the facts of Indian life; but at least, although the British were determined to perpetuate it, Chandigarh is intended to mitigate it. This is inherent in the design of each sector of the city. Each sector is about 500 by 1,200 yards and is enclosed by the broad 'V 3' roads for fast traffic. These form a great grid overlying the whole plan, but while they do not curve and wind as Mayer's streets would have done, they are not—as in a typical American town—absolutely straight. It was Maxwell Fry who persuaded Le Corbusier to give this very subtle curvature to the city grid.

Each sector provides in theory for the twenty-four hours of the day of every inhabitant, with all essential services and many communal amenities. Each sector is built for a population of 5,000, rising in due course to 25,000, twenty sectors giving an ultimate population of about half a million.

A few sectors are set aside for special purposes. Almost the whole of the sector in the centre of the town, for instance, is the business or commercial area. This, although central, does not cut Chandigarh into two halves as it would have done in the Nowicki Plan. Again, one whole sector is devoted to industry and to railway sidings, but this is on the extreme south-eastern edge, the lee side of the town. Other sectors are used predominantly for such things as the university or other forms of higher education, and so on.

The normal sector is of course primarily residential and in every case there is an attempt to mix the classes, the different grades of housing. This is not always successful. The first sector to be developed, for instance, contained an excess of low-grade housing and could easily have become a slum. This was simply because the first task of the planners was to house the lowest grade of worker, the people who were actually making the roads and levelling the ground of the new city. (The same problem at the same time was distorting the scheduled building of Brasilia; it should have been foreseen but wasn't.)

In general, however, it was Le Corbusier's concept of the sector that prevailed. Each sector was free of mechanized traffic, being served by animal transport—bullocks or camels—or by bicycles. Through each sector ran a portion of parkland. Except for the Rajendra Park alongside the Capitol, there is no specific 'park' in the orthodox sense, not in the urban European sense of the word. The Chandigarh parkland wanders through almost all the sectors, a cooling thing as well as a visual thing. It is the perfect expression of the oldest idea in Le Corbusier's vocabulary —the loose and informal pattern of trees and water underlying the quite rigid and geometric pattern of streets and buildings, this latter being the skeleton which holds the thing together, while the parkland is the more sensual flesh on the bones.

This, or something like it, is a theme which had virtually run through his whole life. It had been the basis not only of the early exhibition projects such as the *Ville Contemporaine* of 1922 but —one must always remember—should also have been the theme of Marseilles, if only there had been eight blocks there instead of one. Although Chandigarh is innocent of all high-rise buildings, the theme of all Le Corbusier's most revolutionary planning projects is realized, if in an Indian guise, at Chandigarh. The sector, with fast traffic on the broad and nearly straight streets which are its boundaries, is really the carpet of his *Ville Radieuse* concept. This loose pattern of trees and water is a setting for communal things—things hitherto unknown to the humble Punjabi—such as schools, crèches, library, clinic, swimming-pool, theatre, museum and so on.

For the rest, so far as the ordinary residential sectors are concerned, one must record not only Jane Drew's low-grade housing, but also that of Pierre Jeanneret and of Jeet Malhotra; the excellent middle-class and upper-class housing by Maxwell Fry and M. N. Sharma; a hospital by Jane Drew and a cinema by Maxwell Fry; a health centre or clinic by Pierre Jeanneret; the State Library by J. K. Chowdhury; and various governmental colleges by Maxwell Fry. Aditya Prakash designed a pleasant, cool and salubrious house for the District Commissioner.

Le Corbusier, as we shall see when dealing with the Capitol, had planned a Governor's Palace, in itself a fine and indeed now famous essay in abstract form, a small masterpiece. This was perhaps too grandoise for a modern India moving towards democracy: at any rate that is what Pandit Nehru thought. So the Governor's Palace became the Museum of Knowledge, while Pierre Jeanneret built for the Governor a more modest but still very spacious villa, sparkling and attractive in a lush garden.

These buildings are a few among the many designed and built by the team. They may be slightly unequal in quality, and Le Corbusier, better than anyone, must have known this. He let it go. He knew that he might plan an entire city but that he could not design everything single-handed. Having had the wisdom to give these men and women their freedom, he left them with that freedom; he was there to advise if asked, and he left it at that.

Building methods were as primitive as life itself:

> 'The new capital is the scene of intense activity. Thirty thousand workers—men wearing dhotis and women clad in multicoloured saris—work seven days a week. Machinery is limited to a few bulldozers and concrete mixers. Women pour liquid concrete into wooden moulds. After setting, a slab is removed and carried by hand to the house nearby. Bricks are carried from trucks to building sites in baskets on the heads of erect women, while men mix mortar with their feet. Boys carry water in big leather bags of buffalo hide. Hundreds of men are busy smashing huge boulders into gravel with hammers.'[67]

The university, both architecturally and socially, is felt to be one of the disappointments of Chandigarh. Le Corbusier, as a kind of gesture, designed the studios of the architectural school, but otherwise had nothing to do with the university. Even the siting was a relic of the Mayer Plan. At the time of partition in 1947 the University of East Punjab had been scattered through several cities. It was Mayer who urged that a new university campus should concentrate these various colleges within the new capital, that they might be the force behind a new cultural life in Chandigarh. The Senate, therefore, purchased a whole sector of the city even before the appointment of Le Corbusier. It was on the extreme north-western fringe, and while this may have given scholarly seclusion, it also meant social isolation. Complaints of lack of social or cultural contact between town and university are of course common enough in, say, Leicester or Cornell, but this sort of contact was so desirable in the case of a new Punjabi capital that its absence—so far—has been tragic. Architecturally the entire project was developed under the direction of Pierre Jeanneret and B. P. Mathur, and was carried out in a separate University Architecture Office, which meant that Le Corbusier hardly saw the designs while they were on the drawing-board. The University Administrative Building is effective and clearly influenced by the master. For the rest one can only say that, apart from individual pieces of architecture, there is no real campus. The buildings, whether good or bad, seem disconnected from each other and from the site, as well as from the city. This, combined with the virtual segregation of the sexes and absence of university clubs, has militated against a full university life, whether within the city or within the university itself.

The greatest work that can fall to an architect, short of the city itself, is that monumental group of buildings which symbolizes the life and ethos of the city, whether secular or ecclesiastical; in short the Capitol. That word may once have meant no more than a citadel upon a hill, as in ancient Rome, but we use it here to mean the great symbol which any great city must have—its outward expression to the world, like the tower of the village church seen across the fields. If, in addition, the city is the capital of a state, then its capitol becomes the expression, not only of the city itself, but also of a nation and of its government.

There are a score of such great capitols in the world, spread over five thousand years. In themselves they trace the course of man's thinking. When, in the dawn of civilization, man's obsession was with death, he made his architect build him funerary capitols—tombs and sepulchres—such as the great temples of

Karnak, the Pyramids with their courts and chapels or, on the other side of the world, those temples in Yucatan. And then, later, when man idealized the beauty of his own body, deifying it, he had also to carve it in marble, and all through the Hellenic world, set upon an Acropolis or a headland, were those temple groups—capitols of the city-states—which established the architecture of the West. And then, later still, the priest, who had until then merely cared for the temple and its rites, became a kind of god-king—divine kingship—and his palace became the capitol; the city existed for him and for him alone. There were the Japanese temples at Nara, the Potala at Lhasa, the Vatican, the Escurial, the Doge's Palace on the Lagoons, or the Forbidden City of Peking where the 'River of Golden Waters' meanders among buildings of the most rigid rectangularity, as if Le Corbusier had once been a mandarin architect. All these were capitols or symbols, places wherein some mythical and mummified creature still breathed. With the holy aspirations of the various mediaeval religions, we have capitols or symbols such as, say, Pisa, Carcassonne, the cathedral on its cliff at Durham, the High Hill at Cashel, the City of the Caliphs at Samara, or the mosques in their courts at Baghdad, or chapels in their courts at Cambridge. With the architecture of humanism the capitol as a symbol begins to dwindle; the entire city now strives to become symbolic of itself, of its own secular and commercial life —the skyline of Florence, the Baroque Rome of Sixtus V, the Nancy of Stanislas, Wren's Greenwich and abortive London, Pierre L'Enfant's Washington; and then, above all, the central complex of Paris, classical space under perfect control, with the distance from the Place de la Concorde to the Étoile almost precisely the same as from the centre of Chandigarh to the Governor's Palace.

Such capitols are more rare in modern times. The life of a modern city is too complicated, too conflicting and fragmented to be held within one symbol. At Brasilia, an attempt has been made by Lucio Costa and Oscar Niemeyer, first among Le Corbusier's disciples. The ministries and congress, the Presidential Palace and the cathedral, all with elevated highways and approach ramps perfectly integrated for the first time in history with the total architecture, may yet be seen to comprise the most beautiful capitol in the world, function, abstract form, space and light forming part of a single masterpiece. Whether this capitol is a capital is another matter. The only thing it may be said to symbolize, however beautifully, is governmental administration—the cathedral being subordinate to the ministries. If this Capitol of Brasilia—this one other truly modern fiat city—symbolizes anything, then it is a life that cannot yet be discerned, a life that is at the same time both exotically primitive and modernistically sophisticated, a life that is bursting with creative energy but has yet to be resolved into a culture.

The building of capitols seldom falls to one man. One man—Constantine, Michelangelo, L'Enfant, Penn—may conceive the capitol of their city, but always, with losses and accretions through the centuries, there comes a sea-change. Who built Venice? Who built Rome? Chandigarh will not be different from the others. It has so far been the conception of one man, but that man is now dead. What others may do to his unfinished city is unknown. Life is short, city-building is long.

Nevertheless, while Le Corbusier was only the master-planner of Chandigarh, captain of a team, he was indeed sole architect of the Capitol. These buildings, symbols of Law and Government and of a new India, stand together as a single work of art, no less than a great painting or a great symphony. They are, for better or worse, Le Corbusier's own achievement, the one thing above all others—or perhaps alongside Ronchamp and La Tourette—by which he will be remembered.

The position of the Capitol at Chandigarh was never in doubt. Its site was established, almost without discussion, in the Mayer Plan, to be fully accepted, first by Nowicki and then by Le Corbusier.

As has been said, the main area of the city, lying between the two rivers, or rather the dried-up river beds, was flat and almost featureless except for the mango groves. Here were the two dozen sectors, the housing, commerce, schools and parks. Only to the north-east was the ground a little elevated, enabling a square platform to be contrived about half-a-mile across. Its elevation above the plain was not great but it was enough for one to feel, when in the centre of the city, that the approach to the Capitol was an ascent. Here, on the Capitol platform, among his big buildings, Le Corbusier created some extraordinary mounds or artificial hills. In the city itself the parks, groves and watercourses, meagre as they often are, meander across the rigid arrangement of the street plan. So, here on the Capitol, these hills, apparently so casually placed, provide a similarly loose pattern as a foil to the geometric precision of the buildings, courts, terraces and pools. These hills, moreover, more or less conceal the buildings from the spectator until he reaches the point where the whole group can be seen to advantage—as a single piece of design. There is an analogy perhaps in the use of the Propylaea to conceal the Parthenon and the Erectheion—except from a great distance—until one actually emerges upon the plateau of the Acropolis.

The whole splendid group of the Chandigarh Capitol comprises four main buildings, as well as subsidiary monuments. These four buildings are: 1. The Secretariat, 2. The Palace of Justice, 3. The Assembly, 4. The Governor's Palace.*

These four buildings are grouped not symmetrically but with great formality: the pools, courts, roads and buildings combine to create a subtle mathematical and modulor pattern of rectangles. So far from being actually symmetrical in the old 'grand manner' of Rome or the Baroque, the whole approach from the city to the Capitol is a very cunning arrangement whereby the visitor is constantly turned, as it were, through two right angles so that it is along a fresh axis that he sees the Capitol ahead of him. Only as he proceeds along the last few hundred feet of his walk is he absolutely face to face with the Governor's Palace. Such semi-symmetry as there is at that point is mitigated by the fact that the Assembly to the left and the Palace of Justice to the right may balance each other but are far from being identical, and are not even opposite each other. But all this, in any case, is partially concealed by those artificial mounds until one is at the very heart of the complex—at the psychological point.

The Secretariat not only flanks this approach; it is destined to form part of a line of buildings, banks and so on, which will make of that approach an avenue comparable in some ways to, say, Prince's Street, Edinburgh, or the Rue de Rivoli—a one-sided street.

Once one is within the Capitol one sees that the varying masses of Le Corbusier's buildings are points, milestones, demarcating the Capitol area. In spite of the positive avoidance of any absolute symmetry, this plan, it is clear, is the plan of a great Indian city, devised by a great Parisian. And yet, one must admit, the area of the Capitol is too large. The careful arrangement of the buildings and all the ancillary things around them—the artificial hills,

* *Designated as the Governor's Palace, but ultimately the Museum of Knowledge, as already said.*

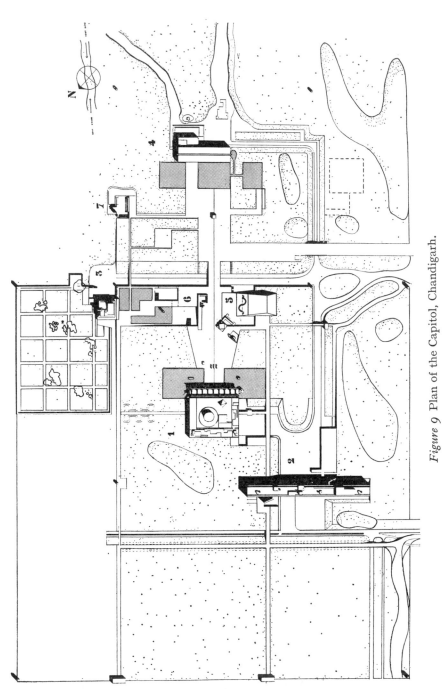

Figure 9 Plan of the Capitol, Chandigarh.

1 Palace of Assembly; 2 Secretariat; 3 Governor's Palace; 4 Palace of Justice; 5 'La fosse de la Considération'; 6 The basins in front of the Governor's Palace; 7 The 'Open Hand'.

the reflecting basins and so on—does almost all that can be done to conquer this desert of paving, probably the largest piazza in the world. The careful and beautiful arrangement, so directly derived from the superb but abortive plan of St Dié, is not wholly successful. The buildings are intrinsically magnificent; they are set in relationship to each other with real genius; the distant Himalayan panorama is superb. And yet, somehow, the distance between the buildings remains too great, even wearisome. We have said that life is short, city-building long: some day perhaps, under some enlightened government, and in some modern manner, these monuments will be linked together, Chandigarh's Capitol unified; some architect now unborn may serve Le Corbusier at Chandigarh as Bernini served Michelangelo in Rome.

The Secretariat, as has been said, flanks the approach to the Capitol from the centre of the city (Pl. 40). Its mass, 775 feet long and 125 feet high, qualifies it to do so. From a distance it appears as a single slab block, tall, long and narrow, but on a nearer approach is seen to consist of six blocks—each containing the offices of a different ministry—lightly divided from each other by an expansion joint. What might be the monotonous character of so large an office building is avoided by the clever variations in the *brise-soleil* patterns (Pl. 41) and by the acroteria or roof top devices which indicate the whereabouts of the restaurant and club. There are also some ingenious sculptural treatments of the rough concrete walls as they come from the shuttering. The entire façade is covered, behind the *brise-soleil* grille, with the 'undulatory glazing' which was also used at La Tourette, but is here found in a more elaborate form: a veil of glass and of sheet-metal ventilators running the full height of the rooms, with an additional veil of copper mosquito net. All this, plus the concrete grille, makes a façade of richness and complexity. The Secretariat, as an administrative office block, is naturally the most utilitarian of the Capitol buildings, but it is impressive when seen against a clear horizon, flanked by the mangoes and reflected in the lake.

The Palace of Justice (Pls. 38, 39) is the best known of all the Chandigarh buildings. It is photogenic. It is also a very real architectural achievement. It is an amazing building, the first ripe fruit of Le Corbusier's reinforced concrete expertise subjected to the catalyst of Punjabi heat and peasant craftsmanship. It is a tall and vaulted building. The roof is lifted clear of the entire structure so that there is always a volume of cool air beneath it. This roof, with great sweeping eaves almost reminiscent of Ronchamp, acts, therefore, as a huge parasol, a protection more from the sun than from the rain. Beneath this 'parasol' are the courts—the High Court and several smaller ones on different levels. These courts are given complete unity externally, and indeed achieve the scale and monumentality of a single large hall. They achieve this very simply by being screened by a large honeycomb grille; the grille, in fact, replacing the wall. If in modern architecture in the West the glass façade has already been substituted for the immemorial wall, then maybe the logic of Indian architecture will be to replace the wall with the sun-breaking grille; a new architecture born of the response of reinforced concrete to tropical heat.

Anyway, the totality is a long building with enormous curved eaves. This unity is broken only by the strong vertical emphasis of the entrance portico; the columns are not, strictly speaking, columns at all, but the ends of the walls which divide the high entrance lobby. The whole building is reflected in a shallow basin with paving taken across as a bridge leading to the portico. The plinth of the building, so to speak, is the long, low shelter— actually an afterthought but a happy one—which provides shade for those waiting to attend the court. The end wall of the building, otherwise blank, bears a single enormous waterspout; in the monsoon season this sends its water splashing down upon a 'fountain of rocks'—actually a basin containing a group of concrete pyramids. The whole structure of this Palace of Justice, like the Secretariat, is as coarse as if it were made of a rocky stone, the concrete being left as it comes from the shuttering in all its unfinished roughness. This contrasts well with the smoother surface of the portico, finished in whites, orange reds, lemons and black.

Internally, at the top of the building but below the parasol roof, there are terraces looking out over the city and towards the mountains. Acoustics—always the most intractable problem of a court of law where many people must speak from different points—is met largely by the use of huge tapestries. Designed by Le Corbusier himself these are rich in colour, Cubist in tradition, the richness here and there caught by a sunbeam finding its way through the outer grille. The largest tapestry, made in Kashmir in five months, has an area of some 7,000 square feet. It hangs behind the seat of the Chief Justice. Eight smaller tapestries hang in the other courts. The Picasso tradition is per-

haps not more familiar to a civil servant in India than to anyone else. There was opposition, but ultimately the Chief Justice,
Jawaharlal Nehru and the Governor of the Punjab hailed these
additions to the treasures of India with delight. They remain in
position.

Mr Peter Blake's description of the interior of the Palace of
Justice cannot be bettered:

> 'Wherever you look, this building offers new and unexpected
> spatial experiences—streaks of sunlight cutting through an
> opening in the structure, unexpectedly lighting up an interior
> concrete wall; ramps, balconies, arches, columns, a patch of
> sky. Curiously enough, most of Corbu's achievements up to
> that time had been in the general area of form and exterior
> space. Here, in the Palace of Justice, Corbu showed himself a
> master of *interior* space as well.'[68]

The Palace of Assembly: Norma Evenson tells us that in 1962,
when the Assembly building was first used, the balance of the
Capitol complex was at last complete. 'Across the expansive
plaza,' she writes, 'two great porticos acknowledge one another,
one (the Palace of Justice) high, massive, vibrant with colour,
the other (the Assembly) horizontal, monochromatic, fragmented
with a series of planar supports for the heavily curving canopy.'[69]

The Assembly is a square building approximately 250 feet
across. On two sides it is enclosed by a *brise-soleil* grille similar
to that of the Secretariat (Pl. 37). Looking across the Capitol to
the Palace of Justice, and taking up the whole of one side of the
Assembly block, is the Assembly portico (Pl. 36). This is a most
impressive affair, although again, as with the Palace of Justice,
'portico' may be a misnomer. The 'columns' have been criticized
for being no more than matchsticks—perhaps mainly by those
to whom the word 'portico' will always mean classical columns.
In fact, of course, these supports of the Chandigarh Assembly
roof are not columns at all; they are the very thin edges of very
deep, fin-like walls whose great depth is always visible, and
effective, when seen in perspective. The roof carried by these
fins is a canopy of very large projection and of upward curve—
again reminiscent of Ronchamp. It is, surely, in the contrast
between the very narrow fins and the very bold sweep of the
roof that one finds the magic of this building.

Internally the great square is a columned hall—a kind of *salle des pas perdus* of nearly a hundred columns, each some forty feet high. On three sides this large columned hall is blanketed against heat by a perimeter of office accommodation which, in turn, is protected by the *brise-soleil*, as are the offices of the Secretariat. 'Immersed'—to use Le Corbusier's word—immersed in the forest of columns of the great hall are two comparatively small debating chambers as well as the big Assembly Chamber itself, a vast circular structure built almost exactly like a cooling tower. This chamber is, therefore, a reinforced concrete hyperbolic shell about four inches thick. This shell or 'cooling tower' rises above the flat roof of the building within which it is 'immersed', proclaiming itself from far off. It gives a broken skyline against the mountains, and this jagged effect is added to by a service tower and by a pyramidical roof immediately over the Governor's council chamber. Shades of the little oratory at La Tourette and of Le Corbusier's old love, as at Marseilles, of a roof-top *jeu d'esprit*! The top of the Assembly Chamber 'cooling tower' is designed to receive an aluminium frame which, said Le Corbusier, 'is a veritable physical laboratory destined to ensure the interplay of natural lighting, artificial lighting, ventilation and acoustic-electronic devices'.[70]

Le Corbusier admitted that the tall, circular pseudo-cylinder of the Assembly Chamber is a difficult form acoustically. This he partially corrected by dividing the upper surface internally into bands of absorbent and reflecting material. These are differentiated by colour, and on this surface there have also been hung some very large acoustic panels, each a most emphatic abstract shape—a quilted plaque. The colour, the panels and the top lighting are probably a distraction to the assembly members below. This is a very dramatic hall; whether it is an ideal debating chamber is another matter.

'*The Palace of the Governor*,' said Le Corbusier, 'crowns the Capitol.' As such, it was never built. It was Pandit Nehru himself who decided that the pleasant and spacious 'circuit house', built by Pierre Jeanneret, was quite adequate as a Governor's residence. Ultimately, therefore, the Capitol site allocated to the Palace will be occupied by those offices which would in any case have been incorporated in the Palace, by state reception rooms and, above all, by the Museum of Knowledge. Le Corbusier's personal interest in the programme for this museum was a considerable consolation to him when he was no longer allowed to build the Palace as he originally intended. The total result, in any case, will be a building not very different in mass or style from the Palace, a building just as definitely conceived for this particular place on the Capitol.

In Le Corbusier's phrase, therefore, whatever the ultimate fate or use of the building, 'The Palace of the Governor crowns the Capitol'. In the sense that the Palace was designed to be the culminating point of the main axis and that it was—if ever so slightly—on higher ground, that statement is correct. The long slab of the Secretariat leads one from the city into the Capitol; the porticoes of the Palace of Justice and of the Assembly, to right and to left, then face each other across the Capitol area; the Governor's Palace should then close the axis. As, so to speak the last building in Chandigarh, it was designed above all things to be a silhouette—a silhouette against the Himalayan sky.

It was designed, therefore, not so much as a Palace as a monument, a piece of three-dimensional form, sculptural architecture *par excellence*, its shape more important than its function. In the Baroque or Classical idiom it might well have been an obelisk, a *temple d'amour*, a triumphal arch or a little palace such as the Trianon. In the eighteenth century it might even have been dubbed a 'folly'. It would have been useless, in the very best sense of that word. It would have been magnificent in the fulfilment of its primary purpose—to crown the Capitol.

Internally the Palace would have been a complex of rooms on five levels. There would have been the underground car-park with a vast suite of reception rooms over, at ground level. This suite would have been mainly of double-storey height, so that the next level would be, in effect, the third storey, the state guest house with a large surrounding terrace. Only at the fourth-floor level would one have found the private apartments of the Governor. The roof, going even further than the Marseilles Building or the Chandigarh Secretariat, would have had loggias, viewing platforms, gardens and sculpture. The whole interior at all levels would have been planned in an extraordinarily free, open and flexible way; the modern 'open plan' developed in the grand manner, the kind of plan which Le Corbusier, on a more modest scale, had invented forty years before. Had the Governor's Palace at Chandigarh been built as originally designed it would have had something of the grandeur—without the pomp—of the Viceroy's House at New Delhi, the modern beauty and freshness of the Planalto Palace at Brasilia and the sculptural strength of Le Corbusier.

Did the whole concept of this Palace go to Le Corbusier's head? He admitted that there was more than one 'crisis' during the development of the plans, and that the building had to be scaled down. 'The heights and sizes, since it was for the Governor, had slipped in on the side of the largest dimensions of the Modulor.'[71] The Palace was, in fact, probably better in a reduced and rather modified form. The model has excellent scale and well repays study as a sculptural essay. The *brise-soleil* grille achieved a new logic—that of the sun-screening slab punched with dark holes. The glass is so far back behind this screen that architecturally, in its ancient role as an element of the façade, it has ceased to exist. The whole thing is now a staccato of black voids in a flat sunlit surface. The arrangement of these slabs—and they have a slight air of nursery blocks about them—builds up almost pyramidically to the strange roof-top acroterion.

The Signs. The major cross axis, from the Assembly to the Palace of Justice—known as the Esplanade—is about 400 yards long. Le Corbusier, very rightly, felt that this was much too long. He also felt that the distance from the Esplanade, on up the main axis, to the Governor's Palace, would be too great. He mitigated both these defects. The main axis, in this last stretch before the Palace, he treated as a remarkable series of platforms and stepped pools. The Esplanade he designed so that it might have spaced along it those sculptural emblems which he called 'The Signs'.

The most startling and fascinating feature of the design for the Capitol, breaking its monotony and giving it emphasis at particular points, was The Signs. These emblems gave scale to the big buildings as well as to the arid spaces; they also stated a philosophy. It was Jane Drew who said to Le Corbusier: 'You should set up in the heart of the Capitol the Signs that symbolize the basis of your philosophy and by which you arrived at your own understanding of the art of city design.'[72] They became keys, therefore, to the creation of Chandigarh. They were all planned to be set up between the Assembly and the Palace of Justice, except for the Open Hand—the largest—which was to be placed a little apart so that like the Governor's Palace it would be seen against the mountains. These signs include the Modulor itself—the gigantic Modulor Man who governs all Le Corbusier's proportions and who, ever since Marseilles, has been incised upon Le Corbusier's walls. There is also the Martyrs' Memorial of India. There is the Tower of the Shade. There is the Harmonic Spiral which gives the Path of the Sun, the twenty-four solar hours. (This, like the Modulor, had become almost a working tool for Le Corbusier as he evolved more and more ingenious methods of bringing sunlight into buildings, the Chandigarh Palace of Justice, the lower church at La Tourette, and so on.) All these Signs were to be of cast concrete, each some twenty feet high and treated with colour, gold or bronze. And there was also to be the Open Hand.

The Open Hand—an astonishing conception—has already been seen in a rather different version, as long ago as 1938, in Le Corbusier's project for the monument for Vaillant Couturier, the Communist deputy. It symbolizes both Man against the World, and also Man in the Modern Age of Opportunity; the Hand that is open both to receive and to give. The actual design is a very remarkable abstract based upon the hand, almost cubical. If it is built it will be over fifty feet high and will be of wood covered with hammered iron. It will be set upon a ball bearing so that it may turn against the sky; as Mr Blake has said, a kind of Atlas 'held up by the Winds'.

The Lake: The Capitol of Chandigarh, lying as it does on an isolated platform on the extreme edge of the city, might well have lacked any softening of its boundaries where it met the arid landscape. To the south-west it was joined to the main city, and on the north-east it had always to be seen against the distant mountains. It was on the remaining sides that something had to be done. To the north-west Le Corbusier established Rajendra Park—still immature—with the rather distinguished Chandigarh Club by Jeet Malhotra. To the south-east is the great lake or reservoir. This was Le Corbusier's personal creation. It came into being out of the whole controversy which raged around the Chandigarh water problem.

It was at first supposed that there was no water anywhere. The mango groves, however, must surely have derived some moisture from those peculiar lunar fissures in which they grew, while something must surely have been left behind each year by the monsoon. In the end water, and very good water, was found at a depth of 250 feet. So far, so good; the town's water supply was assured. But Le Corbusier went further and turned this practical asset into an aesthetic and a spiritual one—the Chandigarh

Lake. In 1955 the Boulevard of the Waters was created on top of the new dam. This dam was two miles long, a curving esplanade some seventy feet wide. The lake itself changed the climate of Chandigarh. The Commemorative Stone, inscribed in Hindi, Punjabi, Urdu and English, reads:

> THE FOUNDERS OF CHANDIGARH HAVE OFFERED THIS LAKE AND DAM TO THE CITIZENS OF THE NEW CITY SO THAT THEY MAY ESCAPE THE HUMDRUM OF CITY LIFE AND ENJOY THE BEAUTY OF NATURE IN PEACE AND SILENCE.

Peace and silence. Le Corbusier, posing as a dictator, created both. The lake was there to assure the people of peace, silence, coolness, quietude and beauty. These things Le Corbusier created by a *diktat*. Motorboats were forbidden. The Boulevard was closed to cars, buses and bicycles. Le Corbusier was determined that the Himalayas by day and the stars of India by night should be reflected in the waters. It was therefore necessary to exclude all street lamps and headlights. Only those little lanterns known as 'camp-fire' lamps were allowed within this domain of silence.

Chandigarh, as has been said, was an intractable problem. The obstacles were almost insuperable. It is still unfinished—perhaps it always will be. It is usually disliked until that moment comes to every observer when the great qualities conquer the dislike. That is why Mr Peter Blake has said that 'words are not adequate to describe the power of Chandigarh', while that brilliant American architect Mr Paul Rudolph, said this:

> 'One approaches the Capitol group across a great plain, the first sight of the buildings is the Secretariat on the left hand, sitting at right angles to the mountain range. In every way it opposes the mountains: the angled stairway, the ramp on the roof, the projecting viewing stand—all of these angles are obviously and carefully conceived to oppose the receding angles of the land masses.
>
> 'Slowly one becomes aware of what appear to be foothills among the buildings themselves, but these subsequently prove to be man-made hills rising out of the plain. The artificial hills are as important to the siting as the buildings, and indeed are an integral part of the whole complex. Indeed the relation of the buildings to the site—also the

manipulation of the site in terms of the various levels of both the geometric depressions and irregular hills—is unsurpassed anywhere at any time. You think you are on the face of the moon. In a sense it becomes one great horizontal plaque. Most of the sunken automobile accesses are not yet there, but the intent is clear.

'As time goes on I am sure that everyone will understand the importance of Chandigarh: people will go there as they now go to the Piazza of San Marco. They will go not because of any individual building but because of the relationship of buildings to site, the environment created, the aspirations of man realized. It is the only grouping of the twentieth century of which I know that makes any sense whatsoever, undoubtedly the century's greatest.'[73]

From Le Corbusier's own pen, in the course of his own life, came many pronouncements. Some were arrogant, a few were dangerously platitudinous, others defiantly propagandist. Some were shattering and perhaps even immortal. Some, as those that concerned Chandigarh, actually came true.

'The materials of city planning are sky, space, trees, steel and concrete, in this order and in this hierarchy.[74]

'I have conceived a great capital for the Punjab, a completely new town, standing on a plain at the foot of the Himalaya. As architect I had a free hand but very little money. This gave great scope for ideas, invention and imagination.'[75]

'The spirit of geometry produces tangible shapes, expressions of architectural realities: upright walls, perceptible surfaces between four walls, the right angle, hallmark of balance and stability. I call it *spirit under the sign of the set-square*, and my description is confirmed by the traditional name of "*allantica*" given to Mediterranean architectural art, for "*allantica*" means antique, based on the set-square . . . strong objectivity of forms, under the intense light of a Mediterranean sun: *male* architecture.'[76]

And that brings us back almost full circle to the man who had, for all his modernity, soaked himself throughout his life in the art of the Mediterranean. It brings us back to his old definition of architecture. That definition was given at a time when most people regarded him as, at best, an ephemeral figure of the *avant garde*. The reader will remember it: *L'architecture est le jeu savant, correct et magnifique des volumes assemblés sous la lumière.* This was a definition that he had formulated under Mediterranean skies, or perhaps only in the pale sunshine of Paris; but it was to come true in the great monuments of Chandigarh, under the burning sun of India.

The impact of Le Corbusier upon the architecture of the world may still be controversial, but that impact is implicit in his whole life, and should have been implicit in this book.

Never before perhaps, not even in the first generation of the Italian Renaissance, have men seen such great changes in so short a time. After all, even the Florentine Renaissance of Brunelleschi and Alberti has left us only a score of great buildings. These stood for no real structural or functional change; they were no more than the outward and stylistic expression of a cultural revolution. Even so it was a century before that style could find even a tentative foothold in the rest of Europe: two hundred years between Brunelleschi's Pazzi Chapel and Inigo Jones's Queen's House at Greenwich. And in the design of cities the delay was even greater: two hundred and fifty years before Bernini could build his colonnades in Rome, three hundred and fifty before men saw the Royal Crescent in Bath. From Le Corbusier's *Pavillon de l'Esprit Nouveau* to Chandigarh was barely thirty years.

Of course one must allow for the speed with which ideas and information travel in the twentieth century; but all the same the Corbu impact, within a single generation, has been terrific. Again, one must not ascribe the Modern Movement too exclusively to one man. On the contrary. Frank Lloyd Wright, the grand old romantic, interpreting his romanticism in terms of modern structure, was probably a greater prophet than the intrinsic quality of his buildings might suggest. Walter Gropius, the teacher whose educational genius, first at his own Bauhaus and then at Harvard, assured the implanting of the new architecture in the minds of a new generation, thereby assured its perpetuity; but that rather than his own buildings was his real contribution.

Mies van der Rohe was at the opposite pole to Le Corbusier. Le Corbusier was the protagonist of reinforced concrete, seeing it as the plastic and sculptural material in which he could realize his own kind of architecture: the rocky, chunky solidity of his Provençal and Mediterranean world, of his masses in the sun. Mies van der Rohe was the protagonist of Hellenic restraint and purity, purity of form, detail and proportion realized through the medium of steel and glass, handled as an Athenian would handle marble.

Clearly, Frank Lloyd Wright was the end of an epoch, while Mies was a rarefied being working for rich and rarefied patrons, creating buildings as if they were Ming pots or Picasso paintings, things not quite of this world. This was magnificent but was unlikely to give birth to a new architecture. Le Corbusier, however, was always 'on the rank', building what he was asked to build, sometimes for quite poor patrons such as the Salvation Army or the Punjabi Government, but always doing it most emphatically in his own manner—or not at all. His career was dogged by frustration, disappointment, prejudice and bloody battles; but in a world that was moving very fast indeed he was always assured of disciples, admirers and patrons. His actual influence therefore, in his own lifetime and probably beyond, has been incalculable.

Le Corbusier was not in any way an orthodox person, and his career does not divide itself in an orthodox and convenient way into juvenilia, success, maturity and so on.

The most marked feature of his life is that certain ideas, specifically architectural ideas, ran through all his work. Those ideas were realized, of course, in different ways at different times. They were never imposed obstinately upon buildings for which they were unsuitable, but their validity was such that in some form or other they were almost always present. What Le Corbusier did was to realize that new technologies, new forms of structure, new materials had all come as an enormous liberation, as the germ from which some great architectural revolution could be born. The old styles had not become obsolete because they were out of fashion; they had become obsolete because, technically, one no longer built that way. And these ideas of Le Corbusier's were not ideas in isolation; they were conceived out of the potentiality of this new way of building; they were its product.

These ideas—the *piloti*, the flat roof, the open plan, the large window and so on—may seem at first sight to be not much more than a series of architectural novelties. In fact—just see what came of them.

In Le Corbusier's earlier houses, the Villa Stein at Garches, the

Villa Savoie at Poissy and so on, the *piloti* meant little more—though it was startling enough at the time—than the obvious fact that it was pleasant (a) to live one floor up among the foliage and with a wider prospect, and (b) that even in those days it was already useful to keep the car underneath the house. The idea persisted, to run through everything he did and to blossom almost out of recognition; to become in due course the recreational undercroft of the *Pavillon Suisse*, or the gargantuan pylons of Marseilles which lift the whole vast building into the air . . . with the children playing underneath it.

The flat roof, popularly the most controversial feature of the earlier modern houses, was developed simply because, when the walls no longer had to respond to the peculiar spans and shapes of the pitched roof above them, the entire plan was liberated. One could plan as one liked, for the joy of the spaces and areas one created. And if the early roof-gardens—in any case really only a by-product of the flat roof—were in fact not used very much, one must also remember that years later we have the crèche, the gym, the pool and the running-track—all looking to the sea and the mountains—at Marseilles; we also have the richness of the terraces and pavilions and sculpture that was devised for the roof of the Governor's Palace at Chandigarh.

It is, moreover, the flat roof, permitting the elimination of dividing walls, which caused the development of the open plan. One was now moving towards the era when one can in effect build anything: Saarinen's T.W.A. Building at Kennedy Airport, with its wide wings: Utzon's Opera House in Sydney, like some yacht putting out to sea; Wright's snail-like Guggenheim Museum; or Le Corbusier's own Philips Pavilion. One was moving towards such an era, but even within four walls it was becoming clear forty years ago that the cellular plan, the division of a building into 'rooms', was no longer a necessity.

That open plan, popularly thought of as meaning that the kitchen is in the living-room, is not of course primarily a domestic thing at all. It may still be controversial but it is now part of architecture throughout the world. At its best one finds it, for instance, in the lovely Planalto Palace at Brasilia, in Mies's beautiful Bacardi Offices in Mexico City, or in Skidmore, Owings and Merrill's United Airlines Offices in Chicago. One could give a hundred examples but perhaps all of them, even if by some devious route, could be traced back to the dusty and abandoned ruin of the Villa Savoie at Poissy. The so-called open plan may now be found not only in the architecture of the 'prima donnas' but also in a score of big airport concourses, hotel lobbies and lush office buildings everywhere, not to mention the Assembly Building at Chandigarh. Air-conditioning, heating, lighting, acoustics and glass walls are all, admittedly, necessary corollaries of this kind of planning—especially glass—but indubitably it all began forty years ago in those villas around Paris.

So much has been said about the use of steel and reinforced concrete in modern architecture that it is sometimes forgotten that the third element, one which plays an equally vital role, is glass. The big span possible in steel is not much use if there is no glass to put underneath it. The history of architecture could be written in terms of glass: the little coloured nodules in the lancets at Chartres: the patina of leaded lights in the Tudor manor: the elegant Georgian pane, and so to the sixty-footer of our own day. Internal transparency—the long vista through the building—became linked with the whole idea of the open plan, just as the large window became linked with the possibility of spanning large openings. Both these things are obvious. It needed Le Corbusier to discover the obvious. Moreover Le Corbusier realized at a very early date that large sheets of glass do not mean just big windows; they mean windows so big that they could no longer really be called windows at all; they must be thought of, in fact, particularly by the designer, as transparent walls. The façade, as had become obvious in the Paris Exhibition of 1937, had ceased to be a wall punctuated by a row of holes framed in carving and called 'windows'. Façade was dead and the entire building, whether small villa or Manhattan skyscraper, could now become a single composition, a single object, 'an arrangement', as Whistler might have said, 'in black and white', solid and void. This was one of the starting points of that revolution in Form and Architecture for which Le Corbusier, far more than any other one man, was responsible.

That was one starting point. The other was concrete. Le Corbusier very quickly realized the plastic potentiality of reinforced concrete. Only during his lifetime did the practice of reinforced concrete become a highly scientific system where the insertion into the concrete of the right kind and amount of steel, and in the right place, made possible those bold winged buildings of Saarinen and Utzon, the spider web bridges of Maillart and the big stadia of Nervi. To start with, Le Corbusier was compelled to use this highly scientific art in a modest way, as for instance in the flat surfaces and curving stairs of his villas. In the *piloti* of the *Pavillon Suisse* (1932) he began to realize it more fully. By the time he used reinforced concrete at Marseilles (1947–52) it had transformed his architecture.

Flat surfaces, abstract form in rectangular compositions—these were the basic elements of the early houses of the twenties. With the honeycomb balconies and the pylons at Marseilles, and the first *brise-soleil* at Rio (1945) the flat composition—Whistler's 'arrangement in black and white' or Ben Nicholson's paintings turned into architecture—had vanished. Henceforth a much richer, more staccato, more sculptural surface appears in all his buildings. By some miraculous chance the hot sun of Chandigarh caused him, almost forced him, to develop the whole concept of the grille and the *brise-soleil* until it became virtually a new kind of architecture in itself.

And this new kind of architecture, the chunky instead of the smooth, has also spread throughout the world, both where the climate demanded the *brise-soleil*, and where it did not. An increase in plasticity, a much bolder modelling, has been avidly seized upon by a whole generation of young architects. Compare the earlier, pre-war work of Maxwell Fry—as for instance in the 1936 Sun House at Hampstead—with his later work in Abadan; compare the famous 1953 Hunstanton school by the Smithsons— all as smooth as the Villa Savoie—with the same architects' Economist Building in St James's Street ten years later, where everything is faceted and modelled. In 1961, in the United States Embassy in Grosvenor Square, London, Saarinen followed his brief in keeping the 'Georgian scale of Mayfair', but not in keeping the flush, smooth façade so favoured both by Robert Adam and, ten years earlier, at General Motors by Saarinen himself. The Architecture Building at Yale, built in 1963 by Le Corbusier's great admirer, Paul Rudolph, or the Tyrone Guthrie Theater, of the same year, built by Ralph Rapson in Minneapolis, are just two other examples.

If Le Corbusier's influence upon architectural form may possibly be dismissed by his adversaries as no more than a fashion, the work of 'all the little Corbs', his influence upon the design of cities cannot be disposed of so easily. That influence will be permanent. It is the product of a lifetime; it is concerned not only with aesthetics and form, but with how men and women live.

It is very easy to say what kind of town it would be nice to live in. According to one's temperament, life in, say, Siena or Williamsburg or nineteenth-century Paris or even Miami, might be delicious. That is not the point. Cities, unlike some buildings, must be real. They are for life as it is lived, and they are for today. Any planner can design in a vacuum. A number have done so and have produced a Welwyn or a Canberra. Le Corbusier never designed in a vacuum. He faced the problem, the eternal modern problem of populations, the sheer pressure of numbers, too many people in too little space. He not only faced it; he turned it to account. In the Le Corbusier city, which we have come across so many times in this book, the 'carpet'—that loose pattern of trees and water, schools and playgrounds—which meanders between the more rigid lines of motor roads and buildings, is not only a foil to the rigidity, and a humanizing of the town, it is also something which, in its turn, needs that geometric skeleton of living towers and elevated highways. The 'carpet' and the towers are a foil to each other; they also make a good town in which to live. Like some of his architectural notions, the idea of the city was always in his mind. Some of his earlier houses seem almost to be designed as if they had to fit into one of his streets. From the first paper project, the *Ville Contemporaine* of 1922 designed for three million inhabitants, right on through the tragedy of St Dié to the sectors and the Capitol of Chandigarh, the Le Corbusier city runs like a golden thread through the tapestry of his life, a perpetual effort to achieve an ideal, to realize a dream. That ideal is now in the world and it is quite certain that we have not heard the last of it.

None of us knows very much about the last years. His wife had always remained right outside his sophisticated existence, but she had given him quietude and affection, the necessary conditions for work. Ironically, as has been said, her death coincided with his greatest triumphs, the triumphs of Ronchamp, La Tourette and Chandigarh. He had to enjoy them alone. He was seventy-seven and perhaps, although it did not seem so, the end came when it should have come.

It is very easy to remember him: the short, sharp sentences, the quick-fire logic, the Gallic gestures. And his appearance: that white and deeply carved face and the long head, so instantly recognizable whether flitting through the Paris traffic in the tiny green Fiat, or in a crowded room. One noticed, too, the spare frame, wiry and athletic. Except for a time during the Occupation he was never ill. He believed in 'the whole man' of the Renaissance, and took a lot of trouble over keeping fit. He would go for a run in the Bois before breakfast, and he was a very good swimmer.

In the August of 1965 he was bathing in the Mediterranean, off St Tropez, when he met with a terrible and fatal accident.

He was born in the mountains. He loved the sun. He died in the sea.

Appendix

THE WORKS OF LE CORBUSIER

NOTE:
    (a) There is often slight inconsistency in dating, as between one source of information and another. This is due to the fact that buildings are variously dated according to the commissioning of plans, the start of building operations, the completion of work, and so on. Where possible the double date is given—the start of work and completion.

    (b) Very few Le Corbusier books are indexed. In this list of works, therefore, some page references are given: (*1*) is to page numbers in W. Boesiger's *Le Corbusier 1910–65* (Girsberger, Zürich, and Thames and Hudson, London); (*2*) is to page numbers in the volumes of Boesiger's *Le Corbusier: The Complete Architectural Works* (Thames and Hudson, London).

    (c) The List of Works is divided into two parts. First, the executed buildings, and second, projects. Projects include not only abortive plans but also various schemes prepared for propaganda or exhibition purposes, to demonstrate a theory or an article. A few sketches, miscellaneous pieces of furniture, etc., have had to be omitted.

EXECUTED WORK

Maison à La Chaux-de-Fonds. 1905.
    Probably Le Corbusier's first executed design.   *1*, p. 22.

Villa à Vaucresson près Paris. 1922.
    Built as the result of exhibiting at Salon d'Automne
    in 1922.   *1*, pp. 18, 32.
     2, vol. I, pp. 48–52.

Maison Ozenfant, Paris. 1922.
    Studio-house for painter.   *1*, pp. 19, 30.
     2, vol. I, pp. 55–7.

Maison La Roche, Paris. 1923–4.
    Difficult site. Special provision for the second
    house on the same site for Le Corbusier's brother,
    Albert Jeanneret.   *1*, pp. 18, 34.
     2, vol. I, pp. 60–77.

Maison Lipchitz, Boulogne-sur-Seine. 1924.
    Two houses for artist-sculptors.   *1*, p. 18.
     2, vol. I, pp. 70–1.

Small villa on Lac Léman. 1925.
    The house Le Corbusier built for his mother,
    who lived there until her death in 1951.   *1*, pp. 18, 38.
     2, vol. I, pp. 74–5.

Pavillon de l'Esprit-Nouveau. 1925.
    A most significant piece of design, built at the
    International Exhibition of Decorative Arts in
    Paris.   *1*, pp. 18, 28.
     2, vol. I, pp. 98–108.

Colonie Pessac, Bordeaux. 1925.
    An attempt to build a small model village of
    standardized houses.   *1*, pp. 18, 42.
     2, vol. I, pp. 78–86.

'*Palais du Peuple*' *de l'Armée du Salut, Paris. 1926.*

1, p. 18.
2, vol. I, pp. 124–5.

The Cook House, Boulogne-sur-Seine. 1926.
A square house in which Le Corbusier's 'Five
Points of Architecture' begin to be realized—the
main living area being on the top floor with views
over the Bois de Boulogne.

1, pp. 18, 48.
2, vol. I, pp. 130–5.

Small house for artists at Boulogne-sur-Seine. 1926.

2, vol. I, p. 122.

Maison Guiette, Anvers. 1926.

1, p. 18.
2, vol. I, pp. 136–9.

Villa Stein at Garches, near Paris. 1927.
A further realization of the possibilities of the
piloti, the free plan and the external stair. A
significant house.

1, pp. 18, 54.
2, vol. I, pp. 140–9.

The Weissenhof Houses, Stuttgart. 1927.
Two houses, derived from the earlier Citrohan
house, and built as part of a 'colony' of houses
in the Weissenhof Exhibition, to demonstrate
the application of industrial methods to
architecture.

1, pp. 18, 50.
2, vol. I, pp. 150–6.

Maison Plainex, Paris, 1927.

1, p. 18.
2, vol. I, pp. 158–9.

Pavillon Nestlé. 1928.

2, vol. I, p. 174.

Villa at Carthage. 1928.
Le Corbusier's first significant study of planning
for climate—the assurance of ventilation and of
protection from sun.

1, pp. 18, 49.
2, vol. I, pp. 176–9.

Restoration of a house at Ville-d'Avray. 1928–9.

1, p. 18.
2, vol. I, pp. 201–3.

Asile Flottant de L'Armée du Salut, Paris. 1929.

1, p. 18.
2, vol. II, pp. 32–3.

Villa Savoie at Poissy. 1929–31.
The most magnificent of Le Corbusier's pre-war
houses, combining his planning and structural
theories with great elegance.

1, pp. 18, 58.
2, vol. I, p. 186;
vol. II, pp. 23–31.

Centrosoyus, Moscow. 1929–33.
The largest of Le Corbusier's buildings at that
date. Built for the Co-operative, it now houses
civil servants—offices, restaurants, club, theatre
etc.

1, pp. 18, 100.
2, vol. I, pp. 206–13;
vol. II, pp. 34–41.

Maison Erazurris au Chili. 1930.

    1, p. 18.
    2, vol. II, pp. 48–52.

Apartment for M. Charles de Beistegui, in the Champs-Elysées. 1930–1.
    An entirely new apartment constructed on the roof
    of an existing building.   *1*, p. 18.
    2, vol. II, pp. 53–7.

Villa for Mme H. de Mandrot at Toulon. 1930–1.
    2, vol. II, pp. 58–62.

Apartment Building—Immeuble Clarté—at Geneva. 1930–2.
    A building for 45 apartments with double heights
    and interior furnishings, nevertheless built entirely
    from standardized elements.   *1*, pp. 18, 62.
    2, vol. II, pp. 66–71.

Pavillon Suisse, Cité Universitaire, Paris. 1930–2.
    This students' hostel was a building of great
    significance and originality. It may be said to have
    turned Le Corbusier into a world figure.   *1*, pp. 18, 110.
    2, vol. II, pp. 74–89.

Cité de Refuge de L'Armée du Salut, Paris. 1932–3.
    A very large and over-elaborate office building.
    Early attempt at air-conditioning.   *1*, pp. 18, 115.
    2, vol. II, pp. 97–109.

Maison Locative, Porte Molitor, Paris. 1933.
    This apartment house is interesting mainly
    because Le Corbusier built the pent-house for
    himself.   *1*, pp. 18, 64.
    2, vol. II, pp. 144–53.

A weekend house at la Banlieue de Paris. 1935.
    A house behind a curtain of trees made as
    inconspicuous as possible, even the flat roof being
    planted with grass.   *1*, pp. 18, 67.
    2, vol. III, p. 134.

Holiday house at Mathes. 1935.
    A very low-cost house, built by a local builder by
    vernacular methods and with a minimum of
    supervision by the architect.   *1*, pp. 18, 70.
    2, vol. III, p. 134.

L'Exposition Internationale, Paris. 1937.
    Project D. Le Pavillon des Temps Nouveaux.
    An ingenious building constructed as a giant tent.   *1*, p. 18.
    2, vol. III, p. 158.

Ministry of Education Building, Rio de Janeiro. 1936–45.
    The most important of Le Corbusier's pre-war
    buildings. His first high-rise building and his
    first use of the *brise-soleil*. In collaboration with
    Oscar Niemeyer and Lucio Costa.   *1*, pp. 18, 126.
    2, vol. III, p. 78

Ideal Homes Exhibition, London. 1938–39.
    This house was the only thing Le Corbusier ever
    built in England.   *1*, p. 18.
    2, vol. IV, p. 14.

Galerie des Arts à l'Exposition de la France d'Outremer, Paris. 1940.
    A very beautifully planned, built and lit
    exhibition.   *1*, p. 19.
    2, vol. IV, p. 91.

Factory for M. Duval at St Dié. 1946–51.
 M. Duval was one of Le Corbusier's few friends
 in connection with the re-building of the town of
 St Dié.   *1*, pp. 19, 136.
                                                                        2, vol. V, p. 12.

United Nations Building, New York. 1947.
 The precise degree of Le Corbusier's responsibility
 for the U.N. Building will always be a matter of
 controversy.   *1*, pp. 19, 130.
                                                                        2, vol. IV, p. 196;
                                                                        vol. V, p. 37.

L'Unité d'Habitation, Marseilles. 1947–52.
 Immediately after the war Le Corbusier astonished
 the world with this building. It also showed the
 first full use of his Modulor System of
 proportioning.   *1*, pp. 19, 138.
                                                                        2, vol. V, p. 189.

House for Dr. Currutchet, La Plata, Argentine. 1949.
                                                                        1, pp. 19, 82.
                                                                        2, vol. V, p. 46.

Chapel of Notre-Dame-du-Haut, Ronchamp. 1950–5.
 This pilgrim chapel on a hill which is a spur of
 the Vosges is possibly Le Corbusier's most
 remarkable work, certainly the most moving.   *1*, pp. 19, 256.
                                                                        2, vol. VI, p. 16.

Chandigarh: establishment of the main plan. 1950–7.
 Le Corbusier was master-planner for this new
 capital of the Punjab, but individual buildings
 were by members of his team.   *1*, p. 19.
                                                                        2, vol. V, p. 112.

Chandigarh: The Palace of Assembly. 1950–7.
 One of the group of large buildings which
 Le Corbusier designed personally for the Capitol
 of Chandigarh.   *1*, pp. 19, 216.
                                                                        2, vol. V, p. 120;
                                                                        vol. VI, p. 94.

Chandigarh: Monument of the Open Hand. 1950–7.
 This remarkable conception dates back to
 Le Corbusier's 1938 project for a monument to
 the Communist Deputy, Vaillant Couturier.

Chandigarh: Palace of Justice. 1952–6.
 With its tall portico and rich *brise-soleil* grilles,
 this is the most impressive of the Chandigarh
 buildings. Also remarkable for its rich interiors—
 with Indian-made tapestries.   *1*, pp. 19, 200.
                                                                        2, vol. VI, p. 56.

Chandigarh: The Secretariat. 1952–6.
 The only high-rise building in Chandigarh.
 Le Corbusier's most elaborate use of his *brise-soleil*
 grille, both for climatic and decorative reasons.   *1*, pp. 19, 206.
                                                                        2, vol. V, p. 136;
                                                                        vol. VI, p. 78.

Chandigarh: The Capitol. 1950–6.
 The general lay-out of the Capitol, apart from
 individual buildings, was worked on for about
 six years. Still incomplete.   *2*, vol. VI, p. 54.

Beach Hut at Cap Martin (Mediterranean). 1952.

1, p. 19.
2, vol. V, p. 62.

Chandigarh: Peasant's house.
    No date—various types built during Chandigarh
    development.

2, vol. V, p. 158.

L'Unité d'Habitation, Nantes-Rezé. 1952–7.
    Basically similar to the Marseilles block but
    without the great *piloti*, and lacking some of the
    social amenities.

1, pp. 19, 148.
2, vol. V, p. 166.

Villa Sarabhai at Ahmedabad. 1954–6.

1, pp. 19, 73.
2, vol. V, pp. 160–5;
    vol. VI, p. 114.

Villa Shodan at Ahmedabad. 1954–6.

1, pp. 19, 73.
2, vol. V, pp. 160–5;
    vol. VI, p. 134.

Maison Jaoul at Neuilly-sur-Seine. 1955–7.

1, pp. 19, 82.
2, vol. V, p. 173;
    vol. VI, p. 208.

Maison de L'Association des Filateurs at Ahmedabad. 1956–7.

1, p. 90.
2, vol. VI, p. 144.

Museum at Ahmedabad. 1956–7.
    A small version of the 'square snail' museum
    such as Le Corbusier would use on a larger scale
    at Tokyo.

2, vol. V, pp. 160–5;
    vol. VI, p. 158.

L'Unité d'Habitation at Berlin. 1956–7.
    For the Interbau Exhibition. The design was
    spoilt by the contractors and disowned by
    Le Corbusier.

1, pp. 19, 153.
2, vol. VI, p. 192.

The Monastery of La Tourette, near Lyons. 1956–9
    The regime of the Dominican monastery,
    functionally and in spirit, was here planned for
    through the medium of a quite untraditional plan.
    A splendid building on a fine site.

1, pp. 19, 266.
2, vol. VI, p. 42.

Pavillon du Brésil, Cité Universitaire, Paris. 1957–9.
    A quarter of a century earlier the *Pavillon Suisse*
    had brought official disapproval; nevertheless
    here is Le Corbusier building for the second time
    in the Cité Universitaire.

1, pp. 19, 154.
2, vol. VI, p. 202.

Museum at Tokyo for the Matsukata Collection. 1958–9.
    The 'snail' plan developed to its full potentiality
    on a very beautiful site.

1, pp. 19, 246.
2, vol. VI, p. 168;
    vol. VII, p. 182.

Philips Pavilion, Brussels International Exhibition. 1958.
An early use by Le Corbusier, for exhibition
purposes, of the hyperbolic-paraboloid roof.

Chandigarh: The Boulevard of the Waters. 1958–64.
The great curving esplanade—free from traffic—
which Le Corbusier created on the dam with which
he had made the big lake in order to bring peace
and beauty to Chandigarh.   *2*, vol. VIII, p. 82.

The Dam at Bhakra in the Himalayas. 1958–65.
Le Corbusier, at the request of the engineers,
gave some architectural form to this dam.   *2*, vol. VIII, p. 158.

L'Unités d'Habitation at Meaux and at Briey-en-Forêt. 1960.
                                                             1, pp. 19, 184.
                                                             2, vol. VI, pp. 180,
                                                             198.

Maison des Jeunes et de la Culture, at Firminy. 1960–5.
This was associated with a stadium for 10,000
people.   *1*, pp. 19, 158.
                                                             2, vol. VII, p. 130;
                                                             vol. VIII, p. 26.

Carpenter Arts Center, Cambridge, Mass. U.S.A. 1961–4.
This building for Harvard University fits very
well into a highly traditional site. Le Corbusier
never saw it.   *1*, pp. 19, 164.
                                                             2, vol. VII, p. 54.

Sailing Club on the Lake at Chandigarh. 1963–5.
Le Corbusier always attached importance to the
calm beauty of this lake and the Club is most
carefully subordinated to the landscape.   *2*, vol. VIII, p. 78.

Exhibition Pavilion at Zürich. 1963–7.
Originally designed as a house, this became for
exhibition purposes, the 'Centre Le Corbusier'.   *1*, pp. 19, 285.
                                                             2, vol. VIII, p. 142.

L'Unité d'Habitation, Forminy-Vert. 1963–8.
                                                             2, vol. VII, p. 135;
                                                             vol. VIII, p. 13.

Chandigarh: Gallery of Fine Arts in the Museum. 1964–8.
                                                             2, vol. VIII, p. 92.

Chandigarh: School of Architecture studios. 1964–9.
This was one of the few buildings, in the main
town and outside the Capitol, which Le Corbusier
designed personally for Chandigarh.   *2*, vol. VIII, p. 102.

Le Musé du XXe Siècle, Nanterre. 1965.
Work on this building was continued by
Le Corbusier's staff after his death.   *2*, vol. VIII, p. 162.

The Stadium, Firminy-Vert. 1965–9.
This youth centre stadium was completed after
Le Corbusier's death.   *2*, vol. VIII, p. 42.

PROJECTS

Ateliers d'Artistes. 1910.

1, p. 23.
2, vol. I, p. 22.

Maison 'Domino'. 1914–15.
A very early example of an attempt to design
prefabricated housing.

1, p. 24.
2, vol. I, pp. 23–6.

Seaside villa. 1916.

2, vol. I, p. 28.

Plan for an abattoir at Bordeaux. 1917.

1, p. 19.

Maison 'Monal'. 1920.

1, p. 25.

Maison 'Citrohan'. 1920.
An early attempt to work out the house with
intersecting volumes—double-height room,
roof-garden, etc.

2, vol. I, p. 31.

House for an artist. 1922.

1, p. 19.
2, vol. I, p. 53.

Housing for working-class. 1922.

2, vol. I, p. 54.

Maison 'Citrohan'. 1922.
A development of the 1920 'Citrohan' project.

1, p. 25.
2, vol. I, pp. 45–7.

La Ville Contemporaine 'City for Three Million Inhabitants'. 1922.
The model was shown at the Salon d'Automne.
The town was of great significance, showing how
early Le Corbusier tried to handle a high-density
city while also giving ample open spaces.

1, pp. 19, 316.
2, vol. I, pp. 34–9.

Housing. 1922.
A new formula for apartment houses, may be
regarded as a precursor of Marseilles and other
Unités d'Habitation.

1, p. 19.
2, vol. I, pp. 40–4.

Villa at Auteuil. 1922.

2, vol. I, p. 58.

Weekend house at Rambouillet. 1922.

2, vol. I, p. 59.

Two town houses at Auteuil. 1922.

2, vol. I, p. 60.

Diagram for standardized housing. 1923–4.

2, vol. I, pp. 68–9.

Villa Meyer, Paris. 1925.

1, pp. 19, 47.
2, vol. I, pp. 87–91.

Plan for a Students' Quarter. 1925.

> *1*, p. 19.
> *2*, vol. 1, p. 73.

The 'Plan Voisin' for Paris. 1925.
This plan showed in a highly formal way
Le Corbusier's conception of the relationship
of high buildings to traffic streets. It was never
meant to be more than a project but led to
accusations that he wanted to destroy Paris.

> *1*, pp. 19, 320.
> *2*, vol. I, pp. 109–17.

Apartment houses. 1925.

> *2*, vol. I, pp. 92–7.

Lotissement d'Audincourt. 1925.

> *2*, vol. I, p. 72.

Minimum housing. 1926.

> *2*, vol. I, pp. 126–7.

The League of Nations Building, Geneva. 1927–8.
The rejection of this scheme—after he had
received a first award—was a scandal and also
one of the great disappointments of Le Corbusier's
life. It may have delayed his recognition as a
world figure by almost twenty years.

> *1*, pp. 19, 94.
> *2*, vol. I, pp. 160–73.

Apartment House. 1928–9.

> *2*, vol. I, p. 184.

The Draeger Printing Works, Paris. 1929.

> *1*, p. 19.

The World Museum (Mundaneum) at Geneva. 1929.

> *1*, pp. 19, 234.
> *2*, vol. I, pp. 190–5.

Low-price housing. 1929.

> *1*, p. 19.
> *2*, vol. I, pp. 198–200.

A house in Brussels. 1929.

> *1*, p. 19.
> *2*, vol. I, pp. 204–5.

'My House'. 1929.

> *2*, vol. III, p. 131.

Porte Maillot. 1929.
An imaginative planning project for one of the
most congested parts of Paris, the western exit—
high buildings, open spaces and elevated
traffic-ways as a setting for a monument to
Maréchal Foch.

> *1*, p. 19.
> *2*, vol. II, pp. 63–5.

Studies in South American Urbanism. 1929–30.
A series of brilliant sketches showing the
potentialities of São Paulo, Rio de Janeiro
and Buenos Aires.

> *1*, pp. 19, 324.

Plan for the development of Barcelona. 1930–2.

             2, vol. II, p. 90.

Study for the development of Algiers. 1930–4.
    Le Corbusier was engaged upon the study of
    Algiers for some four years, and often returned
    to it in various forms.
             1, pp. 19, 327.
             2, vol. II, pp. 140–3,
                 160–9, 174–7.

Study for a Museum of Modern Art. 1931.

             1, pp. 19, 236.
             2, vol. II, pp. 72–3.

Palace of the Soviets, Moscow. 1931.
    This was the result of an international competition
    in which Le Corbusier was awarded first place.
    The rejection of the scheme almost at the moment
    when construction was scheduled to start was a
    disappointment similar to that arising out of the
    League of Nations. It also marked a tragic shift
    in the development of Soviet culture.
             1, pp. 19, 104.
             2, vol. II, pp. 123–37.

Apartment House in Zurichorn. 1932.
    A building with eight apartments sharing common
    services.
             1, pp. 19, 53.
             2, vol. II, pp. 94–6.

Working-class apartment building, Zürich. 1933.

             1, pp. 19, 53.
             2, vol. II, pp. 94–6

The Rentenanstalt Office Building, Zürich. 1933.
    This was an important competition project—
    precursor of many features in both the Ministry of
    Education Building in Rio and the United
    Nations Building.
             1, pp. 19, 118.
             2, vol. II, pp. 178–9.

Town-planning studies for Geneva, Stockholm and Anvers. 1933.
             1, pp. 19, 329.
             2, vol. II, pp. 154–9.

Apartment building in Algiers. 1933.
    Of special interest because of the development
    of the plan on a cliff-side site.
             1, pp. 19, 120–1.
             2, vol. II, pp. 170–3.

Lottery Building in Barcelona. 1933.
             1, p. 19.
             2, vol. II, pp. 195–9.

Studies for the theme of 'La Ville Radieuse'. 1934.
             1, pp. 19, 332.
             2, vol. III, p. 36.

Co-operative Village. 1934–8.

             2, vol. III, p. 104.

Plans for the Residence of a College President in the University of Chicago. 1935.
             2, vol. III, p. 132.

Plans for the development of the National Museums in Paris. 1935.
             1, p. 19.
             2, vol. III, p. 82.

Le Corbusier

Town planning scheme for Hellocourt, Lorraine. 1935.

1, p. 19.
2, vol. III, p. 96.

Swimming-pool at Vagues, Algiers. 1935.

1, p. 19.
2, vol. III, p. 98.

Apartment Building, rue Fabert, Paris (no date)

2, vol. III, p. 102.

Bata shop. 1936.

2, vol. III, p. 116.

Amusement Centre. 1936.

1, p. 19.
2, vol. III, p. 90.

Town plan for the University City of Rio de Janeiro. 1936.

1, pp. 19, 326.
2, vol. III, p. 42.

Planning projects for Paris. 1936.

1, p. 19.
2, vol. III, p. 46.

L'Ilot insalubre No. 6. Paris. 1936.

1, p. 322.
2, vol. III, p. 48.

Studies for a housing exhibition, Paris. 1937.

1, p. 19.

The Paris International Exhibition. 1937.
    Project A: Vincennes.

2, vol. III, p. 140.

The Paris International Exhibition. 1937.
    Project B: Kellerman.

2, vol. III, p. 148.

The Paris International Exhibition. 1937.
    Project C: A Centre for modern aesthetics.

2, vol. III, p. 152.

Bata Pavilion: The Paris International Exhibition. 1937.

2, vol. III, p. 170.

Gratte-Ciel Cartesian. 1938.
    A study for a high-rise building introducing
    significant features.

1, pp. 19, 122.
2, vol. III, p. 74.

Monument to Vaillant Couturier. 1937–8.
    This tremendous and imaginative conception
    was never built but it became the inspiration
    for the Monument of the Open Hand in
    Chandigarh.

2, vol. IV, p. 10.

Town plan for the Pont de St-Cloud bridgehead at Boulogne-sur-Seine. 1938.

2, vol. III, p. 56.

Plan for the development of the Quartier-de-la-Marine, Algiers. 1938–42.
    A brilliant piece of planning upon which

Le Corbusier worked for many years, only to have
it rejected by the Vichy Government. Includes
skyscraper office block with hotel and restaurant
at the top.   *1*, pp. 19, 124.
                                                               2, vol. IV, p. 48.

Development of the Town Centre at Boulogne-sur-Seine. 1939.
                                                               2, vol. IV, p. 24.

Centre for Winter and Summer Sports in the Vars Valley. 1939.
   Hotel, châlets, shops, ski-lifts etc., all beautifully
   subordinated to the mountain landscape.   *1*, p. 19.
                                                               2, vol. IV, p. 27.

Biological Research Station at Roscoff. 1939.
   A complicated planning problem on a site by the
   sea, and involving the incorporation of an old
   house.   *1*, p. 19.
                                                               2, vol. IV, p. 22.

Museum of Unlimited Growth for Philippeville, North Africa. 1939.
   The first of the 'square snail' plans, composed of
   standardized units so that further convolutions
   of the 'snail' could always be added. This project
   was probably the first 'break through' of the
   century into new conceptions of museum design.   *1*, pp. 19, 238.
                                                               2, vol. IV, p. 16.

Maison Clarke Arundel. 1939.
                                                               2, vol. IV, p. 26.

General Plan for Liège Exhibition. 1939.
                                                               2, vol. III, pp. 172–3.

Houses in Dry Construction. 1939–40.
   Metal frame, metal sheet ceiling and external
   cladding panels.   *2*, vol. IV, p. 38.

Standardized house for foreman. 1940.
                                                               2, vol. IV, p. 30.

Standardized house for engineer. 1940.
                                                               1, p. 19.
                                                               2, vol. IV, p. 34.

The 'Murondin' Houses. 1940.
                                                               1, p. 19.
                                                               2, vol. IV, p. 94.

Portable Schools for the refugees in the early days of the War. 1940.
   Le Corbusier did not see why, if the army had
   portable huts, there should not also be portable
   schools. An ingenious failure overtaken by events.   *2*, vol. IV, pp. 100–2.

The Master-Plan for Algiers. 1942.
   This master-plan was only part, although an
   important part, of Le Corbusier's unceasing efforts
   to achieve something worthy of his talents in
   Algiers.   *1*, p. 19.
                                                               2, vol. IV, p. 144.

Le Corbusier

Studies for the 'Linear Industrial City'. 1942.
This plan, like the 'Green Factory' was one
result of the wartime researches of the ASCORAL
Group 'the flowering of the French section of
CIAM'.   *1*, pp. 19, 336.
                                                  2, vol. IV, pp. 72–3.

House on an agricultural Estate at Churchell, North Africa. 1942.
Designed during the war, to be built with native
labour and local materials in a hot Arab country.
The two gardens were to have been irrigated in
the Arab manner.   *1*, pp. 19, 76.
                                                  2, vol. IV, p. 116.

L'Usine Verte. 1944.
'The Green Factory' was another product of
wartime research by the ASCORAL Group. It
would have been a large factory—3,000 workers—
set in open country with workshops open to the
woods and fields.   *1*, p. 19.
                                                  2, vol. IV, p. 76.

Unité d'Habitation transitoire. 1944.
As the war showed signs of coming to an end,
Le Corbusier drew the distinction between
reconstruction and planning—planning was for
the permanent good of the city and the country;
reconstruction might be for urgent but temporary
needs. This scheme was intended to come within
the latter category.   *1*, p. 19.
                                                  2, vol. IV, pp. 124–30.

Plan for St Dié. 1945.
The abandoned plan for St Dié will, like the
League of Nations Building and the Palace of the
Soviets, always remain as one of the greatest of
Le Corbusier's abortive projects. Only in the
Capitol of Chandigarh did he realize something
of the St Dié concept.   *1*, pp. 19, 338.
                                                  2, vol. IV, p. 132.

Plan for La Rochelle-Pallice. 1945–6.
Le Corbusier's plan preserved the old town within
a green belt, created a new linear industrial city
linked to the mole, and created a new residential
city onto the sea.   *1*, p. 19.
                                                  2, vol. IV, p. 166.

Plan for Saint Gaudens, 1945–6.
Natural gas from the Pyrenees may transform and
industrialize a whole district. Le Corbusier's task
was to plan Saint Gaudens as a commercial
centre, introducing 5,000 new inhabitants, while
preserving the fine landscape.   *2*, vol. IV, p. 162.

La Sainte-Baume. 1948.
The underground church and shrine between
Toulon and Marseilles. Although abandoned, this
scheme may have led indirectly to Le Corbusier
being invited to design the Chapel at Ronchamp.   *1*, pp. 19, 254.

Plans for Bogota and for Izmir. 1948–50.
                                                  1, pp. 19, 342.
                                                  2, vol. V, p. 42.

Roq et Rob at Cap-Martin. 1949.
    A housing project using standardized elements.   *1*, pp. 19, 132.
                                                       2, vol. V, p. 54.

House for Prof. Fueter. 1950.
    Professor Fueter of Zürich University had been
    Le Corbusier's patron for the *Pavillon Suisse.*
    Unfortunately he died before this house could be
    started.   *1*, p. 19.
      2, vol. V, p. 64.

Plans for Marseilles. 1950–1.
    When the *L'Unité d'Habitation de Marseilles* was
    under way, Le Corbusier did a number of plans
    for different parts of the city—Le Vieux-Port (which
    had been blown up by the Germans), Marseilles-
    Veyre and Marseilles-Sud.   *1*, pp. 19, 344.
      2, vol. V, pp. 85, 99.

Housing for Strasbourg. 1951.
    1, pp. 19, 134.
    2, vol. V, p. 102.

Steel-framed houses at Lagny.
    1, p. 19.
    2, vol. VI, p. 204.

A competition scheme for low-cost housing at Antony. 1956.
    The replanning of a suburb south of Paris.
    Le Corbusier's scheme—which was rejected—
    concentrated all housing and services in a single
    Unité d'Habitation, leaving the parkland entirely
    untouched.   *1*, p. 19.

A Stadium at Firminy. 1956.
    Eight hundred dwellings in two blocks and some
    smaller houses.   *1*, pp. 19, 158.

A Stadium for Baghdad. 1956.
    1, p. 19.

Church at Firminy-Vert. 1960–5.
    1, p. 19.
    2, vol. VII, p. 136;
    vol. VII, p. 42.

Chandigarh: The Museum of Knowledge. 1960–5.
    The Palace of the Governor, proving too ambitious
    and expensive, was scaled down to become the
    Museum of Knowledge—a project in which
    Le Corbusier took a great personal interest. The
    design for the museum has now been further
    modified and the present design, in model form,
    bears no relationship to the original Palace of the
    Governor.   *2*, vol. VIII, p. 68.

Chandigarh: The Tower of Shadows. 1960–5.
    This, with the Monument of the Open Hand,
    the Modulor Man, etc., was among the 'Signs'
    on the Capitol. It would have been a place of
    meditation.   *2*, vol. VIII, p. 74.

Exhibition Pavilion at Stockholm. 1962.
    1, pp. 19, 282.
    2, vol. VII, p. 178.

Le Corbusier

International Art Centre at Erlenbach-Frankfort. 1963.
    An unusual museum planned for a site in the
    open country.   *1,* pp. 19, 279.
                                                 2, vol. VII, p. 164.

Factory for Olivetti at Rho-Milan. 1963–4.
    Provision for 4,000 employées.   *1,* pp. 19, 169.

Palace of Congress at Strasbourg. 1964.
                                                 1, pp. 19, 188.
                                                 2, vol. VII, p. 152.

French Embassy for the City of Brasilia. 1964–5.
                                                 1, pp. 19, 162.
                                                 2, vol. VII, p. 12.

Hospital in Venice. 1965.
                                                 1, pp. 19, 176.
                                                 2, vol. VIII, p. 132.

Notes

1   Le Corbusier (1960b), p. 44
2   Le Corbusier (1960b), p. 21
3   Le Corbusier (1960b), p. 24
4   Le Corbusier (1960b), p. 30
5   Le Corbusier (1960b), p. 35
6   Le Corbusier (1960b), p. 37
7   Le Corbusier (1960b), p. 37
8   Le Corbusier (1960b), p. 37
9   Le Corbusier (1967), p. 185
10 Le Corbusier (1960b), p. 49
11 Le Corbusier (1954a), p. 29
12 Le Corbusier (1960b), p. 34
13 Boesiger (1960), p. 44
14 Le Corbusier (1960b), p. 34
15 Le Corbusier (1960b), p. 73
16 Le Corbusier (1960b), p. 89
17 Le Corbusier (1960b), p. 106
18 Le Corbusier (1960b), p. 98
19 Le Corbusier (1960b), p. 96
20 *The American Architect*, 1936;
    letter from Le Corbusier
21 Le Corbusier (1953), pp. 52–8
22 Report on the United Nations
    Headquarters by Le Corbusier
    as a member of the French
    delegation
23 Blake (1963), p. 127
24 Le Corbusier (1954a), pp. 165–6
25 Blake (1963), p. 130
26 Paul Rudolph, in *Architectural
    Forum*, 1952
27 Information from Clive Ent-
    wistle
28 Le Corbusier (1960b), p. 304
29 Le Corbusier (1954a), pp. 15–17
30 Le Corbusier (1954a), pp. 18–20
31 Le Corbusier (1954a), p. 56
32 Le Corbusier (1954a), p. 26
33 Le Corbusier (1954a), p. 27
34 Le Corbusier (1954a), p. 37
35 Le Corbusier (1954a), p. 71
36 Le Corbusier (1960b), p. 141
37 Le Corbusier (1957), p. 88
38 Le Corbusier (1957), p. 27
39 Le Corbusier (1957), p. 88
40 Blake (1963), p. 135
41 Le Corbusier (1957), p. 118
42 Boesiger (1960), p. 240
43 Le Corbusier (1957), p. 47
44 Le Corbusier (1957), p. 103
45 Le Corbusier (1960a), p. 172
46 Le Corbusier (1960a), p. 172
47 Henze & Moosbrugger (1966),
    p. 7
48 Henze & Moosbrugger (1966),
    p. 19
49 Henze & Moosbrugger (1966),
    p. 7
50 Henze & Moosbrugger (1966),
    p. 10
51 Henze & Moosbrugger (1966),
    p. 10
52 Henze & Moosbrugger (1966),
    p. 11
53 Henze & Moosbrugger (1966),
    p. 12
54 Henze & Moosbrugger (1966),
    p. 14

55 Henze & Moosbrugger (1966), p. 13
56 Evenson (1966), p. 6
57 Evenson (1966), p. 6
58 Evenson (1966), p. 13
59 Evenson (1966), pp. 14–15
60 Evenson (1966), p. 25
61 Evenson (1966), p. 28
62 Evenson (1966), p. 27
63 Evenson (1966), p. 27
64 Evenson (1966), p. 27
65 Boesiger (1960), p. 184
66 Boesiger (1960), p. 184
67 Achal Rangaswami, in *Architectural Forum*, September 1953
68 Blake (1963), p. 147
69 Evenson (1966), pp. 80–1
70 Boesiger (1960), p. 202
71 Boesiger (1960), p. 206
72 Evenson (1966), p. 86
73 Paul Rudolph in *Architectural Forum*, April 1961
74 Le Corbusier in *Architectural Forum*, September 1953
75 Le Corbusier (1929–70), vol. V, p. 11
76 Le Corbusier (1954a), p. 223

Select Bibliography

A full Le Corbusier bibliography would be an immense document. This one is selective and is limited mainly, although not wholly, to the English language. Almost every book by Le Corbusier himself is included.

Every Le Corbusier building, at the time of its completion, was the subject of articles in professional journals in every civilized country. Such articles can be found in libraries and are not included here. Many other articles, critical or analytical, are, however, listed below.

Books

BLAKE, Peter (1963). *Le Corbusier: architecture and form.* Harmondsworth: Penguin Books
[Extract from (1960) *The Master Builders.* London: Gollancz.]

BOESIGER, W. (ed.) (1960). *Le Corbusier 1910–60.* London: Tiranti.
(1967). *Le Corbusier 1910–65.* London: Thames & Hudson.
See also LE CORBUSIER.

CHOAY, Françoise (1960). *Le Corbusier.* London: Mayflower.

COLUMBIA UNIVERSITY SCHOOL OF ARCHITECTURE (1963). *Four great makers of modern architecture.* New York.

DAMAZ, Paul (1956). *Art in European Architecture.* New York: Reinhold; London: Chapman & Hall.

EVENSON, Norma (1966). *Chandigarh.* Berkeley: University of California Press; London: Cambridge University Press.

GAUTHIER, Maximilien (1944). *Le Corbusier ou l'architecture au service de l'homme.* Paris: Denoël.

HENZE, Anton (1957). *Le Corbusier.* Berlin: Colloquium-Verlag.

HENZE, Anton, and MOOSBRUGGER, Bernhard (1966). *La Tourette: the Le Corbusier Monastery.* Trans. Janet Seligman. London: Lund, Humphries.

HEPPENSTALL, R., and CALI, F. (1957). *Architecture of Truth*. London: Thames & Hudson.

JEANNERET, Pierre. *See* LE CORBUSIER.

LE CORBUSIER (1929–70). *Œuvre Complète*. Zürich: Artemis Verlag.
> Vol. I. *Le Corbusier et Pierre Jeanneret, Œuvre Complète de 1910–1929*. Ed. W. Boesiger & O. Stonorov. 1929; 9th ed. 1967.
> Vol. II. *Le Corbusier et Pierre Jeanneret, Œuvre Complète de 1929–1934*. Ed. W. Boesiger. 1935; 8th ed. 1967.
> Vol. III. *Le Corbusier et Pierre Jeanneret, Œuvre Complète 1934–1938*. Ed. Max Bill. 1938; 8th ed. 1967.
> Vol. IV. *Le Corbusier, Œuvre Complète 1938–1946*. Ed. W. Boesiger. 1953; 6th ed. 1970.
> Vol. V. *Le Corbusier, Œuvre Complète 1946–1952*. Ed. W. Boesiger. 1953; 6th ed. 1970.
> Vol. VI. *Le Corbusier, Œuvre Complète 1952–1957*. Ed. W. Boesiger. 1957; 6th ed. 1966.
> Vol. VII. *Le Corbusier, Œuvre Complète 1957–1965*. Ed. W. Boesiger. 1965; 2nd ed. 1966.
> Vol. VIII. *Le Corbusier: Les dernières œuvres*. Ed. W. Boesiger. 1970. Published in Great Britain as *The Complete Architectural Works of Le Corbusier*, vols. I to VIII. London: Thames and Hudson.

> (1930a). *Précisions sur un état présént de l'architecture et de l'urbanisme*. Paris: Editions Crès.
> (1930b). *Une Maison—un Palais*. Paris; Editions Crès.
> (1934). *Aircraft*. London: Studio Ltd.
> (1938a). *Des Canons, des Munitions? Merci! Des Logis . . . s.v.p.* Boulogne-sur-Seine: Editions l'Architecture d'aujourd'hui. (Monographie du 'Pavillon des Temps Nouveaux' à l'Exposition Internationale 'Art et Technique' de Paris 1937.)
> (1938b). *Peintures, 1918–1938.* (Exposition 30 Nov.–17 Dec. 1938.) Paris. *Le lyrisme des temps nouveaux et d'urbanisme*. Colmar: *Le Point Journal*, special number.
> (1943a). *La Charte d'Athènes, avec un discours luminaire de Jean Giraudoux*. Paris: Editions Plon; 2nd edn (1957) Paris: Editions de Minuit.
> (1943b). *Entretien avec les étudiants des Ecoles d'Architecture*. Paris: Editions Denoël; new edition (1957) Paris: Editions de Minuit.
> (1946a). *Manière de penser l'urbanisme*. Boulogne-sur-Seine: Editions l'Architecture d'aujourd'hui. (Written 1943.) New edition (1963) Paris: Mentreux.
> (1946b). *Towards a New Architecture*. Trans. Frederick Etchells. London: Architectural Press. [*Vers Une Architecture*, 1923.] Reprint of English translation, from 13th French edition, first published by John Rodker, 1927.
> (1947a). *The City of Tomorrow and its Planning*. Trans. Frederick Etchells. London: Architectural Press. [*Urbanisme*, 1925.] Reprint of English translation, from 8th French edition, first published by John Rodker, 1929.
> (1947b). *Concerning Town Planning*. Trans. Clive Entwistle. London: Architectural Press. [*Propos d'urbanisme*, 1946.]

(1947c). *U.N. Headquarters*. New York: Reinhold; London: Chapman & Hall.

(1947d). *When the Cathedrals were White*. Trans. F. E. Hyslop. New York: Reynal & Hitchcock; London (1948): Routledge & Kegan Paul. [*Quand les Cathédrales étaient blanches*, 1937.]

(1948a). *The Four Routes*. Trans. Dorothy Todd. London: Dennis Dobson. [*Sur les 4 Routes*, 1941.]

(1948b). *New World of Space*. New York: Reynal & Hitchcock.

(1950). *Poésie sur Alger*. Paris: Editions Falaise.

(1953). *The Marseilles Block*. Trans. G. Sainsbury. London: Harvill Press. [*L'Unité d'habitation de Marseilles*, 1950.]

(1954a). *The Modulor*. Trans. Peter de Francia and Anna Bostock. London: Faber & Faber. [*Le Modulor*, 1949; 2nd edn, 1951.]

(1954b). *Une petite maison*. Zürich: Girsberger.

(1955). *Dessins* (ed. Maurice Jardot). Paris: Mondes.

(1956). *Les Plans Le Corbusier de Paris 1956–1922*. Paris: Editions de Minuit.

(1957). *The Chapel at Ronchamp*. Trans. Jacqueline Cullen. London: Architectural Press. [*Ronchamp*, 1955.]

(1958a). *Modulator 2*: Trans. Peter de Francia and Anna Bostock. London: Faber & Faber. [*Le Modulor 2*, 1955.]

(1958b). *Le Poème électronique Le Corbusier*. (The Philips Pavilion, Brussels World Fair 1958). Paris: Editions de Minuit.

(1959). *L'Urbanisme des trois établissements humains*. 2nd edn. Paris: Editions de Minuit.

(1960a). *Le Convent Saint Marie de la Tourette*. Paris: Editions du Cerf.

(1960b). *My Work*. Trans. James Palmes. London: Architectural Press. [*Mon Œuvre*, 1960.]

(1967). *The Radiant City*. London: Faber & Faber. [*La Ville radieuse*, 1933, 1964.]

(1968). *Nursery Schools*. New York: Orion Press.

LE CORBUSIER & JEANNERET, Pierre (1927). *Zwei Wohnhäuser von Le Corbusier und P. Jeanneret*. Stuttgart: Wedekind.

LE CORBUSIER & PIERREFEU, François (1948). *The Home of Man*. Trans. Clive Entwistle & Gordon Holt. London: Architectural Press. [*La maison des hommes*, 1942.]

PHILIPS TECHNICAL REVIEW (1959). *The Philips Pavilion at the 1958 World Fair in Brussels*.

TROEDSSON, Carl Birger (1951). *Two Standpoints towards modern architecture (Frank Lloyd Wright and Le Corbusier)*. Gothenburg: Chalmers Terniska Högskolas Handlinger No. 113.

WEBER, Heidi (ed.) (1967). *Le Corbusier. Œuvre lithographie*. Zürich: Centre Le Corbusier.

Articles in Periodicals

ANTHONY, Harry A. 'Le Corbusier: his ideas for cities.' *The American Institute of Planners Journal*, vol. 32, no. 5, pp. 279–88. September 1966. Washington D.C.

ANTHONY, Harry A. 'Potentials of the skyscraper-studded park.' *Columbia University, School of Architecture*: *Four great makers of modern architecture*, pp. 189–95. 1961. New York.

BANHAM, Reyner. 'The last formgiver.' *Architectural Review*, vol. 140, pp. 86, 97–108. August 1966. London.

— 'Painting and Sculpture of Le Corbusier.' *Architectural Review*, vol. 113. June 1953. London.

BRETT, Lionel. 'The space machine, an evaluation of the recent work of Le Corbusier.' *Architectural Review*, vol. 102, pp. 147–50. November 1947. London.

BURCHARD, John Ely. 'A pilgrimage: Ronchamp, Raincy, Vèzelay.' *Architectural Record*, vol. 123, pp. 171–8. March 1958. New York.

CANDILIS, Georges. 'Le Corbusier.' *L'Architecture d'aujourd'hui*, vol. 35, p. v. Juin-Juillet 1965. Boulogne-sur-Seine.

— 'Le Corbusier et notre époque.' *L'Architecture d'aujourd'hui*, vol. 34, pp. 17–31. Avril-Maı 1964. Boulogne-sur-Seine.

CLAUDIUS-PETIT, Eugène. 'Hommage à Le Corbusier.' *Urbanisme: Revue Française 35ᵉ année*, no. 92, pp. 2–11. 1966. Paris.

CORNELL, E. Interpretation of Le Corbusier's manifesto for the new architecture. *Arkitektur*, no. 10, pp. 351–6. 1966. Stockholm.

CROSBY, T. 'To Le Corbusier, despite enchantment.' *Studio*, pp. 52–3. January 1968 (review of *The Radiant City*).

DREW, Jane. 'An exercise in one, two and three dimensions.' *Architecture and Building*, pp. 60–1. February 1959 (review of Le Corbusier exhibition at the London Building Centre).

— 'Le Corbusier—a personal note.' *Town Planning Institute Journal*, vol. 51, pp. 380–1. November 1965. London.

FRY, Maxwell. Speech given at opening of exhibition in Liverpool. *Architect and Building News*, pp. 80–1. 17 December 1958. London.

GASSER, Hans Ulrich. 'The painter, Le Corbusier.' *The Architects' Year Book*, vol. 6, pp. 35–44. 1955. London.

GOLDFINGER, Ernö. 'Le Corbusier.' *Architectural Design*, vol. 35, pp. 474–6. October 1965. London.

HITCHCOCK, Henry Russell. 'Le Corbusier: a preliminary assessment.' *Progressive Architecture*, pp. 232–7, October 1965; pp. 198–201. November 1965. New York.

— 'The evolution of Wright, Mies and Le Corbusier.' *Perspecta*, no. 1, pp. 8–15. Summer 1952.

MALRAUX, André. '. . . celebra l'immortalita di Le Corbusier' (funeral speech). *L'Architettura: Cronache e Storia*, vol. 11, no. 122, pp. 494–5. Dicembre 1965. Milan.

NAVA, Antonia. Book review of 'Quand les cathédrales étaient blanches. Voyage au pays des timides.' *Casabella*, vol. 15, pp. 2–5. Maggio 1937.

NIEMAYER, Oscar. 'Le Corbusier.' *Modulo*, vol. 8, no. 32, pp. 23–4. Março 1963.

PEVSNER, Nikolaus. 'Time and Le Corbusier.' *Architectural Review*, vol. 125, pp. 159–65. March 1959. London.

ROBERTSON, Howard, and YERBURY, F. R. 'Problems of the interior—I and II rooms and furnishings by Le Corbusier and Jeanneret and Charlotte Perriand.' *The Architect and Building News*, vol. 123, pp. 18–20, 2 January 1931; p. 117–19, 16 January 1931. London.

ROWE, Colin. 'The mathematics of the ideal villa—Palladio and Le Corbusier compared.' *Architectural Review*, vol. 101, pp. 101–4. March 1947. London.

STIRLING, James. 'Garches to Jaoul. Le Corbusier as domestic architect in 1927 and 1953.' *Architectural Review*, vol. 118, pp. 145–51. September 1955. London.

SUMMERSON, John. 'The "poetry" of Le Corbusier.' *The Architect and Building News*, vol. 162, pp. 4–6. 5 April 1940. London.

ZERVOS, Christian. 'Qui bâtira le Palais des Nations à Genève?' *Cahiers d'art*, 2me année, nos. 7, 8 and 9, pp. I–XVI. 1927. Paris.

UNSIGNED

'Anéantissement d'un esprit, d'une culture, avènement d'un autre esprit, d'une autre culture.' *L'Esprit Nouveau*, no. 22, pp. 19–22. Avril 1925.

'The City of Tomorrow. Corbusier revisited.' *Country Life*, vol. 103, pp. 104–5, 23 January 1948. London.

'City of tomorrow and its planning.' *Architectural Review*, vol. 66, pp. 135–8. September 1929. London. And *Creative Art*, vol. 5, pp. 612–24. September 1929.

'Corbu: Tribute to a Master.' *American Institute of Architects Journal*, vol. 44, no. 4, p. 14. October 1965. New York.

'Five questions to Le Corbusier.' *Zodiac*, no. 7, pp. 50–5. 1960. London. And *Bauen und Wohnen*, no. 3, pp. 45–7. 1963. Munich.

'Furniture by Le Corbusier and Charlotte Perriand.' *Architectural Design*, vol. 36, p. 361. July 1966. London.

'If I had to teach you architecture.' *Architectural Design*, vol. 29, pp. 86–7. February 1960. London. And *Focus*, vol. 1, no. 1, pp. 3–12. Summer 1938.

'Intuitive flash and reasoned argument.' *Architecture and Building*, pp. 368–372. October 1956.

'Last works of Le Corbusier.' *Architectural Record*, vol. 139, pp. 187–94. April 1966. New York.

'Le Corbusier' (notes on his life and works on the occasion of his winning the Royal Gold Medal). *Building*, p. 41. February 1953. London.

'Le Corbusier.' (W. Gropius on Le Corbusier. José Luis Sert on Le Corbusier.) *Connection*, pp. 18–25. Winter 1966. De Kalb, Illinois.

'Le Corbusier accepts royal gold medal.' *The Architects' Journal*, vol. 117. p. 451. 9 April 1953. London.

'Le Corbusier addresses the students of the A.A. School.' *Architect and Building News*, vol. 193, p. 17–18. 2 January 1948. London.

'Le Corbusier at Harvard—a disaster or a bold step forward?' *Architectural Forum*, vol. 119, pp. 104–7. October 1963. New York.

'Le Corbusier: his impact on four generations.' *RIBA Journal*, pp. 497–500. October 1965. London.

Select Bibliography

'Le Corbusier, muralist.' *Interiors*, vol. 107, pp. 100–3. June 1948. New York.

'Le Corbusier receives honorary degree of Doctor of Laws, Cambridge University, June 1959.' *Architects' Journal*, vol. 216, pp. 44–5. 20 August 1959. London.

'Le Corbusier, a symposium.' *Architectural Association Journal*, vol. 74, pp. 254–62. May 1959.

'Le Corbusier: a tribute.' *Architectural Forum*. October 1965. New York.

'Le Corbusier and Pierre Jeanneret.' *RIBA Journal*, vol. 38, p. 404. 2 May 1931. London.

'Le Corbusier's day dream.' *Arts and Architecture* (Los Angeles), pp. 16–17, 30–1. September 1963. (Lecture by E. N. Rogers at Columbia University.)

Lecture by Le Corbusier on the occasion of the A.A. Centenary on the Golden Section. *Architects' Journal*, vol. 107, p. 36. 8 January 1946. London.

Presentation of the Royal Gold Medal to Le Corbusier. *RIBA Journal*, vol. 60, pp. 215–18. April 1953. London.

Index

Index

Index